BEING
PAKEHA

BEING PAKEHA

An encounter with New Zealand and the Maori Renaissance

MICHAEL KING

HODDER AND STOUGHTON
AUCKLAND LONDON SYDNEY TORONTO

Typeset by Sabagraphics Ltd, Christchurch.
Printed and bound by Singapore National Printers Ltd for Hodder &
Stoughton Ltd, 46 View Road, Glenfield, Auckland, New Zealand.

Contents

For my family, past and present —
a community of living and dead —
and especially for Eleanor Frances King, 1916-1988

Author's Note

THOSE WHO CAN, do; those who can't, write about what they used to do. I've always believed people should wait until retirement age before embarking on memoirs. An unexpected coincidence of factors produced this book, however.

In 1984 my last surviving grandparent died aged 94; I entered my fortieth year; and I came under fierce attack from some quarters for my work in Maori history. At the same time I had to endure a lengthy convalescence. Unable to work on other projects I brooded, took notes of my brooding, and re-read old letters and diaries. Because of the events that preceded and accompanied my illness, much of the brooding was of a stock-taking kind. For more than a decade I had been writing about origins and connections in the lives of others. But who was I, who was my family, where did we come from and where did we belong? What did it mean to be Pakeha in New Zealand? It seemed an appropriate time to address myself to such questions.

In addition to recollection, I was helped by my earlier work: the journals I have kept intermittently since school days, interview notes made as a journalist and historical researcher, letters, and (in small part) material published elsewhere. Wherever I quote dialogue in what follows, I have relied on a contemporary record.

The result focuses on elements of personal and national identity. Much more has happened to me that I hope eventually to write about — from causing a whole street to be torn up when I was three (I had flushed a sack of lemons down the toilet and blocked 200 yards of sewerage pipe), to my unwilling participation in the last polio epidemic. But those events do not belong here. This is selective and ethnic autobiography, a book about belonging and not belonging.

A criticism by a Maori correspondent that I have 'used' people I know to make implied statements in this book about Maori-Pakeha issues distressed me. In a sense, of course, it is unavoidably true: an autobiographer can only draw on his own encounters and relationships. But the purpose in so doing is to construct a readable and honest narrative and to point up matters of significance to the wider New Zealand community. The balancing factors are that I admire and respect the people about whom I have written; and that one can only be true to the truth one has experienced, not to that experienced by anybody else. In the Maori-Pakeha context, this book is about Being Pakeha, not Being Maori. The latter is for someone else to write.

Michael King

Families, like trees, grow and develop with their surroundings. Seeds are blown by the wind and new trees are born elsewhere. Roots sink into the ground from which the new tree draws life. Children, like branches, stretch out. Families and trees have similar destinies.

Mirella Ricciardi, *African Saga*

Do you remember all that? Well . . . there are good aesthetic reasons why this should not be wiped from the record eternally. No one would put so much heart into things doomed to be forgotten and wasted. Or so much love.

Saul Bellow, *Humboldt's Gift*

INTRODUCTION

A View From the High Ground

FOR THOSE CONCERNED about questions of personal and national identity — about the evolution of cultural themes — the generation since World War Two has been the most interesting in New Zealand's history. For those actively involved in defining the issues, it has been an exciting and sometimes dangerous period in which to live. This book recounts what it felt like to grow up in Pakeha New Zealand in the 1940s and 1950s and then to encounter the Maori renaissance of the 1970s and 1980s. It is an experience which has already embraced thousands of New Zealanders, and which will ultimately be shared in some form by all of them as Maoridom waxes in influence and exerts pressure on the national life.

To be Pakeha in the 1940s and 1950s was to enjoy a way of life that changed beyond recognition in the succeeding decades. At the outset, for almost all of us, Britain was Home, the centre of an Empire of which our country was the most far-flung Dominion. The visit of the reigning monarch was one of the highlights of our primary school years. 'Girls were girls and men were men', in the words of the popular song, and each sex was allocated a set of pre-determined roles. Families were nuclear: mother and father (married), with three or four children. Inflation and demonstrations were things that happened abroad or in history. Criminals seemed a remote class, and neighbours were invariably of European descent and Christian.

Unless you were Maori, it was possible and forgivable in the forties to view New Zealand as a single-culture society. The country's major institutions were based on European models, the systems of government and law derived from Britain, the dominant values were post-industrial revolution, Western and Christian. Most New Zealanders accepted this package without question, and new immigrants, such as displaced Continental Europeans, were expected to conform to it. So were Maori when they moved out of their rural enclaves into the nation's towns.

Suspicion and hostility fell upon those who behaved differently or spoke any language other than English. New Zealand's xenophobia was intensified by the fact that the country lacked borders with any other.

Nobody could be said to be responsible for the social pattern: like all forceful cultures, it simply carried individuals and communities along like a river. The factors which might have disturbed its course lay upstream. The European colonists' crimes against the Maori — the wars of the 1840s and 1860s, the major land grabs, the setting up of institutions designed to limit or annihilate the practice of Polynesian values in New Zealand — most of these had occurred in the nineteenth century. In the twentieth, Maori and Pakeha had lived by and large in separate parts of the country, segregated geographically and socially. When Maori did come to the cities they tended to behave like Pakeha. They were only embraced by Pakeha New Zealand when they became All Blacks, and (in times of crisis) soldiers.

The pattern changed drastically after World War Two, however. A trickle of Maori migrants to the towns and cities in search of work and opportunities for material betterment became a stream, and the stream a torrent. For the first time in New Zealand since the nineteenth century, the country's two major cultural traditions collided and generated the white water of confusion and hostility. Nobody was prepared for this outcome. Maori experienced discrimination in accommodation, employment and hotel bars. They were confronted by a world that was aggressively European in orientation at the very time that they had severed bonds with many of the sources of their own culture — traditional marae, hapu and extended families. Many of them became marginal people, weakened both by what they had relinquished and by what confronted them. They were soon disproportionately represented in the ranks of convicted criminals, problem drinkers and (when the economy slumped) the unemployed. All this led civic planners and back-fence gossipers to eventually recognise and discuss what they regarded as 'the Maori problem'. It must have been a Maori one, they assumed, because it had not been apparent until the Maori became urban; it was they who had altered the status quo, not the Pakeha.

12

Most Maori who succeeded in Pakeha-defined New Zealand in the post-war years (and there were many) were prepared to diminish or submerge their Maoriness. They learnt to play Pakeha games according to Pakeha rules. They were congratulated for so doing by Pakeha compatriots who spoke with pride about the adaptability of 'our Maoris'. In popular idiom, it was a high compliment to speak of Maori who were good mixers among Pakeha as 'real white men'. The groundwork for such behaviour had been laid by the Maori parliamentarians, Maui Pomare ('there is no option but to become Pakeha') and Peter Buck. Those who remained Maori in the towns and cities, and risked opprobrium for doing so, followed other early models — Apirana Ngata and Tau Henare, for example, in whose company Pakeha political colleagues generally felt uncomfortable, believing those men had chips on their shoulders because they emphasised injustices and lack of Pakeha sensitivity to Maori feelings and needs.

But the saddest group — and the most vulnerable — were the children of Maori urban migrants who felt neither Maori nor Pakeha, and who were accepted as neither. It was members of this group who, in their insecurity, had most difficulty coping with family life, with city life, with a largely unsympathetic Pakeha bureaucracy; and it was this group that swelled the ranks of Maori school drop-outs, convicts, psychiatric patients and gangs. And — in another manifestation of discontent — it was other members of the same group who first led the fight to recover and revalidate Maori identity in New Zealand and to put down specifically Maori cultural roots in the Pakeha-oriented towns and cities. They did this especially by establishing supra-tribal Maori organisations and urban marae. They eventually carried the majority of Maori opinion with them to the point where, in the 1980s, a Maori leader could say: 'Now we are eyeballing Pakehas: we want our share of the national life and resources.'

By the mid-1980s it was again possible — as it had been in the eighteenth century — to be Maori anywhere in New Zealand and to be assertive about and proud of that identity. A genuine cultural renaissance was under way in the towns and in the countryside. People who had suppressed Maori backgrounds, inclinations and values, now expressed them forcefully. Parents who had been brought up to speak only English began to learn the language of their ancestors and to ensure that their pre-school children did so. In addition to the mushrooming of marae in the towns, those in rural areas were renovated and revived. Spokespersons for Maori interests began to force their way into the variety of bureaucracies that controlled New Zealand life, from the Auckland Regional Authority's planning committee to the New Zealand Historic Places Trust. There was, said Ranginui Walker, a revolution facing New Zealand in the 1980s. In any enterprise involving Maori, Maori demanded control. 'No longer are Maori leaders content to remain as silent partners in such matters,' wrote Sidney Moko Mead. 'They expect to participate directly in the negotiations and they want to speak for themselves. . . . [This] is new. It is also exciting for the Maori people because it is evidence of the return and the rise of mana Maori. . . .'

The return and rise of mana Maori had consequences for Pakeha as well as for Maori. For the first time since the mid-nineteenth century, it led to a widespread Pakeha awareness of Maori values and aspirations as being often separate and different from Pakeha ones. It impelled Pakeha to examine their consciences and their institutions to see if New Zealand was indeed, as many Maori alleged, a racist society. And it required adjustments in New Zealand life: a restructuring of institutions to accommodate Maori needs and values, and a preparedness to share decision making with people whose criteria were not Pakeha.

If the assertion of mana Maori was an accomplished fact by the late 1980s, the process of Pakeha adjustment to it was not. This latter process had barely begun. And it was proceeding at different rates in different areas of the national life. The guardians of the education system were among the first to begin to make changes; guardians of the law among the last to even consider them. Some individual Pakeha responded by learning the Maori language and trying to equip themselves with Maori views of New Zealand experience and knowledge of Maori protocol. Others withdrew into their professional and suburban enclaves and resisted efforts to change their personal lifestyle

14

or the national one; an outgoing Prime Minister said it was time to speak up for the superiority of British traditions in New Zealand — to recognise that Pakeha had contributed more to New Zealand life than Maori. It would be a long time before such divergent Pakeha responses would be reconciled. Meanwhile, cracks in the edifice of Pakeha racial and cultural superiority added to the momentum of the Maori cultural revival.

This book is one Pakeha's eyewitness account of the events which generated these issues. It is not an autobiography *per se*: but is necessarily autobiographical. In describing experiences common to most Pakeha New Zealanders, it tries to place these experiences in cultural and historical context. It is *not* a Pakeha view of Maori history; but it becomes a personal account of Pakeha-Maori interaction, because only at the points of such interaction can Maori things be defined as Maori and Pakeha as Pakeha; only in situations of contrast can contours be sought, light and shade become apparent, positives be defined against negatives.

I make no apology for use of the terms Maori and Pakeha. Some have argued that there is no 'Maori' culture in New Zealand, only an amalgam of New Zealand Polynesian tribal traditions. This was once so, in the eighteenth century; it is no longer so. In the twentieth century, without relinquishing tribal feeling, most Maori have come to accept their identity and destiny as one people. Others regard Pakeha as a pejorative expression and opt for European; I cannot agree that it makes sense to identify as European those whose physical and cultural origins are one, two, or even four or five generations removed from Europe. Nor can I accept that the terms 'black' and 'white' have place or meaning in the New Zealand context. There are few New Zealanders whose skin is black (and none of them Maori); and there are even fewer among the non-Maori population who are truly 'white'. Even more inappropriate are such related expressions as 'the white mind', which some commentators have begun to use to describe perceptions of non-Maori. Minds do not have colour, black or white. The use of such expressions oversimplifies reality and imports into New Zealand a rhetoric spawned in other countries to describe the clash of other cultures.

15

By contrast, the words Maori and Pakeha have meaning, relevance and appropriateness in the context of New Zealand life and history. Maori (from 'tangata maori' — ordinary people) denotes the descendants of the country's first Polynesian immigrants. Pakeha denotes non-Maori New Zealanders. The terms are indigenous to New Zealand, and usually neither is pejorative. Both offer a kind of shorthand to describe two broadly separate though not homogeneous traditions: that of New Zealand Polynesians, in which information tends still to be transmitted orally, values communally rather than individually based, and prestige measured by what one distributes rather than by what one accumulates; and the originally Western and European tradition which includes emphases on literacy, on individual rights, and on material acquisition. The categories, I emphasise, are broad and not mutually exclusive; there are many Pakeha whose values and lifestyle bear little relation to the Western stereotype, just as there are Maori who have relinquished or not encountered Maori traditions. But they do represent actual cultural options, two different forces in New Zealand by which people can choose to organise their lives.

Some New Zealanders of European descent object to the use of the word Pakeha, regarding it as a term of abuse, or as an unwelcome label laid upon them by a culture that is alien to them. These are the people who live in this country but who prefer to be called 'Europeans', 'Caucasians', 'Non-Maori' — or simply New Zealanders. Do they have a case?

First, there is the word Pakeha itself. We shall probably never know its original meaning or where and when it was first coined. Assemble a group of Maori kaumatua or language experts and ask them the origin of the expression and you get a variety of answers: it is derived from a word for flea; from a word for white clay; from pakepakeha, the fairy people with fair skins; or from the same word meaning outlandish; or it was a corruption of the expression that Maori allegedly heard most frequently from the first English-speaking sailors who socialised with them: 'Bugger Ya'.

What *can* be said with confidence is that — whatever its origin — the word Pakeha now means non-Maori, or refers to a person of predominantly European descent; or to the English language (korero Pakeha). It *can* be used as a pejorative expression, as can the word Maori in some contexts. But most often it is not. Most often it is simply a descriptive word applied to people and things 'in New Zealand that derive originally from outside New Zealand, especially from Europe; even more especially — because of the nature of our history — from the United Kingdom.

To me it is the obvious word to describe such things. 'New Zealand' is often too general a term, because — as I have indicated — there is no single coherent national culture which gives New Zealanders a shared vision of themselves and of the world. 'European' is inadequate, because many of those things and people we call Pakeha are several generations removed from Europe. 'Caucasian' is an inaccurate and racist term. And 'non-Maori' is a negative description or definition, indicating what something is *not* rather than what it *is*.

'Pakeha' on the other hand is an indigenous New Zealand expression that denotes things that belong to New Zealand via one major stream of its heritage, things that are not Polynesian. But it also denotes — for me — things that are no longer European. Things and people that *derive* from abroad but which, through the transformation of history and experience, through their proportions and combinations, are now unlike their sources and antecedents.

To give you some examples: the music of Bach and Beethoven is European, not Pakeha; the music of Douglas Lilburn and From Scratch is Pakeha, not European. The stories of Chekhov and Roald Dahl are European; those of Sargeson and Crump are Pakeha. The films *Amadeus* and *Diva* are European, *Smash Palace* and *Vigil* are Pakeha. *Paradise Postponed* is European; *The Fireraiser* is Pakeha. A field or meadow is a European concept; a paddock a Pakeha New Zealand one.

Let me stress this. To say that something is Pakeha in character is not to diminish its New Zealand-ness, as some people imply. It is to emphasise it. It is simply a more detailed, more finely focussed definition of something New Zealand. If I say that Mira Szaszy, Sonja Davies, Lani Tupu and Wally Hirsh are all New Zealanders, then I am telling the truth. But if I say that Mira

Szaszy is a Maori New Zealander, Sonja Davies a Pakeha New Zealander, Lani Tupu a Samoan New Zealander, and Wally Hirsh a Jewish New Zealander, then I am giving you information about those people that is more specific, more useful and more interesting than the initial description.

The next thing to consider is whether or not there is such a thing as Pakeha *culture* in New Zealand. By culture, of course, I don't refer simply to the arts, especially to the 'high arts', as some people do when they use the term. I refer to the basis of the relationship between the individual and society, the values and the rituals through which people perceive and feel their identity; and by which society accepts or rejects them — for culture, by its nature, is both inclusive and exclusive. It includes the arts, of course. But it also includes experience of history and the themes of history, it includes going to school, what is taught at school, going to church, playing sport or music of one's choice, membership of the RSA — and so on. It includes using language in a manner that is not identical to the manner in which that same language is used elsewhere.

In the sense that I have just employed the word, *of course* Pakeha New Zealand and Pakeha New Zealanders have a culture. It may not be coherent or tightly cohesive. Its ingredients may not be exclusive. But the combinations and proportions in which those ingredients come together are exclusive. This is emphasised by the manner in which Pakeha New Zealanders have too often closed ranks against people from other races and cultures, from Horis to Chows, to Poms, to use the language of exclusion. And it is less offensively illustrated by the experience of New Zealanders *outside* New Zealand.

More and more New Zealanders are travelling and have travelled. That process turns a minority of them into expatriates, blurring their sense of identity. The majority, however, see with the perspective of distance contours in New Zealand life — especially Pakeha New Zealand life — that are not so visibly apparent at home.

And there is a further point. While Maori are Maori and Pakeha are Pakeha, each has been influenced by the other and had his or her culture shaped by the other. One essential ingredient of

18

Pakeha-ness, as far as I am concerned, is contact with and being affected by Maori things: Maori concepts, Maori values and Maori language. As I note in this book, the Maori presence in New Zealand has given the land on which we live an historical echo, a resonance it would entirely lack had the Maori not come here first, lived here first and named things first. When I go to a new place, or visit a familiar one, I instinctively look first for the shapes on the land and the middens that indicate where the first inhabitants of that place chose to make their home and gather food. I am drawn to and comforted by the psychic residue of their presence.

My brush with these things doesn't make me Maori. But they are part of the experience that makes me Pakeha, experience I could not have gained in any other part of the world. Pakeha-ness includes for a growing number of people, even those who are affected by being negative about it, some experience of Maori history, values and views of life.

For many Pakeha people, including myself, the inclination and indeed the need to define Pakeha-ness has been given momentum by the current Maori cultural renaissance. The confidence with which many Maori have been able to say who they are and where they come from has led many Pakeha to ask precisely the same questions about themselves and to join (for example) local branches of the New Zealand Genealogical Society in growing numbers.

For me, the exploration of roots has led to a deeper understanding of my genetic and cultural inheritance; and — perhaps paradoxically — to a deeper feeling of sympathy for and identification with the tangata whenua of New Zealand in their post-colonial travail.

Three of my grandparents were Celts — two Irish and one Scot. Great-grandparents on both sides of the family had spoken Gaelic. That language, however, was eventually obliterated for us by the cultural imperialism of the English in what they chose to call the United Kingdom. The tribalism of which my family had been a part was shredded by the armies of Montrose in Scotland and Cromwell in Ireland. The final violence to the Celtic pattern of my ancestors' lives was accomplished by the combination of rural famine with the industrial revolution, which uprooted my antecedents from the villages and clan territories where they had lived for centuries, deposited them in the slums of industrial cities, and finally drove them to seek new lives and fresh opportunities in New Zealand. This process is not unlike that to which the Maori have been subject for the past 150 years.

This book does not set out to accuse or to allocate blame. It is a view from the high ground of the 1980s. Things apparent to us now were not visible in the 1940s and 1950s, even less so in the 1920s and 1930s; people cannot be blamed for what they did not know. They can, perhaps, be blamed for what they don't know today, if their ignorance of the nature and history of New Zealand society is wilful and results in a perpetuation of inequalities and injustice. The key to redressing imbalances and reconciling past misunderstandings is knowledge; and the first step towards knowledge is self-knowledge. I begin, therefore, with an account of Pakeha origins. I end with what I trust will be ground for a closer understanding between Maori and Pakeha.

No reira, kia ora tatou. Kia hora te marino, kia whaka papa pounamu te moana, kia tere te karohirohi. May calm be widespread, may the sea lie smooth as greenstone, may the warmth of summer fall upon us all.

CHAPTER ONE

Immigrants

IN A COUNTRY inhabited for a mere one thousand years, everybody is an immigrant or a descendant of immigrants. Such descendants are heirs to history and traditions carried from their country of origin in addition to those generated in their country of birth. In the case of my own family, three out of four grandparents were of Celtic descent: two Irish and one Scot. The fourth was English, Northumbrian. I was fortunate to know the three who made the journey half-way round the world to New Zealand in the second decade of the twentieth century.

The one I didn't know, my father's father, was an Irish-Glaswegian descended from refugees from the potato famines. Both his parents had been born in Ireland. He himself was a handsome man, a spirits salesman, described by my grandmother as an extrovert. His antecedents were all Irish and Catholic: Gleesons, Cassidys, Lynches and others. When the Great War broke out he and his five brothers volunteered immediately for service in Kitchener's army, my grandfather joining the First Battalion of Gordon Highlanders. He was killed in France less than a year into the fighting, at the Battle of Loos in September 1915. He was 27, my father 11 months old. This left my Scottish grandmother a widow with two children in the Gorbals. But the war which had brought this disaster also brought an escape.

My grandmother was rescued from potential poverty in Glasgow by a New Zealand soldier born in Hokitika. He too had volunteered at the outbreak of war, joining the First Otago Infantry Regiment. He survived the Gallipoli campaign and then fought in France, where he was wounded at Armentieres and Citernes. After being in hospital for the second time he was posted to the reserves in England. On leave in Glasgow he met my grandmother and persuaded her to marry him before he was due to leave Britain in 1919. He brought her out to New Zealand with her two children on the SS *Ionic*, and they lived initially at Otahuhu in Auckland. Widowed a second time, my grandmother was left to bring up her children in an unfamiliar country, in circumstances that became so harsh as the Depression deepened that neither she nor my father could bring themselves to talk about them in subsequent years.

Deprived of an Irish grandfather on that side of the family, we had our tough Scottish Presbyterian grandmother. Gran was born Martha Lyon in 1889. Her other ancestors were Lamonts, Walkers, Kerrs, Cunninghams and Toners. Her first home was in St Clair Street, St George's Cross, a two-roomed apartment in a sandstone building that housed her parents, two brothers and three sisters. Her mother died when she was five, and she did not get on with either her father or her stepmother. Her only happy memories of childhood were of the new clothes that arrived each Christmas from her dead mother's relatives, the Walkers; and — when she was nine — seeing Queen Victoria pulled through the centre of Glasgow in a carriage. Occasionally, she spent holidays with her mother's brother at Dunoon on the coast of the Firth of Clyde. Otherwise her recollections of Scotland were uniformly grim. She left school to work in Deacon's Tobacconists when she was twelve. Later, she was a clippie on the Glasgow trams. She married at eighteen to escape her father's unhappy home.

Grandmother King was a strong and brave woman. But to her the past was something to defeat and transcend. She survived by working hard, and by disregarding the series of misfortunes life dealt her. She was unsentimental about Scotland and about the Highland background of her ancestors, who had come to Glasgow to seek work in the city's growing industries after the forcible breaking up of the clans by Cromwell and Montrose. Her father, Hugh Lyon, had been a slater, as had his father and grandfather before him. All this she told me once and refused to repeat. 'Why do you want to know? It's past. Over. We came here to forget all that.'

She brought up my father and my aunt in this manner, and they inherited her determination, her sternness, and her unwillingness to remember. By the time her grandchildren knew her she was a Scot in accent only (although that accent grew stronger with age). She didn't want to talk about the old country;

she told few stories about her family or her past, other than her glimpse of Queen Victoria in 1898. Her chief skills seemed to me (because I was the most persistent) ones of diversion and concealment. 'How old are you, Gran?' 'As old as my tongue and a little bit older than my teeth.'

Yet even while she shut out conscious recollection, it was her Scottishness that had long since determined her character — especially her dourness, her thrift, and her conviction that you expressed loyalty and love for your family by *doing* things, not by talking about those virtues. You provided your dependents with the necessities of life by working hard, and you did unto others as you would have them do unto you. You did not make a fuss about such matters nor seek praise for them.

If she wasn't a reminiscing grandmother, she compensated by being an active one. She knitted prodigiously for us: everything from cardigans to slippers. With fertile hands she grew vegetables, fruit and flowers from seeds she prepared herself. Every corner of her sandy section at Miramar bloomed with carnations, jonquils, daffodils and Christmas lilies. She told us which flowers brought good luck inside the house (carnations) and which brought bad (arum lilies, like peacock feathers). She scrubbed her back and front doorsteps daily and we always had to step *over*, not on them. Her front room, perpetually darkened by curtains and old photographs, was reserved for the most serious occasions, such as funerals. When we visited or stayed with her we lived in the kitchen, where she fed a wood-fire stove. On such visits she made crisp oatmeal biscuits and hid sweets for us to find in the garden. She cured her grandchildren's warts by rubbing steak on them and burying it under a full moon. All these habits, I realised later, were those of a survivor. And Gran survived. She lived on her own until she was over 90. She resisted innovation: she never wanted a refrigerator and was only persuaded to take the telephone late in life. When she died it was in her 95th year. Our sense of loss was heightened by the fact that she had been so actively with us for so long.

The sense of tradition, though, of belonging to a culture and a clan, came overwhelmingly from the other side of the family.

My mother's parents had been born in Hexham-on-the-Tyne in the north of England. But there too was an Irish strain, and it dominated their lives. My great-grandfather, Peter Tierney, came to Northumberland from Clew Bay in County Mayo in 1857, and later married Isabella Lafferty in Hexham. With this background, Ireland was as much home to my grandmother as Tyneside — more so, in fact, because it was the source of the family's history and religion. Asked her identity, Nellie Tierney, later Smith, always said Irish. The feeling was intensified by her father's tales of Mayo and by the intensely Irish nature of Catholicism in Hexham. The nuns who spoiled her at St Mary's School did so because they were Irish and regarded her as a fellow exile in a foreign land; they read her their letters from 'home'. The priest who ministered to them and performed her marriage, Father Patrick Mackay, was also Irish. At home the family of eight children sang together like angels for entertainment, and nearly always Irish songs that reflected the propensity of the Irish in Ireland to weep for its troubles; and those away from the 'dear ould Sod' to weep for their exile:

It shines thro' the bog, thro' the brake, thro' the mire land,
And he called it the dear little Shamrock of Ireland,
The dear little Shamrock, the sweet little Shamrock,
  the dear little, sweet little Shamrock of Ireland.

Grandmother Smith still sang these songs throughout my childhood, praising both places she loved, Ireland and Hexham, in a voice that trembled with nostalgia and loss:

Oh bonny Tyneside, I see thee once more
After long years of exile away from thy shore.
Through far foreign countries, a rambler I be,
And much have I suffered, and much have I seen.
Though I've been in lands where a brighter sun shone,
Yet I ne'er saw a country as fair as my own.
And I never have seen, in my wanderings wide,
A place I like better than bonny Tyneside.

Another source of that vibrato I heard so often could have been ambivalence. For while she celebrated Hexham as the most beautiful spot on earth, she did so more as an outpost of Ireland than as part of England. The English, she reminded us, had been the cause of more suffering in Ireland than in any of their colonies elsewhere. They had tried to stamp out Celtic culture, the Gaelic tongue and the Faith. Oliver Cromwell headed her list of history's villains. And when she sang 'The Mountains of Mourne', she knew a verse which had been banned in her early years in New Zealand:

> I've seen England's King from the top of a bus
> I never knew him, though he means to know us.

These Irish-English grandparents came to New Zealand separately after their marriage in 1910: Oliver Smith to find a job and a house, Nellie to join him a year later when he was settled in Wellington. After giving up painting and paper-hanging because of lead poisoning, my grandfather became assistant-stationmaster at Porirua and my mother and her brother and sister grew up there in a house on the large Mungavin Farm. Unlike my father's family, they relinquished none of their past. They had emigrated to better themselves, not to forget. They kept in touch by letter with the seemingly vast clan whose first generation — my grandmother's brothers and sisters — diminished steadily throughout my childhood as death carried them away. Both grandparents were planning a return journey to Hexham and Newcastle when my grandfather died in January 1953.

I knew him only slightly. Grandfather Smith was the son of a regular soldier in the British Army, who had served in India and who late in life became a shoemaker in Hexham. His mother was a Burnup, an old Hexham family. When I stayed with them, in Ngaio, Grandad was usually at work in town, or in the vegetable garden at the back of the cottage at weekends. Photographs show him looking as old in his forties as I remember him at sixty-five. He spoke with what I later recognised as a Tyneside accent that rendered one-syllable words as two: 'gey-et' for gate, 'wr-rick' for work. And he retained his northern dialect: 'hinny' as a term of endearment, 'canny' as a compliment, 'our Michael' to distinguish members of the family from outsiders. Thrown together in the evenings in front of a coal fire, while my grandmother made steak and kidney pie, scones ('butter biscuits') or rice puddings, we played dominoes as he had done at Home, knocking when we couldn't put one down. I was seven when he died and I inherited his pocket watch, his pen knife and his dominoes.

Grandmother, however, née Tierney, was the source of family lore, like the seannacae she knew about from her father's childhood in County Mayo. She was the teller of stories, the singer of songs, the keeper of the family album. She told us all — her children, her grandchildren, her great-grandchildren — who we were and where we came from. Then, having told us, she kept reminding us. She had been a great beauty. I have a photograph of her taken at the Meeting of the Waters on the Tyne just before she left Hexham in 1911. She wears a lace blouse and long skirt. One elbow rests with nonchalance on a willow branch, the other hand encloses a cluster of leaves. Behind her the Tyne runs smooth and clear over well-worn stones. Both the place and the face are redolent of peace.

Her father, Peter Tierney, had died three years before the picture was taken. She told us he had come to Hexham to work for the Kirsopp and Leadbitter families, local Catholic gentry who owned estates in England and Ireland. In Mayo he had looked after their horses. In Hexham, at the Spital, he became their chief gardener. He married Isabella Lafferty after the death of his first wife in 1873. My grandmother was one of five children from the new union. Her father continued to work at the Spital, and Lady Katherine Bates, the Leadbitter's only child who inherited the estate, became my grandmother's godmother (they were a recusant family; Lady Bates' father had been High Sheriff of Northumberland and her husband, Sir Charles Loftus Bates, commanded a Northumberland regiment). The Tierneys lived at Chareway Cottage, one of the Spital estate houses, which in the seventeenth and eighteenth centuries had been Hexham's house of correction or prison. The larger part of the home had been the warder's quarters.

In addition to her Irish history — which always stressed the persistence of Catholicism in the face of Protestant persecution

— my grandmother was soaked in Hexham's past. The town was old and had a lengthy reputation for independence, one of the factors that made it a refuge for Catholic families after the Reformation. The Romans had settled close by at Corbridge and Hadrian's Wall was only a few miles to the north. Hexham flourished in Saxon times, initially as a centre for Celtic Christianity ('God's people have worshipped here since 674 A.D.' proclaims a notice in Hexham Abbey). After the restoration of Latin authority, it was the seat of the great bishops Wilfred and Acca, who built there what was described as the finest church north of the Alps. For two centuries it became virtually independent of the rest of the English Church and its clergy married and bequeathed Church property to their heirs. It was sacked by the Danes and the Scots and survived. It was a starting point for the Pilgrimage of Grace, the uprising that resisted Henry VIII's Dissolution of the monasteries. It was the home of the Earl of Derwentwater, one of the leaders of the Jacobite Revolt of 1715. And it was the scene of the Hexham Riot against militia recruiting in 1761.

Although the great abbey that still towers over the town belonged to the Church of England in my grandmother's youth, it had been Catholic for four centuries prior to the Dissolution, and the district's subsequent history made Catholic families such as the Leadbitters, the Gibsons, the Bates, and my grandmother's feel more secure there than they would have done elsewhere in England. The other monument my grandmother spoke of frequently, because it contained the tombs of St Cuthbert and the Venerable Bede, was Durham Cathedral, twenty-five miles to the south-east. She once described it to me in detail: three great Norman towers rising off the peninsula formed by the river Wear, the older Galilee Chapel, the tombs of the saints. 'It must have been wonderful to see all those things,' I said to her. 'Eee, we never went inside,' she said. 'It's in Protestant hands now.' Right till the time she died in 1971, she spoke of the Reformation as a setback soon to be rectified.

There were other places in Hexham sacred in family lore, shrines we could all describe without having seen them as a result of my grandmother's stories: Tyne Green, where her brothers and sisters and cousins had played; the Sele, the park where they walked and courted; the Meeting of the Waters where they picnicked; Swallowship, a beech forest glade with bluebells underfoot, to which they walked on Sundays; the Spital, the manor house surrounded by large gardens kept by my great-grandfather. Eventually I was to see them all in a pilgrimage 'Home'. In childhood I saw them in my imagination and in her photographs. Indeed, so fondly did my grandmother describe them, and with such nostalgia, we often wondered why she and my grandfather emigrated.*

It was, of course, to improve material prospects, for themselves and their children. Most of the family who remained in England never quite succeeded in breaking out of the twin shackles of class and lack of opportunity. Her brother Teddy — who developed trench feet in World War One and kept returning to Lourdes in search of a cure — became a postman. George spent his life in coal mines, and Jim (how we loved to hear about him) played the harmonium on market days, drank, and at one time was a sheep stealer, hanging carcasses in the old cells in the house of correction. Uncle Jim was the black sheep that every family was supposed to have; but we also knew that, though Teddy was reputed to be the saint, Jim was the one who was with each of his parents when they died, and he stayed with his mother at Chareway Cottage long after the rest had departed. The only other members of the family who could have been said to have led adventurous lives were Lizzie, who went to America and finished up as cook for the Morrow family, parents-in-law of Charles Lindbergh, in Michigan; and Kitty (named after Lady Bates) who married a Scottish policeman.

Years later, in 1976, I went to Hexham. The stone cottage had been three-quarters demolished to make room for buses to turn into a new terminus. The fragment that remained contained

---

*Much of the nostalgia for the places she knew and loved was evoked in a long poem her brother Teddy wrote in the 1920s. It ended:

Now as I've travelled o'er with you,   With dear old Hexham-on-the-Tyne,
This place I love so dear,   So wonderful and grand,
I think that you'll agree with me   And that no spot was better named
No other can compare   The Heart of all England.

the old cells my grandmother had described, with narrow windows and jagged bars like teeth. A Newcastle cousin and I picked the lock on the heavy remaining door so that we could get in to test the ambience of the old family home (the first time, his father said, he had heard of anyone trying to break *into* prison). There were no ghosts. It was cold, dark, and ankle deep in dead pigeons.

The lane along which my great-grandfather had walked to and from the Spital, and which the Bates family used when they drove to Mass in a brougham, was still there. But it was sealed in asphalt and lined with terraced houses. As we stood there mourning the mutilation of Chareway Cottage, an old woman in tortoiseshell glasses hobbled up to us and said, 'It was a pretty house. Did ye never see it?' I hadn't, of course, except the fragments that appeared in family photographs. The woman was from one of the terrace houses but had lived in the lane all her life. I told her my grandmother's name. No, she hadn't known her, she'd gone to New Zealand too early. But she remembered Granny Tierney, the matriarch, who had died there in 1924. And she had been well acquainted with Uncle Teddy and Uncle Jim. 'Eee,' she said, 'the Tierney boys. They were such canny lads.' The Geordie 'canny' is far more warm and approving than the same Scottish word. 'Aye,' she said, walking away and still remembering, 'such canny lads.'

My mother was born in Wellington, just before the family shifted to Porirua in 1916. Her stories — and she was as communicative with us as her own mother had been — took up themes where my grandmother's left off. If my grandmother had learnt to be Irish in England, my mother achieved the same identity in New Zealand in the years following the First World War. In addition to family (an older brother and sister), the first people she knew were the O'Malleys — six Irish sisters who had sworn on their parents' death beds that they would stay with one another rather than marry. And they did, living first in a large house in Tinakori Road and later (in my childhood) in Northland, Wellington. They were my grandparents' closest friends and they kept the flame of Irish awareness strong in the family, especially during 'the Troubles' in Ireland between 1916 and 1921. In spite of ruthless persecution, the O'Malleys stressed, Ireland and the Irish had never lost their dream of independence; and when the Saorstat Eireann was declared in December 1921, they had succeeded in establishing the only Celtic state in the modern world. The first adult discussions my mother remembered were of this issue, and of Sinn Fein heroes and Black and Tan villains.

Irish questions were defined more sharply in Porirua after the formation in Wellington of a strong branch of the Protestant Political Association.* Local members were quick to accuse the Irish of disloyalty to King and Empire (in Ireland and New Zealand), and tended to make Catholics scapegoats for anything that went wrong in the community, from floods to accidental fires. In the midst of the Troubles, my mother's sister Mona came home from school with instructions to write a short essay on the Union Jack for homework. 'Right,' said my grandmother. 'I'll tell you what to put.' And she sang while my aunt copied:

Red is the colour of the blood we've shed
In making England's name.
White as the snow have our motives been
In spreading England's fame.
Blue is the colour of our naval lads,
The finest that the world has ever seen.
And if you want another colour to compare with all the rest,
Old Ireland sends its little bit of green.

The family waited to hear the result of this mild assertion of Irishness. The headmaster, a PPA stalwart, read the essays himself to the assembled school. He came to my aunt's and recited it with obvious approval until he reached the last two lines. Then he stopped, frowned, put it at the bottom of the pile and never finished it.

At home, the family sang for evening and weekend entertainment, just as my grandmother's had done in Hexham. There were English regulars, especially 'The Blaydon Races' and 'The Miner's Dream of Home' ('I saw the old homestead and

---

*Founded in Auckland in 1917 by the Rev. Howard Elliott, a former Baptist minister, to fight 'rum, Romanism and rebellion'.

faces I love/I saw England's valleys and dells/I listened with joy as I did when a boy/To the sound of the old village bells.') But, as for the previous generation, the favourites were Irish: 'The Rose of Tralee', 'Danny Boy', 'A Little Bit of Heaven', 'The Wearin' of the Green', 'Believe Me If All Those Endearing Young Charms'. Every 17 March, the whole family, green, yellow and white ribbons flying, took the train into town to join the O'Malleys for the St Patrick's Day celebrations organised by the Wellington Irish Society: Mass in the morning at the Basilica; the parade through town mounted by the society and the Catholic schools, with floats featuring green-caped colleens singing and dancing jigs; a gymnastic display at Newtown Park to tunes such as 'Oft' in the Stilly Night'; and a concert in the evening at the Town Hall.

It was the O'Malley sisters too who helped prepare my mother for end-of-year school concerts in the Porirua Hall. This was the major annual event in the village, attended by the whole community. My mother had confidence and a sweet voice, and nothing would do but that she should sing Irish songs. On the most memorable occasion, when she was to do 'The Dear Little Shamrock', Annie O'Malley helped my grandmother prepare a costume. Little Nellie Smith wore green satin shoes, stockings dyed green and a green sateen frock. Then she was wired up with three huge paper leaves, also green: one fitted behind the top of the head, and one on each arm. Whenever the words 'from one leaf shall branch like the shamrock of Ireland' recurred, my mother raised both arms and became a shamrock. Protestant Political Association notwithstanding, she drew encore after encore. 'Everybody accepted us as Irish and there were times when they did so kindly.'

Because of the proximity of Takapuwahia Pa, Porirua School had a large Maori enrolment. Generally, the two communities — Maori and Pakeha — remained separate, but on friendly terms. There was complete integration only at school itself — in class, in the playground and in sport. My mother was taught five stones (later knuckle bones), string games and poi by Maori girlfriends. She also remembered concert items which would have embarrassed a later generation but caused hilarity among Maori

31

and Pakeha pupils at the time. One was the performance of 'Ten Little Nigger Boys', 'the Pakeha boys wearing charcoal, the Maori boys as is'; another was Manawa Pohio reciting:

God made the niggers
He made them in the night.
He made them in a hurry
And forgot to paint them white.

Integration finished with the school day. At the gates Pakeha students turned right for Porirua proper, Maori turned left and headed back to the pa. There were relationships that cut across this de facto segregation, however. My grandmother was especially close to the Wineera family. Te Okoro (Jack) Wineera, father of my mother's school friend Stan, had married in London before being killed in World War One. His widow Gertrude came to New Zealand after the war and married her brother-in-law. Gertrude, starved of English news, formed an attachment to my grandmother, who in turn formed an even closer friendship with old Mrs Haana Wineera, Jack's mother, and visited her regularly at the pa for cups of tea. Both my grandparents went there for weddings.

For the Irish in Porirua, the greatest source of their culture was — as it had been for the previous generation — the Church. The village was part of first the Lower Hutt and then the Johnsonville Catholic parishes. The parish priests, Dean John Lane and later Father Michael Griffin, were Irish. The curate appointed to Porirua, Father James Henley, had Irish parents. The parish priests were as loyal to their country of origin as to their Church: indeed, they scarcely differentiated between the two. They were as much for de Valera as they were for Christ and they gravitated most strongly towards their fellow-Irish parishioners. They were also chauvinistic about the culture of Ireland — proud of the early independence of the Celtic Church; proud of the learning kept alive in Irish monasteries in the Middle Ages; proud of the missionaries who had carried Celtic Christianity to England, Scotland, Brittany, the German states, the Ukraine, and even Southern Italy; and proud of recent Irish history that had sent the sons and daughters of the Isle of Saints around the world, with nuns and priests in their wake, to light the candle of faith in Protestant or heathen lands.

Church activities also dominated the family's social life. There was Mass every Sunday. Confession was held in the church once a month, during which my grandmother and her friend Mrs Sloane would swap hats so as to confuse the priest in his darkened cubicle (to whose advantage, the family never knew). There were weekend parish picnics, usually to Plimmerton Beach on the special excursion train (2s 6d return). Here, each family ate its own food together but joined other parishioners for swimming in modest costumes, egg and spoon races, sack races, three-legged races, and treasure hunts, in which practically the whole beach was dug over in search of buried coins. Religion also brought more serious obligations. Once a year my grandmother and Mrs Sloane walked miles to a remote farm to visit what was ominously referred to as 'a lapsed Catholic' (and an Irishman at that). The object was to keep the potentially damned man in touch with the Church, and to collect a donation for parish activities. The husbands and children, who always accompanied the women on this expedition, were never allowed to set foot inside the offender's gate. They waited at a distance and played and picnicked.

A generation later, my brother and sisters and I were heirs to the Irish Catholic tradition. It was as natural a part of our lives as it had been in my mother's and grandmother's. The priests we listened to each Sunday and Holy Day of Obligation had Irish accents and Irish names: O'Connor, Clancy and McGrath. At the age of five, I was enrolled at the Brigidine Convent in Ngaio. There too the nuns were first or second generation Irish. The Irish brogue of my first teacher sounded alternately beautiful and threatening as she told cautionary tales about what happened to those who kept the Faith and those who lost it. The saints we learnt about were Irish: Bridget, Brendan, Colomban, Kilian, Patrick himself (though born, of course, in England) and even De Valera, sometimes spoken of in the same breath. We heard stories about the frightful deaths of English monarchs who had persecuted Catholics and the Irish. We were told that the souls in purgatory would haunt us if we didn't pray for their delivery. The nuns said that one of the signs of the end of the world would be the sinking of Ireland under the sea, to deliver it from the temptations of the Anti-Christ. And we were warned of the conspiracies of Masons and asked if our fathers were Hibernians. The school roll was by no means made up entirely of Irish descendants. But there was a sense of community, a strong degree of homogeneity. We were all European, Catholic and taught by Irish nuns. We saw nothing incongruous about singing lustily on 17 March:

Hail Glorious St Patrick, dear saint of our isle.
On us thy poor children
Bestow a sweet smile.
And now thou art high in thy mansions above,
On Erin's green valleys look down in thy love.

Spiritually and socially, our lives were a continuation of that which my mother's parents had lived in Hexham, my paternal grandfather's family in Glasgow, and my mother in Porirua. We were all descendants of the Irish diaspora — a people scattered by invasion, plunderings, murder, religious conflict, rebellions and famine; but a people secure in their history and identity, both of which were strengthened by family lore and a continued flow of priests and nuns out of Mother Ireland.

We were New Zealanders, but Irish New Zealanders. Although statistics may have lumped us among the almost ninety percent of the population descended from the European migration to New Zealand, we did not feel like members of a majority. Nor did we feel part of a wider group and culture that had displaced an indigenous people and shredded the formerly seamless robe of their culture. Because we — my siblings and myself — saw no Maori at this time, we had no concept of race; simply of Irish and Scots versus the rest. We did not encounter other ingredients in New Zealand life until we left the suburbs of Wellington. By that time, I was six years old.

CHAPTER TWO
A New Zealand Family

IN EVERY SENSE, my mother and father had lived far more exposed
lives than that which they later constructed around their children.
For my father, the distance from the Gorbals to Wellington had
been more than a question of geography: it involved a journey
through occupations and class; from marginal living to relative
security. Both parents had encountered a wider diversity of people
than we did in childhood and adolescence. Both had at times
lived close to Maori communities and had Maori friends — my
mother at Porirua, my father at Te Kumi near Wairoa and at
Takapuwahia in the days when he used to tramp from the pa
over Colonial Knob to Kaumanga, south of Titahi Bay.

By 1933 they both lived in Wellington, and they met after
my father saw and admired her from a tram in Willis Street.
Lewis King was then nineteen and working for Charles Haines
Advertising. Nellie Smith was seventeen and still a pupil at
Wellington Girls' College. It was the way she carried herself
and wore her uniform and medals that caught my father's
attention. Accustomed to creating opportunities (he had left
school at thirteen to make his way in the world) he discovered
through a mutual friend that she played table tennis for a Ngaio
club. He was a sub-lieutenant in the Royal Naval Volunteer
Reserve, which also had a team. It was a simple matter to arrange
for the RNVR to challenge Ngaio to a tournament. When the
visiting team arrived at RNVR headquarters in Hinemoa Street,
he appropriated Nellie Smith on the pretext of showing her
the building and its equipment. My mother, flattered, scarcely
knew what was happening. Thus began a five-year courtship.

Their activity, of course, was circumscribed by the conventions
of the time. They were allowed to go picnicking in my father's
bullet-nosed Morris Cowley, provided a chaperone went too. They
enjoyed long Sunday hikes after my mother had already walked
from Ngaio to Wadestown and back for early Mass. Most of
their destinations (Pencarrow Light, Butterfly Creek, Kaitoke

Forks) my father knew already from his excursions with the Hutt Valley Tramping Club. On Sunday evenings, he — who was not musical — had to endure recitals in the Smith family parlour. My aunt and uncle, who were then receiving singing lessons from the distinguished operatic bass Signor Lucian Caeseroni, performed 'Bird Songs at Eventide' in duet. Then Bernie would sing 'Your Tiny Hand is Frozen' solo, Mona 'You Are My Heart's Delight', and Nellie, with conviction, 'The Curse of an Aching Heart'.

Their own aches were relieved in 1939, when they were able to marry. Lewis was by this time an accounts executive in the fledgling New Zealand advertising industry. He was also a lieutenant in the RNVR, in which he had learned naval discipline, seamanship, navigation and how to use weapons. Two major events marked their first year together. The birth of their first child, my sister Louise; and, earlier, New Zealand's declaration of war on Germany. With hundreds of thousands of others, they listened to the broadcast in which an ailing Prime Minister Savage voiced his Government's stand in words that became as familiar to New Zealanders as parts of Churchill's speeches later in the war:

> Both with gratitude for the past and with confidence in the future, we arrange ourselves without fear beside Britain. Where she goes, we go, where she stands, we stand. . . . We march forward with a union of hearts and wills to a common destiny.

The Second World War (always to us *the* war) was the dominant event for my parents' generation. For the participants, it represented an escape from a neighbourhood to an international event; for most it was the one great epic in their lives. Success or failure in it followed them long afterwards, for those lucky enough to return did so among men they would know for the rest of their lives. For the next generation, too, the war was pivotal. So many events would be marked with pre- or postwar labels, and the values emphasised in our childhood were those that had evolved as a result of the austerities, social disruptions and emotional deprivation of war.

All that, however, lay in the future. In 1939 neither the consequences nor even the outcome of the international crisis were apparent. The men and women who chose their response did so blindly. Whatever reservations some New Zealanders had (and there were many in the New Zealand-Irish community, including the Prime Minister himself, who had fears about the brutalising effects of war), my father had none. His RNVR training had been undertaken in the belief that the fascist menace in Europe would lead to conflict. His own father had been killed fighting Germans in 1915; he was prepared to risk the same outcome twenty-five years later. Britain was threatened and hence the Commonwealth. He saw it as *dulce et decorum* that he should defend from aggression the land of his birth and the country of his adoption.

The majority of New Zealanders — from Cabinet to men and women in the street — shared this view. It was perhaps the last war in which the issues seemed to be clear, the cause just. Ethnic differences — between Maori and Pakeha, between Irish and English, between (even) German and British New Zealanders — were submerged as men volunteered for war service. It was typical of the country's unanimity that two of the highest-ranking officers should have the names Freyberg and Kippenberger; and that the 28th (Maori) Battalion should win a reputation as the most vigorous fighting unit. The smell of khaki was in the streets again and, as my mother noted, 'we all thought the boys looked marvellous in uniform'. Jingoism was abroad, as it always used to be in countries that did not suffer invasion-jingoism that anaesthetised separation and loss and hid what was to come.

In May 1940, my father sailed for Britain with the First Naval Draft and the Second Echelon of the New Zealand Army, which included the Maori Battalion,* on the converted luxury liner *Aquitania*. He returned thus to the land he had left as a five-year-old. For the next six years my mother was, like thousands

*As a result of this voyage he formed lifelong friendships with Bill Ngata, son of Sir Apirana; Wiremu Herewini, later Director of Maori Welfare; and Charles Bennett, knighted in 1975 after his term as President of the New Zealand Labour Party.

of New Zealand women, a solo parent with a child that did not know its father. That father compensated for absence as best he could with a continuous flow of letters and photographs datelined 'somewhere at sea', according to the rules of wartime censorship. In fact he was sailing on destroyer escorts with East Coast, Atlantic, English Channel, Russian and Mediterranean convoys. In 1940 and 1941 he was with HMS *Weston* and *Berkeley* (the latter was scuttled during the Dieppe landings).

From August 1941 to March 1943 he sailed on HMS *Onslow*, taking part in fifteen convoys to and from Russia and the epic June 1942 convoy to Malta. He covered American landings for the North Africa campaign and took part in two Combined Operation raids on Norway. The first was an assault on the Lofoten Islands; the second a raid on Vaagso Island in the Norwegian fiords which destroyed fish factories, oil tanks and 16,000 tons of shipping, and resulted in the capture of a large number of German servicemen.

Like most New Zealanders, my father was reticent about the war, especially talking to those who had not shared the experience. And he was never guilty of saying anything that could have sounded boastful. But there is no doubt that he had what was called 'a good war': he survived, the navy became a second home, and he discovered in its training and its long traditions (he went twice to the gunnery school in Portsmouth, for example) a substitute for the secondary and tertiary education which the Depression and his family circumstances had denied him. It made him the equal of men with whom he would not otherwise have *felt* equal, many of them with vastly different class and educational backgrounds. On top of this, he was respected, liked and decorated. The extent of his success comes to light in war histories, illuminated by the objectivity of other people's observation. In *73 North, The Battle of the Barent's Sea*, for example, Dudley Pope writes:

Onslow's First Lieutenant . . . was Lt Lewis King, a New Zealander, a man small of stature, humble of his capabilities but very much liked by everyone. The crew would do anything for him — a cause for perpetual astonishment so far as King was concerned. He bore the nickname of all first lieutenants, 'Number One'.

He was awarded a DSC for his part in the Barent's Sea Battle, which took place as *Onslow* was escorting a convoy to North Russia. The ship was hit three times by eight-inch shells from the German heavy cruiser *Admiral Hipper*, resulting in heavy loss of life and the outbreak of dangerous fires. The official history of the Royal New Zealand Navy notes:

> Although Lieutenant King . . . had been first lieutenant in the leader for one month only, he exercised complete control when the ship was seriously damaged. . . . A fire raged as a result of two hits forward; the forward fire and repair party had been wiped out; the ship had to remain at action stations and it suffered a 20 per cent loss in personnel through casualties. Despite these severe handicaps, by personal demonstration he showed his untrained assistants exactly what he required and the serious fires were under control in remarkably short time. Nearly the whole forepart of the ship was on fire at one time or another; nevertheless after four hours he was able to report to the bridge that all fires were extinguished and a collision mat in place over the hole in the ship's side. He continued unceasingly to attend to the safety of the ship and the welfare of the ship's company. Her safe arrival in harbour 24 hours later is testimony to his sound judgement and untiring efforts. In courage and leadership he set a fine example to his men and that their morale remained as high as ever is a tribute to their first lieutenant.

The Russian convoys were by far the most testing of his war experiences. The latitudes were equivalent to those in which Antarctic expeditions were conducted, and they sailed in the depth of winter as well as in summer. My father wrote later of 'the intense, penetrating cold, the continual struggle to prevent icing up of superstructure, rigging and decks, the huge seas and the storm conditions to be met north of the Faroes and Iceland'. Added to these horrors were the determination of the Germans to prevent supplies getting through, the concentrated attacks by U-boat wolf packs, almost unceasing persecution from the air, and the constant threat of enemy surface ships. The Germans had an overwhelming advantage in the form of bases for both air and sea attack along the whole of the Norwegian coast, around North Cape and practically into Kola Inlet. The combination of extreme weather and unceasing attack made it virtually impossible for personnel to relax and imposed a dreadful physical and mental strain, especially on ships' companies who had to face these convoys again and again.

While my father was on *Onslow*, my mother was taken as a guest to Miss Eileen Stace's spinning circle at Eastbourne, on Wellington's eastern bays. She spoke to the women about Lewis's letters from the Russian convoys and showed them photographs of the ship's iced superstructure and of the crew in sheepskin garments. Members of the group were so moved by the stories and shocked by pictures of what seemed to be wholly inadequate clothing for Arctic conditions that they invited my mother to join the circle and at once directed all their efforts to items for *Onslow*'s crew: pullovers balaclavas, seaboot stockings and patchwork rugs made from woollen squares. My mother stayed with the circle for the remainder of hostilities and members subsequently returned to spinning and knitting garments for every man from Eastbourne who had gone overseas.

In the latter stages of the war, my father joined HMNZS *Achilles* for the expected battle with Japan in the Pacific. Again, his outstanding performance was noted by others. Dr Donald Stafford Matthews, the ship's Principal Medical Officer, wrote in *Medicine My Passport*:

> We had in Lieutenant-Commander Lew King . . . a brilliant gunnery officer who stands out in my memory as the most conscientious and efficient officer with whom I served. . . . Nothing gave me more confidence than watching the way in which Lew and his boys disposed of the balloons tugged by planes in practice shots. Some Jonah had pointed out that it only takes a few seconds from the moment you spot a Kamakazi coming out of the clouds till it hits your deck; yet I felt that if twenty of them descended on us Lew would hit the lot.

Achilles survived attacks and spent the last three weeks of the war within sixty miles of the Japanese coast. The crew visited

Nagasaki only two months after the second atomic bomb was dropped, and my father described it as 'an area like the Hutt Valley, completely flattened but for factory chimneys sticking up in the distance'.

As I eagerly told anyone who would listen (until it visibly shocked the nuns orchestrating our morning talks at school), my father had been away at the war for nearly six years by the time I was born. I never thought to mention — and did not know until I was older — that he had been home on short leave nine months before my birth. Nevertheless he was still away when I was born in December 1945, and he only got back to Wellington for Christmas that year by hitch-hiking rides on Australian aircraft between Japan, the Philippines and Australia. He flew the final leg, 13½ hours from Sydney to Auckland, in the bomb blister of an RNZAF Catalina.

From early 1946 we lived together as a family for the first time in a house in Ngaio. Lewis King returned to work at Carlton Carruthers with his name added to the list of directors. The war was over; yet the fact that it had occurred conditioned our lives for years afterwards. Decorated in the service of King and country, my father would never share the ambivalence towards England that our Irish background and Catholicism inculcated from other directions. Like most ex-servicemen, he continued to seek and enjoy the friendship of former comrades-in-arms through organisations such as the Returned Services Association, the United Services Officers' Club, and the Navy League. He was party to the masonic intimacy of combatants which outsiders neither understand nor share.

At home the effects of war showed in the determination of both our parents to create 'the idyll of suburban domesticity' to compensate for the lost years. Three of us — myself, my brother Terry, my younger sister Geraldine — were born within six years of war's end. My father worked hard, physically and mentally, to ensure that we owned our family homes and enjoyed gardens around them. My earliest memories are of him with tools, building a bridge over a fern-covered gully at Ngaio, and helping him rake mown lawns. My mother worked equally hard to establish an ordered domestic routine — clean and tidy house, regular nutritious meals, emotional security — according to the division of parental roles accepted at that time. As children we *were* secure, we were happy.

Of course there were difficulties, and they too were a consequence of that six years of combat and absence. My father — himself fatherless — had difficulty bonding with his children and relating to them in a relaxed manner. This was especially so in the case of my older sister, who 'had grown accustomed to his absence in the first six years of her life. With each successive child the relationship grew closer, reaching the intimacy we had all hoped for in the case of the youngest, Geraldine. There was a suggestion too in the early years of peace that my father more than once preferred the mateship of male companions — with its accompaniment of social drinking and outdoor activities such as rabbit and duck shooting — to the occasionally raucous disorganisation of life at home with small children. In spite of the best of intentions on all sides, the gap between naval and domestic life was too wide to be bridged instantly and easily. Added to all this were the usual tensions created by children asserting their own identities and independent behaviour in the face of a parent returning home daily from an emotionally demanding job and expecting quietness and conformity. My mother dealt with these difficulties common to most families by being all things to all of us and smoothing the waters deftly whenever they became troubled. Her versatility and her compassion seemed (and still seem) boundless.

At the end of 1951, when I had completed one year at the Brigidine Convent in Ngaio, we made a break with suburbia. We moved further away from Wellington to my mother's old stamping ground on the west coast of the North Island. Throughout her childhood, her family had picnicked and gathered shellfish and mushrooms from around the near-deserted second arm of Porirua Harbour, Paremata. It was then an estuary edged by farmland and two tiny villages, Paremata itself and Pauatahanui. She and my father had driven there during their courtship, before the road bridge linked the north and south sides of the harbour. When I was a pre-schooler we picnicked there too, and on one occasion we spent a summer in a rented house there. In 1951 we shifted to the peninsula known to local Maori as Te Rapa a te Whai (the stingray tail) and to Pakeha as Golden Gate. It was almost halfway between Paremata and Pauatahanui. We remained there until I was twelve, living at first in a cottage on the beach popularised twenty years later by poet Sam Hunt as Bottle Creek; and then in a larger home my father built on top of the peninsula. They were the most memorable years of my life.

A sense of history comes from three ingredients: early habitation, evidence of that habitation, and stories about it based on the evidence. Paremata had all three. Rare for a New Zealand locality, it had been occupied sporadically over nearly a thousand years; the imprint of the people before was as visible on the rural landscape as the rise and fall of the tides around it. In the 1950s the remnants of moa hunter camps — moa bone (which the then Dominion Museum identified for me), argellite tools, drill points, even human burials — were exposed whenever wind and sea shifted sands in the dunes at the mouth of the harbour. A huge canoe anchor there, a drilled boulder, was reputedly that of the Polynesian navigator Kupe. It was removed to the Dominion Museum for safe keeping. At least two terraced pa sites and half a dozen kainga on the flats faced the inner harbour and disgorged shells, hangi stones, and fragments of artifacts as banks and beach fronts eroded. Our near-neighbour Jack Barry dug up stone tools and midden remains from his garden. Another neighbour, Pop Carter, found adzes on the ridge above our house. At the end of the point, where it jutted deep into the harbour, the Ngati Toa chief Te Rangihaeata had kept a lookout in the 1840s, which surveyed the harbour for almost 360 degrees. Back in the domain on the other side of the harbour stood our own version of Stonehenge: the crumbling remains of Fort Paremata, the most spectacular relic of the British effort to drive Rangihaeata and the Ngati Toa out of the harbour in 1846 in retaliation for their harassment of Pakeha settlements in the Hutt Valley. Close by, on the Plimmerton side, the site of Thom's Whaling Station was marked by enormous bleached ribs and vertebrae that poked from the sandhills. The space between was littered with patterned crockery shards and old bottles, possibly from Boddington's Public House which had opened at about the time the barracks went up.

All these things interested me profoundly. A solitary child, I walked, rowed and cycled around the harbour and explored every site. I kept my eyes on the ground in front of me as a matter of habit, looking for artifacts and other signs of early human activity. I sought out knowledgeable locals such as Pop Carter (whose father had owned a sawmill near Pauatahanui in the nineteenth century, and who remembered the Tarawera eruption), Cliff Porter, captain of the 1924 'Invincible' All Blacks, and old Elisabetta Vella at Plimmerton, whose husband Marino had owned Mana Island, and who had been shipwrecked in the *Wairarapa* when she arrived in New Zealand from Bussin on the Adriatic in 1894.*

My obsession with local history intensified when my father procured copies of Stephen Gerard's *Strait of Adventure* and James Cowan's *The New Zealand Wars and Pioneering Period*. In Cowan I found a detailed account of what had happened militarily in the neighbourhood in 1846. It was supplemented with maps, photographs, and descriptions of combat that enabled me to pinpoint and stand on each site; and once standing there, to imagine that I was experiencing what had happened there. I discovered that on the very point on which we lived, Lieutenant McKillop from HMS *Calliope* had run a gunboat ashore, fired on a reconnaissance party led by Rangihaeata, and then been driven off after a hectic exchange of fire during which his mounted brass gun exploded, injuring more of his own men than Maori. I lay in the earthworks behind the Pauatahanui Anglican church, which had been built over Rangihaeata's pa. I cycled up the Horokiri Valley and then climbed Battle Hill to find Rangihaeata's rifle pits and (at the bottom) the graves of Imperial troops killed fighting there. These experiences did make history live for me. I *felt* the presence of people who had gone before. I saw them

---

*Twenty years later I got to know kaumatua who were able to tell me the history of the area from Ngati Toa perspectives: Te Oenuku Rene, Rongopai Davis, Harata Solomon. As a child I had no entree into the Takapuwahia and Hongoeka communities, though both my parents had known people at the former before the war.

in a kind of Arthurian world that was not in Camelot but (literally) on my own doorstep.*

By the 1950s Maori no longer lived around our arm of the harbour. But there were still kainga at Porirua (Takapuwahia) and Karehana Bay (Hongoeka). A small number of children from both communities attended St Teresa's School in Plimmerton, to which I had transferred in 1951. Some of them (Hemi and Wera Henry, Frances Aratema) had Maori names; others (Michael Rikit, Ellisons, Loves, Fitzgeralds) did not. Like most children of primary school age I had no racial feeling, but I rapidly became aware that Maoris were 'different'. Most were darker than the rest of us although one, Paul Fitzgerald, had red hair and freckles. They talked about and sometimes brought to school food with which we were unfamiliar — tuna, kina, puha, cress. They took for granted skills that the rest of us utterly lacked, such as being able to gaff eels in the creek that ran under the pines alongside the school. At morning talks they spoke about hui and tangi they had been to with their families. And once, during Social Studies, some of the Hongoeka girls demonstrated poi dances and stick games.

I remember becoming interested in these differences, especially when I began to associate them with the Maori sites around the harbour. The realisation grew slowly that these children were related to the people who were here first, before 'us'; before my grandparents emigrated from Britain, before — even — Abel Tasman and Captain Cook 'discovered' New Zealand. Certainly I had no negative feelings of my own about them or their dissimilarities, nor did I inherit any.

Gradually, however, I became aware of the fact that other people reacted differently, especially adults. A lady along the beach screwed up her nose when I told her about the stick games and poi. 'Dirty Maoris,' she said. It shocked me. I didn't ask her why she said that, I was just disappointed that she did not share my enthusiasm. And yet she was interested and encouraging about everything else I did and spoke about. Later I became aware

---

*So important was Cowan to my growing love of history that I was delighted when the Government Printer asked me to write an introduction to a new edition of *The New Zealand Wars* in 1983.

that although we all played together in the school grounds, the Maori children were not invited home to play with Pakeha children, nor to their birthday parties. I thought this odd, but I sensed it would be embarrassing to ask anybody why this was so. In the case of my own home it was not an issue. Because we lived halfway round the harbour — far from Plimmerton or Porirua — I never asked anybody home except one or two children of immediate neighbours. We were too remote. Nor, then, did we have Maori neighbours, nor did this surprise us. Maoris lived in pa like Hongoeka or Takapuahia, not in Pakeha villages or suburbs.

One afternoon, though, walking home from Paremata railway station, I saw a boy who lived in the fishing community in Hobson Street, between the railway line and the harbour. He stood naked on the Paremata Boating Club slipway watched by about ten other public school children. He crouched down and defecated over the edge into the water. Then, to applause, he dived into the harbour. I told the lady along the beach about this too on the way home. Her reaction again surprised me. 'Of course,' she said, wrinkling up her nose. 'Dirty Maoris.' It hadn't occurred to me that this boy was Maori (he was). Nor that there was any relation between what he did and being Maori. Nor that his performance merited the same reaction from this woman as the Maori dances and games had provoked. It was all very puzzling. But it was the beginning of an awareness that some Pakeha had negative and even hostile feelings towards Maori, simply because they *were* Maori.

Rather than worry about the peculiarities of the adult world, however, I pursued my own interest in history and wildlife. My father continued to buy me books as my reading ability increased. I added A.H. Reed's *The Story of New Zealand*, Harry Dansey's *How the Maoris Came to Aotearoa*, Peter Buck's *The Coming of the Maori*, W.R.B. Oliver's *New Zealand Birds* and David Graham's *A Treasury of New Zealand Fishes* to my bedside shelves. I also had A.W.B. Powell's wonderful *Native Animals of New Zealand*, covering everything from shellfish to bats. All these, along with Cowan and Gerard, I had read and largely committed to memory by the time I was eleven. I continued to look for artifacts and even found one at school after a tractor had ploughed the paddocks behind the classrooms.

Walking over the long, up-turned sods one lunchtime, I saw something smooth and green, about the size of a penny. I got down on my knees and scraped the soil away from it. It turned out to be an argellite chisel, exquisitely polished. Greatly excited, I rushed over to one of the nuns to show her. She was indifferent. 'Did you bring that from home?' she asked me. 'No,' I said. 'I found it just now. In the ploughed paddock.' 'Oh,' she said, and turned to deal with the next child trying to attract her attention. I was deflated momentarily, but my excitement soon rekindled. I was confirmed in the belief that there could be no more exciting occupations than those of archaeologist or historian.

Word of my collection of artifacts and curios spread around the district and some adults encouraged me and added to it. My father procured old coins from his branch of the Bank of New South Wales; an elderly neighbour, Hartley Myers, gave me a Maori carving and some spears from New Guinea; Jack Barry gave me some small stone tools; Mrs Hornig next door gave me a Roman coin; and — most surprising — our second parish priest, Father John Kavanagh, gave me a beautifully carved nineteenth-century mere in return for weeding his garden. It had been given to him years before when he was a Maori Missioner in Hawera. He also offered me a greenstone pendant, but I could not accept it.

At school, these pursuits were tolerated rather than encouraged. At times I felt that some of the good sisters (of the Congregation of St Joseph of Nazareth, an order founded in Australia) resented children who knew more than they did about specific topics, as if such knowledge undermined their authority. One nun in particular disparaged everything I said as far-fetched and strapped me frequently. Two, however, Sisters Isadore and Andrew, encouraged my precociousness and clearly favoured me. In Sister Isadore's case it was my pursuit of religious studies that most pleased her and she was convinced that I was destined for the priesthood. 'Remember me in your first Mass,' she said, 'or I'll come back and haunt you.' She told us often about one of her former pupils, Father Emmet McHardy, who had gone as a missionary to the Solomon Islands and subsequently died from malaria. She believed him to be a saint and expected his canonisation in her lifetime.

The sisters were on the whole more interested in church history than in that of the secular or local variety. In addition to teaching the basic curriculum, they took up the themes in religious education to which I had been introduced by the Brigidines in Ngaio: the glories of Ireland and her saints, the wickedness of the English persecutors of both Irish and English Catholics, the need to maintain devotion to practices such as the rosary and the nine first Fridays. Although all but one of these nuns had been born in New Zealand, most were second or third generation Irish. The school roll was again crammed with Irish surnames: Boyles, Carmodys, Duffys, Herlihys, O'Sullivans, Fitzgeralds, and many others. It was no wonder that the public school children called us Micks or Doolans. Some of those families — Murphys, Bradeys, Mulherns, McManaways — had been among the first settlers in the Pauatahanui Valley immediately after the war of the 1840s. The complete identity in our minds of Irishness and Catholicism was reinforced by the fact that our priests were without exception Irish, and by the poems drilled into us in class. One, taught by Sister Alocoque, went:

I see His blood upon the rose;
And in the stars the glory of His eyes;
His body gleams amid eternal snows
His tears fall from the skies.
All pathways by His feet are worn;
His strong heart stirs the ever-beating sea;
His crown of thorns twines with every thorn,
His cross is every tree.

And that was the work, not just of a poet and mystic, but of an Irish politician who had signed the Declaration of Irish Independence in 1916: Joseph M. Plunkett.

Politics were never far from these religious considerations. Father Peyton told us during the great Rosary Crusade in 1954 that Communism, the expansionist creed of Russia and China, would sweep through Western countries and bring about a new

Left: *My father's father, an Irishman off to war in Scottish uniform as a Gordon Highlander.*
Above: *Martha King, a widow in Glasgow.*

The Gorbals: the Scotland that the family abandoned.

Nellie Tierney on the bank of the Tyne, 1910.

My father at Te Kumi near Wairoa, 1923, with friend Rangi.

My grandmother's photo of Hexham Abbey.

*The Spital in 1906:
a centre of Catholicism in
Northumberland and
a hiding place for priests
during the years of
persecution.*

Below left: *Chareway Cottage, the
family home in Hexham, in 1908.*
Below: *My mother, Nellie Smith.*

A church picnic at Plimmerton. My grandfather pours tea; next to him are my grandmother, Aunt Mona, Uncle Bernie and girlfriend.

Lewis King and Nellie Smith picnicking at Titahi Bay around 1938, with Bobby, my father's fox terrier.

My mother and father with Louise, shortly before he left for Europe on the Aquitania.

Conditions on HMS Onslow *during Russian convoys: my father stands in front of ice-encased shells and a gun barrel; and the superstructure covered in ice but for the A/A gun kept ready for instant action.*

Family picnic at Karehana Bay, 1948.

The cottage on the beach, Paremata.

St Joseph's Church, Pauatahanui.

Waiting for the Queen: (from left) Sharon McArthur, Michael King, Gaye Allen, Terry King (in clothes matching his brother's).

With my brother, camping near Eketahuna, 1956.

Silverstream: trees, ivy-covered walls and a sense of tradition.

Dark Age if we did not say the rosary daily. Our Lady of Fatima was said to have given the same message to the children to whom she appeared in Portugal in 1917. Worse, the nuns warned us the Blessed Virgin had confided a secret revelation to these children, which they had communicated to the Pope and which was not to be transmitted to the rest of the world until 1960. The sisters believed that this Fatima 'secret' foretold global nuclear war and the end of the world. When Pope Pius XII read it, he was reported to have spent a whole day pacing in his garden repeating, 'Dear God, no.' For me at least, this story was a source of frequent nightmares.* We also prayed for a Catholic restoration in England and a united Ireland ('that Ireland, long a province, be a nation once again'). And, in the most dramatic statement of potential Irish-Catholic independence in New Zealand, we were told that our senior pastor, Archbishop McKeefrey, would ask Catholics not to fight again on behalf of their country if the Government did not grant state aid to Catholic schools. This was part of the 'Hear the Case' campaign organised nationally by the Holy Name Society in 1956.

All such sentiments were in harmony with the Irish feeling that emanated from my mother's side of the family. But some of them, particularly the suggestion that Catholics should not take up arms, were strongly at variance with my father's code of honour. It was on such occasions that I felt that to be Catholic was to be different from the community at large, and that it involved risks. After Benediction on Sunday evenings we sang lustily:

Faith of our Fathers, holy Faith,
In spite of dungeon, fire and sword.
Oh how our hearts beat high with joy
When e'er we hear that glorious word.
Faith of our Fathers, holy Faith,
We will be true to thee till death,
We will be true to thee till death.

---

*1960 came and went and no Fatima secret was divulged. A Church spokesman, Cardinal Joseph Ratzinger, said later that it was not published so as 'to avoid confusing religious prophecy with sensationalism.'

It all seemed sound enough and grand enough when we raised the rafters of the old wooden church at Pauatahanui, and when Father Jeremiah McGrath elevated the sparkling monstrance over his six-foot-four-inch Irish frame. But in bed at nights, going over it, I prayed that the 'true till death' part of the contract would not involve 'dungeon, fire and sword' in my case. Going to the dental clinic was such torture that I feared I would renounce my faith immediately at the first hint of a drill, let alone at the prospect of fire and boiling oil.

Worshipping at Pauatahanui was one of the great joys of my childhood. Mass was said there only once a month (on other Sundays we went to the new and more prosaic church next to the school at Plimmerton). On the charmed days we drove around the harbour early in the morning, the water as flat as sheet-steel. We looked for herons and the ripples of mullet trying to outrun kahawai. The church itself, built in local wood in 1878, stood next to cabbage trees, kowhai and pines on a hillside above Stace's Flat.

In spring and summer the sacristy doors were thrown open, and we could see pasture and trees outside behind the altar. Families who had built the church — the Abbotts and the Murphys — had their own pews. The bachelors of the district all gathered at the back, beside the organ. The windows were not stained glass but papered, with peeling pictures of Christ and assorted saints donated by others among the district's established families — O'Connells, Bradeys, Vellas and Mulherns. The church was redolent of age, sanctity and unadorned beauty. In later years I could never smell incense or burning wax without that simple, solid building and its occupants coming forcefully to mind.

Also fixed in my recollection is Father McGrath's heavy brogue booming from the altar: 'What doth it profit a man if he gain the whole world and suffer the loss of his soul?' In this aspect he was as powerful and frightening as an Old Testament prophet. But when he made the parish announcements the blarney took over and he was a considerable entertainer. 'Now ye wouldn't believe it, but people have been phonin' me and askin' what time Midnight Mass is. Midnight Mass! Midnight Mass this year

50

is the same time it's always been, twelve o'clock midnight. And it will be a sung Mass featurin' Caruso and McCormack, in the form of Father Clancy and meself. So tie up yer yappin' dogs before ye leave home.'*

It would be misleading, however, to imply that all this placed us outside the mainstream of non-Catholic New Zealand life. We *were* taught New Zealand history in social studies, although I later recognised it as history of a highly ethnocentric kind: New Zealand had not existed until European navigators discovered it; English missionaries brought Christianity and civilisation to an 'uncivilised' Maori; the Treaty of Waitangi was 'the fairest treaty ever made between Europeans and a native race'; and the 'Maori Wars' were caused by those same natives becoming resentful, sullen and insolent. All this and more the sisters took from *Our Nation's Story*. We never heard a Maori interpretation of this story. It was years before I knew there was one. Of the things that had happened on the very doorstep of the school, Te Rauparaha's arrest at Taupo Pa, for instance, the sisters knew nothing and showed no interest when I raised them in morning talks.

This general view of 'white man's history' was reinforced from other sources. From the time I was in hospital with polio at the age of nine, my Scottish grandmother bought me a subscription to *Eagle* comic, which I read eagerly every week. The message there was that Europeans were strong, noble, intelligent and trustworthy; non-Europeans were swarthy, slant-eyed and treacherous. On the pages of *Eagle* Winston Churchill fought 'savage' Pathan tribesmen (defending, as it happened, their own territory); Cortez slaughtered Mexicans because they did not want to submit to the King of Spain; Texan rangers, fighting Indians without firearms, 'killed six startled braves with one hand in a few seconds'; Luck of the Legion thrashed the Touareg, 'the most devious and dreaded tribe in the desert'; and

---

*Father McGrath always addressed my parents as 'Your Majesties'. Years later, after he had resisted the reforms of the Second Vatican Council and vowed that he wasn't 'sayin' no Protestant Mass', he was appointed to Ohakune, which he referred to as 'Siberia'. He was eventually knocked down and killed by a bus on a visit home to Dublin.

Storm Nelson in the Pacific dealt with 'Kanakas' who were simple and comical and spoke idiot English. I'm uncertain as to how much we were influenced at the time by such stories; re-reading them as an adult I found them riddled with racial arrogance.

In addition to Irish poems, the nuns had a weakness for a variety of New Zealand ones designed to make us appreciate our own country. One began:

Land of the moa and Maori
Land of the kowhai and kauri.
Land of waving grain
Nourished by gentle rain.
Land of blue mountain, hot lake and fiord
Land of volcano, majestic and weird.

Another stirred memories of Anzac:

There are lines of buried bones,
There's an unpaid waiting debt.
There's a sound of gentle sobbing in the south.

Unlike the Paremata and Plimmerton public schools, we did not have Anzac or Trafalgar Day ceremonies; we didn't even have a New Zealand flag. When we marched around the playground for 'drill' it was to nothing more martial than a cracked '78' recording of *Waltzing Matilda*. But I was very much aware of the presence of war in recent New Zealand history. There were my father's experiences, of course, occasionally re-lived when he had associates from the war at home; and commemorated when he went off to the Dawn Parade on Anzac Day wearing his medals. And there was old Mrs Hornig next door, bereaved as both a wife and mother.

Fran Hornig had no immediate family and I often did my piano practice at her place after school to keep her company. She had a darkened living room with an old walnut piano, whose ivory keys were yellow with age. On it sat portraits of two men in khaki, frozen in youth, and with what looked like an expectation of death in their faces. The sepia one was her husband, killed at Gallipoli in 1915; the other her son Colin, killed in the North African desert in 1942. Both pictures had faded RSA poppies wedged in a corner of the frames. Both men's service medals lay on the mantelpiece. Of her double tragedy, Mrs Hornig said little directly. But she talked about Colin a great deal, and about the promise he had shown as an engineer; and often when I arrived at the door I could see she had been crying. She baked scones while I played the piano and I loved her like a third grandmother.

In 1953, when the young Queen Elizabeth and the Duke of Edinburgh visited New Zealand for the first time, we were encouraged to be as loyal as children throughout the Dominion. The nuns handed out brass Coronation Medals and badges distributed by the Department of Education before school broke up for the summer holidays. Paremata Bridge was decorated with red, white and blue banners. We lined up along it with miniature Union Jacks and New Zealand flags in our hands when the Royal entourage was imminent, on its way south from Paraparaumu Airport to Wellington city. Then we waited. And waited. As we stood there, loyally holding our flags and bladders, the huge sign on the hill reading 'Greetings From Paremata' blew into the harbour and lay there floating, face down. At last, more than an hour late, a line of black cars sped across the bridge. We just managed to spot the Daimler with the Royal Standard on the front. But after it had flashed past we realised that the figure waving on our side had been a man in uniform. We had seen the Duke, not the Queen. Our disappointment was acute, our resentment bordered on rebellion.

My older sister, Louise, was boarding at Sacré Coeur Convent in Wellington and home only on Sundays and holidays. This fact, plus the six years difference between us, meant I did not get to know her until much later. But the rest of us were close and happy as a family. My mother remained at home to look after us, and my brother and younger sister started school three and six years behind me. Usually we walked to Paremata station, caught the train to Plimmerton, and came home the same way. On hot days my mother would pick us up in her Fiat convertible and take us for a swim after school at Plimmerton. The beach then was sandy (and safer) than the harbour and we stood on tiny soles as we waded out towards Mana Island.

Usually after school I amused myself, the gap between my brother and myself being too wide at that age for companionship (although, to my annoyance, we were often dressed in matching clothes). If I wasn't exploring the harbour and historic sites, I was fishing. I had learnt to handle dinghys from the time I was six, and checked out all the likely fishing spots within rowing distance of the house.

My clearest memory from this time is a composite one, based on the excitement of dozens of solitary expeditions. More than afternoon fishing, I liked to get up before dawn and make my way down to the beach through the macrocarpas and pines. I can't smell those trees now, or walk on pine needles, without recalling such excursions. I collected the oars, rowlocks and fishing gear from the boat shed, then walked the short distance to the water's edge, across sand and shell. By this time the sun would be lighting the crests of the hills around the harbour, and they seemed to hang in the sharp clean air. The boat would be anchored knee deep, in still water that reflected the surroundings as faithfully as a mirror. Here and there kahawai and mullet mottled the surface and sharpened my impatience to be on the water. Often the air was so cold that the sea felt warm when I stepped into it. As I walked through the shallows, small flounder preceded me, kicking up mushrooms of sand. When I reached the dinghy I would lay the oars in place, deposit the rod and bait, and haul myself in. Then up with the anchor and away, pulling quickly on the oars.

I loved the dip of the blades, the creaking of rowlocks, and the whisper of water along the sides of the boat. The sun would be coming up over Pauatahanui as I slipped past the bleached shellbank we called Cockleshell Island. Finally, in the channel where the water ran green and deep, opposite Moorhouse Point, I threw the anchor over the bow and paused until it gripped. Then I baited the rod with mullet, released the line into the depths, and waited with exquisite anticipation. Soon I'd feel the pecking of mullet, the sucking of trevalli, or the sudden pull of kahawai. Sometimes I got small snapper, occasionally stingray (which usually broke the trace) and once, unforgettably, a kingfish.

I scarcely ever came home empty-handed from these early morning trips. The ones after school, though, were less lucrative.

Regardless of what I did in the late afternoon, fishing or visiting Mrs Hornig, I always reached home in time for the radio serials at 5.45: *Superman*, or the *Air Adventures of Biggles*. On Sunday nights, in front of the fire after our baths, we listened to the radio together: *Take It From Here, Journey Into Space*. Radio was our major link with the outside world. Its personalities — Aunt Daisy, Selwyn Toogood, Dr Turbott, Harry Squires, Uncle Tom and his Children's Choir — became as well known to us as members of the family. I found deep security in these rituals, especially in sitting close to the fire, smelling the salt wood burn and looking deep into the flames and incandescent coals.

On Friday nights, under pain of sin, we were obliged to eat fish. In fact it was no hardship. We regarded it as a treat; my mother varied its preparation, from battered fillets, to fish cakes, to whitebait fritters. Sundays were organised around church and my sister's visits home. My father cooked breakfast while the rest of us were at Mass, after which we collected Louise and her school friends from the train. Then we sat down to a midday roast dinner — lamb, pork or beef — and spent the afternoons recovering from so much eating. After a high tea of lamingtons, upside-down cake or chocolate eclairs, the girls were put on the train for school, or we drove them back. Coming home in the car we sang, as in previous years, usually Irish songs. 'The Wild Colonial Boy' was our special favourite.

When Patrick O'Hagen made periodic tours of the country I went with my mother and Irish grandmother to hear him sing in the Wellington Town Hall. He helped keep the Irish memory alive, and he added to our repertoire of songs to sing in the car or at family parties:

'Tis well I know that often folk keep wonderin',
When in my eyes a far-off look they see.
What is the cause of all my consolation?
What is this dream so very dear to me?

That dream was still Ireland, and it was as heavily nostalgic for my grandmother as it had been when she was a girl. The further she got from Ireland, in distance and in time, the more nostalgic she became. When we gathered with aunts and uncles and cousins on her birthdays, Uncle Bernie sang *Mother McCree* for her and the tears rolled down her cheeks. Every 17 March my mother and father threw St Patrick's Day parties and invited all their friends, Irish and non-Irish. Again the familiar songs were sung around the piano in our living room. That same day the girls at Sacré Coeur were divided into two teams for an annual cricket match, the Irish versus the World.

Occasionally we went on holidays in one of a succession of family cars: the Humber Hawk, the Standard Vanguard, the Vauxhall; occasionally, because living at Paremata *was* like a holiday. Nevertheless we toured Northland one year, arriving at Opononi only weeks after Opo the dolphin had been killed; another summer we stayed at Taupo; we camped in thick bush behind Eketahuna, where we woke to the dawn chorus and cooked on a fire and where once I saw my father shoot a deer before breakfast; we went to Cape Kidnappers to see the gannets. Sometimes on weekends, to vary the home routines, we took a billy, tea and sausages and walked round the open coast, south from Titahi Bay to Kaumanga; or north from Karehana Bay towards Pukerua. Then we gathered wood and built a fire and made tea as the sun went down behind the South Island.

Although I belonged to the Forest and Bird Protection Society, my father and I did most of our bird watching together around the harbour, especially at the Pauatahanui end. We saw terns, godwits, banded dotterels and black swans. White-faced herons, migrants from Australia and rare at that time, began to nest around the estuary in the early 1950s. Thirty years later they were common throughout the country. Each winter a solitary white heron also visited, but always left for Okarito as the breeding season approached. Out to sea, when we went fishing off Kapiti and Mana in the launch of a retired farmer friend, we spotted petrels, giant petrels and gannets, and on one occasion a mollymawk. There were more exciting fish there too: cod, tarakihi, hapuku, barracuda and conger eels, and the snapper were far larger than those that schooled inside the harbour.

In recollection, those first years at Paremata (I kept returning as an adult) seemed the longest and the slowest of my life. They were Wordsworthian in their simplicity and setting. Indeed, when my parents announced shortly after I turned twelve that we were moving to Auckland, it did seem that a glory had passed from the earth, at least from my earth. The rest of my adolescence felt flat and anti-climactic. But those six impressionable years generated in me a relationship with the sea, a love of wildlife and a passion for New Zealand history. And these were to remain with me, wherever I lived subsequently.

CHAPTER THREE
Gaps in the Spectrum

THE HILLS AND the estuary at Paremata had contained our lives, and every feature of the landscape there was known to me. Auckland, by contrast, was a sprawling mystery. Not only was it far larger than Wellington, the only other city I knew from experience, it was hot, humid and cosmopolitan. I had stayed there once before. In 1953 my parents visited Australia on business at the invitation of the Sanitarium Health Food Company. They were to leave from Auckland and my brother and I to stay with an aunt and uncle and cousins there. We travelled up on the 'Limited' and the whole journey was an adventure: my first sight from a train of the wild coast between Pukerua Bay and Paekakariki; the guard folding down the beds in our sleeper and making them up; the blue light that glowed all night like a huge precious stone; waking up at National Park and seeing Ruapehu moonlit, like a lantern; the near riot at Taumarunui as non-sleeper passengers fought for refreshments; the cups of tea and wine biscuits in the morning; and, finally, rolling into Auckland past the Orakei Basin, Judge's Bay and the grimy shunting yards.

Aunt Mona, my mother's sister, lived at Takapuna. I was to go to school at the brick convent in Devonport with my cousin Anthony. Terry was too young. First, however, we saw my parents off to Sydney on the *Monowai*. They were high on the ship's deck, we were below on the wharf. They tossed down streamers for us to hold while a loudspeaker played 'Auf Wiedersehn' and 'Now Is the Hour'. Just before the ship moved off a crane on rails drove between the passengers and the spectators and severed all the streamers. It seemed a bad omen for a journey.

I can recall little of the six weeks at school there. The nuns seemed more forbidding, because they and their habits were unfamiliar. Occasionally we were allowed to buy a meat pie and a custard tart for lunch, all for one shilling. Far more memorable were the trips into the city. We caught the ferry from Devonport and always ran to the front, to sit at the bow and feel the spume on our faces. Auckland was beautiful from the water — both the metropolis on the city side, with buildings that dwarfed Wellington's; and the Edwardian cluster of Devonport, looking like postcards of an English seaside resort. We poured over the gangway at the Ferry Building at the foot of Queen Street. I had never seen crowds the size of those that thronged the main thoroughfares. In the Farmers' at Hobson Street we spoke to Hector the parrot (who talked back), and rode pedal cars on the open roof. Thoughtlessly, I once tossed a half-eaten toffee apple over the edge and was frightened to go outside again in case I had killed somebody. On weekends we drove in the Belgrave's Prefect to North Shore beaches to picnic and play: Cheltenham, Takapuna, Milford. Unlike the coast around Wellington, there was lots of clean sand and the swimming was always safe. All that was an interlude, however, a kind of holiday. We knew we were going home.

In 1957, Auckland was a shock. We were going to remain there; there was, apparently, no prospect of escape. And it was as much of a contrast with Paremata as any place could have been. We lived at Kohimarama and then Remuera. Apart from the families on each side of us, we knew no neighbours. There was no sense of community — no feeling that I could drop into anybody's place on the way home from school and be welcome. Weekends, formerly a tranquil time, were now pierced by the roar of motor mowers and the sharp smell of cut paspalum. I was enrolled at Sacred Heart College as a day pupil in Form Two.

In the city, there were more Maori and Pacific Islanders than I had seen previously. At school, my cultural experience was extended considerably. My class included Dalmatians (Miocevich, Devcich, Marinovich, Markovina) and descendants of the Bohemian community from Puhoi (Schollums and Rzoskas). We also had Indians, Arabs, Poles and Italians. There were descendants of Irish families, among the students and on the staff, but they seemed a minority among the more exotic immigrants. The traditions of the college, though, were New Zealand (the most honoured old boys were All Blacks*) and French (the Marist

*The most popular, who visited the college and spoke to us, were Maori, Pat Walsh and Keith Davis. Later, I came to know the grandmother who had brought Davis up, a tattooed kuia named Tutengaehe from Matapihi.

Brothers had been established in France in 1817). While still immersed in the religion in which I had been brought up, the flavour was nothing like that I had encountered in Ngaio and Plimmerton. The college's adopted saints were Blessed Marcellin Champagnat, founder of the Marists, whose statue stood in the grounds; and St Peter Chanel, the French priest martyred at Futuna in 1841, a piece of whose bone had been acquired for the college chapel (along with a fragment of the 'true cross').

The atmosphere was rugged and masculine, as if school authorities had decided that boys brought up by nuns needed in adolescence a strong antidote to female role models. I boarded in Form Three and, with the rest of the college, rose early from the dormitories and went fasting to Mass in the new brick chapel. The accepted manner of receiving and returning from communion was with arms folded and faces stern. School began with assembly in the gymnasium (also new, also brick), the singing of the *Salve Regina*, and stirring addresses from the Brother Director, who had a genius for double entendre ('Who knows the daily travail of boys who, like St Paul, must wrestle with themselves? Who can tell the saga of a boy's struggle to get a grip on himself?'). We listened with suppressed, manly faces, and stored our giggles for the brief interlude between assembly and classes. Discipline was harsh, the cane used frequently for the most minor offences. There was little contact with staff outside the classroom, other than at rugby and cricket, neither of which I played. Sports results and commentaries dominated the school magazine. Scholarship was not despised, but it came a poor second to physical activities in school esteem. Piety came third. The one truly virtuous boy in our class was persecuted viciously by his peers and bore the punches and the succession of broken glasses stoically. Poor saintly Brother Luke, an Irish octogenarian who came to lead us in the daily rosary in the last year of his life, was mocked savagely, most of the class stamping their feet in unison as he faltered into our room.

At home too, new influences were breaking into our previously close and quiet family life. Louise had finished school and was attending university part-time. She brought home rock and roll records and boyfriends. One taught me to play the guitar, and almost overnight I abandoned John McCormack and Patrick

O'Hagen in favour of Elvis Presley, Paul Anka and Tab Hunter. I grew a Bill Haley kiss curl. But by the time I had trained the lock of hair onto my forehead, he and the Comets had been overtaken by other stars. Soon with the aid of Brylcream, I was trying to cultivate a kind of Elvis Presley cowlick at the front of my hair and a duck's tail at the back; this combination was made difficult by the school's insistence on short back and sides.

I evolved a brief interest in Grand Prix racing, largely because the New Zealand driver Bruce McLaren lived a couple of houses up the road. I not only got to know him (his family ran the local service station), but stars such as Stirling Moss and Jack Brabham came and went from his house during the New Zealand racing season. We attended the first New Zealand Grand Prix at Ardmore and saw the English driver Ken Wharton killed when his Monza Ferrari rolled and crashed.

I did not abandon my previous pastimes, however. I missed the former proximity of the sea like an absent lover; long before, I had marked in my copy of *The Wind in the Willows* the passage that read, 'There is nothing — absolutely nothing — half as much worth doing as simply messing about in boats.' At Cornwallis, where we visited friends with a bach, I was able to mess about in and fish from small boats again. Those same friends, the Blakeleys, also introduced me to skin-diving (as it was then called) and we chased and speared parore and crayfish at Whatipu and Leigh. On one unforgettable day we surfaced at Leigh to find a large shark cruising between us and the beach, and we had to make for the rocks on an overloaded skiff. The shark, however, was more attracted to a dog that had gone knee-deep in the water to bark at it. Auckland's collection of volcanic pa also interested me and I rode my bike to each one in turn and sketched their terraced defences. I read all I could find about the city's history and filled my scrapbook with articles and pictures about early Auckland and New Zealand wildlife. At college, I excelled in art, social studies and religious knowledge. Deprived of Paremata (though we still had the cottage there, tenanted), we began taking family holidays at Mount Ruapehu and visited a then sparsely populated Coromandel Peninsula in the summer.

The Blakeleys, with whom we also went ski-ing and camping,

had three beautiful and athletic daughters. I fell in love with Justine, the oldest, who had been born the same day as I. I wooed her as best I could but she didn't seem to notice. I would rush to Remuera Road twenty minutes early for my school bus so as to intercept her cycling to St Cuthbert's in the opposite direction; she thought it was coincidence. I sketched a drawing of her house as a gift, but she didn't recognise it. I worked hard at guitar practice so I could nonchalantly toss off Buddy Holly and Elvis Presley tunes; she preferred 'Tom Dooley'. On one dreadful day at Cornwallis, she joined the other children in a parody of a Rogers and Hammerstein song: 'Oh what a horrible morning, Oh what a horrible day, I've got a horrible feeling, Michael is going to play.' I ached for her companionship; but it was three years before, during a school holiday on Ruapehu, I summoned the courage to hold her hand. To my astonishment she reciprocated with warmth though correctly and chastely.

That three-year period in Auckland was, for me, a frenetic interlude. So much happened, and so quickly, that I subsequently remembered little in detail. By 1960 my parents had shifted back to Wellington with Terry and Geraldine, and my father established his own business in the city in which he had lifelong associations. I was transferred as a boarder to St Patrick's College, Silverstream, and the pace of life seemed to slow again.

The move from Sacred Heart to Silverstream — virtual home for me for the next four years — was as marked a contrast as the shift from Paremata to Auckland. But this one seemed for the better. The college lay on a 1400-acre farm bisected by the Hutt River. It had been opened on its original site in 1885 by Marist priests trained at St Mary's College in Dundalk, Ireland, and it retained a strong sense of history and scholarship.* Portraits of former rectors lined the long, dim corridor inside the front entrance. The very titles of the school's officers (prefect of studies, procurator, spiritual director), the identity of the communal rooms (refectory, parlour) and the names of the rectors themselves,

---

*The old college at Cambridge Terrace, Wellington, shifted to Silverstream in 1931. The Cambridge Terrace establishment remained in use as a day school, then moved to Kilbirnie in 1979.

were all redolent of nineteenth-century Ireland. The traditions had been transplanted by the first rector Dr Felix Watters, whose Jesuit brother was president of University College in Dublin when James Joyce was a student there. Initially, Irish history had been a separate and compulsory school subject. (True to his Faith and his country to the last, our Dr Watters had returned to Ireland to be shot dead during the Easter uprising in 1916.)

When the college transferred to the Silverstream site, the traditions accompanied it. Thirty years on, it seemed as long established as a European abbey. The bricks were ivy-covered; the interior wood panels dark-stained; the desks, many of them transferred from the old college, scarred with the graffiti of three generations of students; the locker rooms rank with the odour of hoarded food. Unlike Sacred Heart, the staff seemed cultured and approachable — they *shared* our life rather than supervised it, from morning Mass to Saturday night movies (always Westerns, which the rector regarded as manly entertainment). While rugby, cricket, athletics and boxing featured prominently in their respective seasons, spiritual, academic and artistic activities were given equal weight and old boys honoured for scholastic achievements in addition to sporting ones. Although I made few close friends at Silverstream, being still by preference as solitary a person as I had been at Paremata, I felt far more at home there than I had at school in Auckland. I, even, in what seemed a more sane atmosphere, enjoyed athletics and rugby.

The pattern was set on my first day. The rector, Father Maurie Bourke, had a chronically bad back. Unable to sit comfortably, he strode up and down as he interviewed students in the dark corridor outside his office. His kindness was masked by an Olympian aloofness. 'Er, what's your name?' he asked me as I ran to stay alongside him. 'Michael, Father,' I said. 'Speak up boy, I don't hear.' Louder: 'Michael, Father.' 'Oh no, boy, we don't collect first names here. What's your surname?' 'King, Father.' 'I don't hear.' Shouting: 'King, Father.' 'That's better. We had a boy here whose mother wanted him to be called Milton, short for Hamilton. They'd called him Ham at his old school. I just called him Wright. The other boys called him Baldy. Er, what do you think of that?'

That same morning, having prised out of me the information that I was interested in history, he lent me leather-tooled books from the rector's private library, including first editions of Edward Tregear's *The Aryan Maori* and S. Percy Smith's *Hawaiki; the Original Home of the Maori*. In two years at Sacred Heart nobody discovered this concern of mine let alone encouraged it. Later, two gifted English teachers, Noel Delaney and Bernie Ryan, cultivated in us an abiding appetite for literature and taught us to read discriminatingly. They also nurtured my interest in writing and criticised the resulting essays sympathetically and constructively. 'Fine writing' was discouraged; but good writing — clear, crisp, direct communication — was valued highly. Writers too were esteemed, and the act of writing represented to us as an honourable craft. A fourth priest, Father Kevin Maher, listened to my poetry and read his own to me, mostly about college life:

> Here is the pulse of youth, the urge
> Of waking life; green clovered fields,
> And bees gold-dusty in the yellow gorse
> By the slow river
> Drowsily moving down along the hills.
>
> Here on a summer's day below the School
> The white-clad figures move upon the green
> With clap of bat on ball; or by the water's edge
> Lithe bodies poise a moment and are gone
> With shout and laughter; or by twos and threes
> Companies idle down the river road
> And smoke of camp-fires drifts up in the wind.
>
> Here have been other boys in other days
> Young as these are, as urgently alive,
> Who knew these fields, the river and the hills,
> And swam and played and knew no thought beside . . .
> And by them all this ground was sanctified
> Because, unquestioning, they went away
> And laboured, fought and died, for little things . . .
> To save for these the freedom of the hills,
> The white-clad figures, and the river's song
> And slow smoke rising through a summer's afternoon.

The 'slow smoke rising through a summer's afternoon' was more than hyperbole. It came from 'down the river' where we were allowed to stroll, loll, read, boil billies, toast bread, cook sausages, even put up huts — if we could scavenge sufficient building materials. And all this among gorse, bracken, manuka and punga, alongside deep swimming holes. Across the river, there were extensive patches of second-growth bush. It was an environment that complemented a love of literature. We often took our work down there, to read and swot amid the sights and quiet sounds of natural surroundings. Over the crest of Mount Cecil to the west, still on school property, I could sit under a macrocarpa and look down on Paremata Harbour. As I did so, feelings of loss — far too complex to be explicable to myself or to others — welled up inside me. It was then that I cried for my family, for the grandfather who died when we lived there, for the childhood spent in view of the water, that seemed in memory to have been perfect.

Drawn more strongly than ever to books and the world of books, I became at first a librarian and ultimately head librarian — an excuse to browse among volumes when I might have been assigned other duties. The master in charge, Joe Cudby, also introduced us to music by playing Beethoven, Bach, Brahms, Chopin, Tchaikovsky and Sibelius records as we worked there. Apart from piano lessons, it was my first substantial introduction to 'real' music and seeded another passion that was to be lifelong.

My other hobby, outside sport, was oratory and debating, promoted strongly by the college in its effort to produce forceful defenders of the Faith and to sustain its output of successful lawyers and judges (one of whom, Sir Timothy Cleary, was president of the old boys' association while I was there). I still have notes for some of the earnest speeches by which, weekly, we sought to right the ills of the world and keep sleepy adjudicators awake: 'Will the rising hopes of Pacific nations be satisfied by educational and social development from the West? Or will they remain underprivileged, resentful, an easy prey to anti-Western agitators and nationalist extremists who will turn the ground swell of rising expectations into a tidal wave?'

Strangely, we recognised social problems only beyond our own borders. We were smug about New Zealand's achievements and the example that we imagined the country set to an imperfect world. I underlined approvingly a passage in the school magazine's editorial:

> [This] is an age of opportunity, when hard work and natural ability can guarantee a satisfying and rewarding career. It is — for us in New Zealand — an age of security, in which distress or poverty are dim memories of thirty years ago, in which the children of any family can confidently expect a 'normal' world of comfortable homes fitted with modern appliances bordering on luxury, of educational opportunities unlimited, of new clothes, and presents and holidays by the beach or in the country, a family car, and a feeling of being 'as good as everybody else' . . . it offers openings and rewards to young manhood, accomplishment and serenity in middle-age, security again in advancing years.

So it seemed to us at that time. We saw no gap between rich and poor (indeed, it was far less apparent everywhere then than it was twenty years later), no broken homes, no alcoholics, no homosexuals, no psychiatric cases, no Maori experiencing discrimination, no people under stress. We saw only people like ourselves: Catholic, middle-class, largely Irish in origin, all comfortably provided for. We presumed we were a microcosm of New Zealand and of the world as it ought to be. And if the world was not like that, it was largely the world's fault.

There were smatterings of other ethnic groups among the student body, but not to the extent that there had been in Auckland. We had descendants of the early Italian fishing communities (Barnaos, Criscillos, Meos, Zames), the odd Pole, one Fijian Indian, a few Samoans, and a handful of Maori. The patchwork of their backgrounds, however, had been covered by the levelling blanket of Catholicism. We never discussed the place of minority cultures in New Zealand life, we never saw evidence that these individuals had histories that differed from our own — except very occasionally in the case of the Maori students.

The Maori contingent included three Te Heuheus, sons of the Ngati Tuwharetoa ariki Hepi; one Mariu, also Tuwharetoa;

two Takarangis, from Wanganui; and Maurice Ormsby, whose grandfather and great-uncles were leading elders of Ngati Maniapoto. Maurice was one of my closest friends in the sixth form and I went back to Te Kuiti with him one summer and met his grandfather. But I did not think of him as 'Maori' (I doubt if he did at that time, either). He was rather a Pakeha of Maori descent. The interests we shared tended not to be my historical ones, but arguing literature and religion and, by complete contrast, hanging around milk bars trying to pluck up the courage to speak to girls. We also edited and wrote the student paper (as distinct from the official school magazine), *The Silverstreamer*. After three issues it was closed down by the rector on the grounds that we had exceeded the limits of discretion and good taste. And so we had, cheerfully.

The Te Heuheus and Takarangis *were* Maori, and sometimes through them we had glimpses into a world very different from our own. They were Maori speakers, for example. Timi Te Heuheu composed a school haka and then taught it to us — not as part of a programme of multi-culturism (there *was* no such programme) but as another of the college's rugby barracking chants. The Te Heuheus also referred to their family history in oratory competitions. I remember the whole school gripped with attentiveness one night as Timi told the story of Te Heuheu Mananui, a giant of a man eventually killed in a landslide on the shore of Lake Taupo in 1846. I had never been on a marae, and the story was told in English; but I later recognised that Timi's eloquence, gestures and command of his audience came straight from a Maori oral tradition and from years of witnessing whaikorero.*

Apart from these aberrations, the culture of the college was predominantly Irish and Catholic in character. The staff list was a roll call of Irish names, New Zealand Irish: Doohan, Delaney, Bourke, Ryan, O'Fagan, Cudby, Brogan and so on. Two of them, Pat Abbott who visited to conduct a retreat and Stewie O'Connell who taught, were members of families that had founded the parish and built the church at Pauatahanui. Our secular hero

---

*Not long out of school, Timoti Te Heuheu stood unsuccessfully as a National candidate for Western Maori in the 1966 general election.

was also Irish and Catholic, but not a New Zealander. We followed the political career of John Fitzgerald Kennedy with mounting excitement. He articulated an idealism with which we could identify ('ask not what your country can do for you, but rather what you can do for your country'); and he succeeded in a society that was, like our own, predominantly non-Catholic and materialist. He was a model in public life with whom we could identify more intimately than with any closer to home. We were devastated by his violent death in my final year at school. The day he was shot was the day my older sister Louise was married. Although we tried to keep the news from her, it hung over the occasion like a cloud. Knowing nothing at that time of Kennedy's private life, we consoled ourselves with the conviction that assassination probably ensured his sainthood.

In general, the Irishness of the college was not as raw as that which had characterised our days at convent school. Silverstream's traditions were remembered, historical, and intellectual. Where those in my childhood had been characterised by superstition, anti-English prejudice and a black-and-white view of morality (men were either saints or sinners, abstainers or alcoholics, celibates or libertines), Silverstream introduced me to the Ireland of Newman, Hopkins, Joyce, Yeats, Shaw and Frank O'Connor. Religion was discussed with heavy doses of theology and philosophy rather than by anecdote and precept. Those of us going on to university were expected to be able to hold our own against a host of atheists and hedonists — not with the rosary and pious ejaculations alone, as the nuns would have armed us, but by logical exposition and historical knowledge.

The daily Christian Doctrine class was set aside to instruct us in the Faith and to discuss the multitude of things that interested us most, but which the Department of Education thought too controversial for the curriculum (sex, behaviour, values, politics). In theory we were free to discuss anything as the equal of our teachers; in practice, discussions remained within the bounds of orthodox conclusions and polite exchanges. If they did not, there would be tension and accusations of impertinence. Trouble was usually avoided, however, by the greater knowledge or more sharply honed debating skills of the Christian Doctrine master.

I recall a characteristic exchange between Ormsby and Father George Head, a learned man and, when he did not feel threatened, a kindly one. On the previous occasion, Maurice had been asked to leave the class because he insisted (truthfully, I had been there) that his parish priest spent most of his time in the pulpit asking for money. This incident had left both pupil and teacher edgy, feeling the need to score a decisive tactical victory. The opportunity came during a discussion on immortality. Father Head had outlined the Thomistic teaching on the nature of the soul: man is capable of forming universal ideas, he forms judgements, he reasons things out, he reflects; therefore his soul must be spiritual, because he performs spiritual activities and distinguishes between what a thing is and what it does; therefore it must be immortal, because being spiritual it cannot cease to exist. Before he could reinforce this with scriptural evidence, Ormsby interrupted: 'What about Bertrand Russell?' 'What about him?' said Father Head tartly. 'He's one of the greatest minds of the twentieth century. He says he can find no evidence that human faculties operate independent of the living body. Or the dead one. Shouldn't we take his arguments seriously?'

We all moved forward on our seats, scenting a battle. But Father Head was not upset on this occasion. He knew where he was going. 'And what,' he asked in turn, 'is Bertrand Russell?' Ormsby, on his guard for a trap, hesitated. 'He's a philosopher,' he said at last. 'One of the most admired of our time. He's re-defined Western thought.' 'Well, well, Ormsby,' said Father Head, smiling now. 'You obviously have access to information denied the rest of us. Where precisely did Lord Russell acquire his qualifications in philosophy?'

Ormsby was caught now. He didn't know such a detail, and he was too astute to take a guess. Worse, he could tell by George Head's expression that there was no answer by which he could extricate himself. Father Head waited a long time, to emphasise the completeness of his victory. Then he appealed to the rest of us. 'Do any of you know where Bertrand Russell became a philosopher?' Continuing silence. 'Well, of course, he didn't,' said Father Head, now in control. 'He's neither a philosopher nor a theologian. His degree is in mathematics. And you don't expect competence from a mathematician on theological matters any more than you'd expect a croquet player to make a good All Black. Always look at a person's qualifications before you consider the merit of his arguments. Then consideration may well prove unnecessary.' It was a rout. None of us dared raise the next obvious debating point: how did George Head's letters in music qualify *him* to engage in philosophy? Christian gentlemen could only go so far. . . .

The other area in which strong conservatism — puritanism, even — lay behind the facade of reasonable discussion, was sex. And this attitude too, perhaps, was as much Irish in origin as it was Catholic. Most of the staff, in their roles as teachers of Christian Doctrine and confessors, spoke of sex only as a problem. Heterosexual relations were lumped together in discussion with masturbation and homosexuality, and one was left with the feeling that all were equally unfortunate; or, at the very least, that the married state was inferior to a life of celibacy. Perhaps this was a consequence of the subjects being raised by celibates.

The view of marriage represented to us at that time seemed bleak. Its primary function was described as the procreation of children; its second as 'the allaying of concupiscence'. The third was an expression of love between two people. Birth control was deemed sinful because it interfered with that primary function. This was tidy but — it seemed to me — a warped perspective. What prompted a couple to become attracted to each other in the first place? A conscious wish to be involved in procreation? Or a natural sexual interest that led to love and a wish to express that love in every way possible? The third option always appeared to me a worthier one than that of mere procreation, because it involved whole people as distinct from a mere linking of sexual organs. In fairness, I recall classes in my final year in which Bernie Ryan put a very different perspective on sex to that to which we had become accustomed. He suggested that the so called sins of the flesh — fornication, masturbation — were not so considered because they were ugly, animalistic or unhealthy; but because they involved debasement of a symbol of love and trust. And, redressing an imbalance I had been conscious of

70

throughout my secondary school days, he assured us that sins of intellectual malice, pride and hypocrisy were far more serious than sins of mere physical inclination. All of which helped one come to terms with the body again, instead of regarding it as an enemy and the instrument of the devil.

Another blast of fresh air in my senior years was an extraordinary lay brother, Augustine, a former seaman with a postgraduate degree in science. His cerebral conversation was curiously at variance with the tattoos on his arm, accidentally revealed when he wrote formulae on the blackboard. Aug taught physics and mathematics. But he also read Kung and de Chardin, and he discussed with us (as if we were adults) the need to revise theology in the light of advances in biochemistry, molecular physics and palaeontology. He accepted evolution as a plausible hypothesis, for example, when most of his colleagues were dismissing it as a discredited theory. It was absurd, he kept stressing, to reject scientific evidence because it seemed to conflict with theological propositions; theology too should be open to searching speculation. Aug's erudition and fair-mindedness, the same qualities in a recent Cambridge graduate, Gerry Arbuckle, Bernie Ryan's cheerful positiveness and Spiro Zavos's argument-provoking history classes — these did far more to prepare us for the world we encountered after college than did the negative conservatism of many of their colleagues.*

Beyond the arena of cerebral jousting, however, was the spiritual heart of the college. And this beat strongly and frequently. We rose at 6.00 every morning for Mass, which in pre-Vatican Council days was entirely in Latin. We heard it either *en masse* in an intimate chapel (a converted dormitory) or served it individually in tiny oratories in which all the ordained staff consecrated and consumed the Eucharist daily. In addition there was Benediction of the Blessed Sacrament every Sunday evening; sung High Masses on feast days with an array of deacons, sub-deacons, acolytes and servers; Requiem Masses when staff died; and frequent rosaries and private visits to the chapel for prayer and meditation,

---

*I am speaking, of course, of the late 1950s and early 1960s. Recent evidence leads me to believe that the liberals subsequently got the upper hand; when I was at school, however, they were under siege.

especially during the forty-hour expositions of the Blessed Sacrament.

The early Masses were hard work, especially in winter; it would be cold and dark and we were often little more than half-awake. My favourite ritual was Sunday Benediction, performed at dusk on days when we had been down the river and felt close to nature and close to God. With the celebrant's ornate vestments, the gold radiance of the monstrance, the hymns with their organ accompaniment and the thurible releasing incense, it was an intoxicating combination of sight, sound and smell. The words of the hymns were beautiful in themselves, and mysteriously powerful in translation.

Tantum ergo Sacramentum	*Lowly bending, deep adoring*
Veneremur cernui:	*Lo! the Sacrament we hail:*
Et antiquum documentum	*Type and shadows have their ending*
Novo cedat ritui.	*Newer rites of grace prevail.*

Being a Marist institution, we gave special emphasis to closing prayers that honoured the Blessed Virgin on her Feast Days. These invocations too seemed like poetry of the purest kind:

Hail Holy Queen, Mother of Mercy
Hail our Life, our Sweetness and our Hope.
To thee do we cry, poor banished children of Eve.
To thee do we send up our sighs,
Mourning and weeping in this valley of tears.
Turn, then, most gracious advocate,
Thine eyes of mercy towards us,
And after this, our exile,
Show unto us the blessed fruit of thy womb, Jesus.
Oh clement, oh loving, oh sweet Virgin Mary.

Whether from a love of words and ritual, a strong sense of the sacred or from the rising of adolescent hormones, I found profound consolation in these exercises. They seemed then — as I think they would now were I still able to practise them in that manner — to bring me to the shore of some ocean of spirituality. They apprehended a life beyond the physical, felt but not seen; a permanent fixture beyond the measurement and decay of time. I still believe in the existence of such a reality. Later, I was to glimpse it less frequently, and to doubt that Catholic ritual was the only vehicle in which to approach it, as we believed then.

At the time, though, I was moved greatly by the life and rituals of the Church and gave serious thought to becoming a priest. It seemed the only way to grasp a vision that one would otherwise only glimpse; and it seemed the only way to retain it against assaults of the material world and the appetites of the body, all of which diminished that feeling of proximity to the eternal. My father, however, was horrified at this idea; my mother, probably because of his reaction, not encouraging. I was persuaded to at least try the world and the flesh before I renounced them. And so, armed with prizes in history and Christian Doctrine and good marks in English and French, I entered Victoria University in 1964 with a Bachelor of Arts course laid out before me like a map. I chose my subjects according to my known inclinations and aptitudes. I had no precise idea about what I would become at the end of the process: priest, teacher or writer, perhaps, or some combination of all three.

University life was a surprise and a joy. Interests which had been encouraged but practised narrowly at college were mainstream activities at Victoria. The cultural options were distractingly varied. For the first two years I lived at home, worked hard at my subjects (history, English, French, political science), was an active member of the Catholic and Debating Societies and wrote for *Salient*, the student paper, and for the New Zealand Student Press Association. My initial friends were involved in the same activities: Bill Jeffries, Anna Rutherford, Mary O'Regan, Tony Haas and Hugh Rennie; and Peter Kingston, who widened my knowledge of music and accompanied me to concerts. I also made close friends among the Asian students, especially an Indonesian named Arief, with whom I kept in touch until he was killed in student riots back in Djakarta. In the winter holidays I skied. In summer I worked for the Parks and Reserves Department of the Wellington City Council: one year I cleared blackberry from the whole of Karori Cemetery; another I took two months to level with a hand rake a hillside that was to become the Makara Lawn Cemetery.

As I had been at school, however, I was aware of cultural gaps — in both the curriculum and in student activities. I was unable to study Maori language or culture, as I had intended, because these subjects were not then available. There was only one New Zealand history paper, a general one, at stage one. All the clubs were run by Pakeha students like myself, most of them male; the only minor exception was the disproportionate level of involvement of Jewish students, of whom I knew six (Haas, Paul Peretz, Barbara Cowan, Sue Markham, Monique Bloc and Linda Sacklin.) I knew only one Maori student, Kiri Haira; and one Samoan, Lei Lelaulu who eventually edited *Craccum* at Auckland University.

Reading for New Zealand history, I was lent a marvellous essay by Ruth Ross, called 'The Autochthonous* New Zealand Soil'. It seemed to confirm what I already felt about the gap between Maori and Pakeha understanding; and about the apparent futility of trying to bridge it, at least at university. Mrs Ross was writing about her first contact with the Maori community into which she had moved, at Waiwhao on the Hokianga Harbour. As wife of the new schoolteacher, she had been invited to a twenty-first birthday party. 'For all the friendliness and noise there was an underlying formality to proceedings, but the rules which guided them were unknown to us and we were uncertain what to say and how to say it, what to do and how to do it.'

The Rosses met an old man named Tu, their nearest neighbour. A widower who lived by himself, he had been introduced to them as one of the senior elders and an authority on local history. So they asked him the name of the terraced hill visible behind them.

'Maramarua,' he said. Then, 'Ae, Maramarua.' The conversation, if such it could be called had lapsed. His English seemed fairly limited. Our Maori was nil. We stood there in front of him in a silence we hoped was companionable but which on our side at least was a little uneasy. Then he began to

*Autochthonous: relating to the original or earliest known inhabitants.

sing. And as he sang in his grating harsh old voice he shifted his weight from one gumbooted foot to the other jabbing his walking stick at the soggy winter turf. No one took any notice of him, the background noise of men talking, women laughing, kids yelling continued without check. On and on he sang, tunelessly — at least to our ears. Then as suddenly as it had begun the waiata ended. 'That's why that place is called Maramarua,' he said, and walked away. So now we knew. Or if we did not, whose fault was that? In the Maori world the speaker speaks. Understanding is the business of the listener.

Subsequently, I was to have experiences that paralleled this one. At university, however, I was simply made more aware of how little we learned that would help us understand such encounters in our own country. English papers prescribed few New Zealand books and no Maori literature. In history, Europeanists such as Peter Munz denied there was any such thing as Maori literature ('Where are the books?') and therefore anything Maori worth studying. This view was not entirely shared by New Zealanders such as John Beaglehole and Mary Boyd, but their professional interests and teaching seemed to be more Pacific than New Zealand-oriented. I always felt this state of affairs to be wrong in a New Zealand university, especially in view of what was happening in history, prehistory and Maori language at Auckland University; but I got little support from other students when I argued the matter — amicably — with lecturers such as Peter Munz.

As far as wider culture was concerned, however, it seemed an exciting time to be loosed on the world with a minimum of responsibilities. I attended all university concerts and those of the New Zealand Symphony Orchestra when they performed in Wellington. The Drama Club was active on campus and included such gifted writers and performers as Roger Hall, David Smith, Caroline Harding and Deirdre Tarrant. So-called creative writing was undergoing something of a slump, at least in comparison with Auckland at the same time; after Albert Wendt left university and Michael Amato withdrew from student social life, there were few accomplished writers about, though Bob Lord (later a playwright), Michael Heath and Denis List were producing interesting experimental work. Jim Baxter appeared occasionally, usually invited by the Catholic Society, but disappeared to Dunedin on a Burns Fellowship in 1966. To talk writing with practitioners, it was necessary to head for pubs such as the Duke*, where Alistair Campbell, Harry Orsman, Phillip Wilson and others held court on Friday nights.

Parties were characterised successively by Beatles music, folk, and then folk-rock. Lennon and McCartney were the pop heroes of my early university days, Bob Dylan the star of the later period. The folk idiom brought with it an awareness of social issues that was also fed by the movement against New Zealand involvement in the Vietnam War. A half-Jewish, half-Irish girlfriend of the time, Linda Sacklin, belonged to a folk trio that cut its own record (John, Geoff and Linda). I accompanied them on Saturday night gigs to coffee bars such as Monde Marie — owned by the formidable and flamboyant Mary Seddon, one of the Capital's great hostesses** — and Chez Paris. Some Saturday nights Peter Kingston and I put on lounge suits and narrow black ties and, with partners, made up foursomes to dance at the Caltex Lounge. This was a highly respectable, non-licensed hall over a service station in Lower Taranaki Street, where the resident band was Tony and the Initials. We did the twist and rock and roll, and evenings invariably closed with a cheek-to-cheek rendition of 'I Left My Heart in San Francisco'.

Marijuana, then known as pot, was just beginning to appear on the party scene, and we experimented with it with caution. It did little for me. Most of us were into alcohol and cigarettes, and they seemed injurious enough without introducing further pollutants into the body. Doctors such as Erich Geiringer and Carol Shand were just beginning to prescribe the pill to unmarried women, and this slowly affected attitudes to pre-marital sex, making it safer, less anxious and hence more prevalent. People still got pregnant, however.

---

*. . . of Edinburgh, on the corner of Willis and Manners Streets; since demolished.
**I once saw her eject a drunk Black American sailor from the premises in a performance that would have done credit to a Sumo wrestler.

The Catholic scene too was in a state of ferment. I worked with Peter Gibbons from Auckland University to establish a national Catholic magazine called *Insight*. Pretentiously, it aimed to make Christians 'aware of and interested in the modern church', and 'to give information and promote intelligent discussion of the various aspects of the church today'. Our early contributors included Jim Baxter, Pat Lawlor, W.H. Oliver, Fathers James Kebbell and G.H. Duggan, and even Bishop Reginald Delargy. We were astonished when, after four issues, the magazine was closed down by Archbishop Liston (it was published from Newman Hall, the Auckland Catholic students' hostel). In a letter to myself and other contributors, the Archbishop said: 'I deprecate the publication of so much superficial and brash writing . . . the giving as an address of Newman Hall, which as bishop I have provided for university students . . . is a sad infringement of hospitality.' I wrote to Archbishop Liston and explained the purpose of the magazine, quoted letters of praise we had received from other clergy (including bishops) and asked which articles he found superficial and brash. I was dashed to receive neither acknowledgement of nor reply to my letter.

Jim Baxter commented to me in a letter from Dunedin that the incident was a probable misuse of pastoral discipline, and that he had written about it for *The Tablet*. 'This is my way of fighting for the laity — most of all for the rights of the young laity. None of these old warhorses would dare have me on personally for the way I write, though they may not like it — because they know they'd expose themselves to ridicule in the eyes of the literate protestant community. But I know bloody well the young laity who have grown up in the Church get a very different treatment — and believe me I fight on their behalf with gladness and love, and grateful for the trust shown in me by you and several others.'

The promised article in *The Tablet* never appeared. For me the whole episode was redolent of the differences I had encountered between the anti-intellectual Irish traditions of the nuns and Marist brothers, and those of the Marist priests. The dichotomy was to appear again and again, as long as I remained involved in Catholic activities.

In my third year I left home, went flatting with David Shand and Paul Peretz, and became more heavily involved (too involved) in student politics. I followed Alister Taylor as secretary of the students' association, a virtually full-time job for which I was not paid.* It was an exhilarating year. For once I had an overview of student life and some involvement in all aspects of it (since applications for club grants and use of the Student Union Building had to come through the association). The year before, Taylor had organised what was thought to be the first student march in New Zealand, in support of higher bursaries. In 1966, with Hugh Rennie's help, I organised the first anti-South African demonstration originating from the university.

The occasion was the banning order served in May on the president of the National Union of South African Students, Ian Robertson. As was common in such cases, no reason was given for the ban. Robertson himself was a conservative, supporting American involvement in Vietnam, for example. The action against him was clearly an attempt to undermine NUSAS's anti-apartheid activities. On grounds of student solidarity, and bearing in mind the close sporting connection between New Zealand and South Africa, we decided to object. The Victoria association sent a letter to the South African Prime Minister, we circulated a protest petition, we conducted a twenty-four-hour vigil outside the South African Consulate in Wadestown, and we tried to present our petition to the South African consul (who would not receive us; we were reduced to having to push it through a gap in the front door when somebody opened it inadvertently).

It was all low-key, but it produced virulent reactions, for and against our protests. Letters to the editor in the Wellington papers praised us for our conscience and condemned us for interfering in the affairs of a country about which we knew nothing. To my parents' discomfort, the press releases had gone out in my name and I appeared on television explaining the association's stand. My father, then a member of the Returned Services Association's Dominion executive, warned me that the Security Intelligence Service took an interest in such activities, and that the general public believed they were communist-inspired.

---

*My successors were.

I was active in demonstrations against New Zealand involvement in the Vietnam War the same year, having first believed that it was justified. By 1966, as one corrupt South Vietnamese regime followed another and civilians were dying in large numbers from saturation bombing and defoliation, it seemed to me that we were on the wrong side — or that no side was the right one. It was not a just war. Curiously, I *was* approached by an SIS agent. He was ostensibly a fellow student who worked part-time for 'the Justice Department'. He had an unending supply of American Camel cigarettes, then difficult to procure, and he came into my association office for long conversations. They always turned eventually to the anti-Vietnam movement and to the individuals involved; and to Corso (on whose national publicity committee I sat). He constantly sought appraisals from me about the likely political allegiances of activists in both organisations. I told him nothing and eventually refused to discuss Vietnam with him. The following year he was exposed as a member of the SIS by a Sunday paper and left university.*

Student politics, like student journalism, was a business in the mid-sixties. We regarded our responsibilities as serious in themselves, but also as a dry run for careers in the world beyond university; indeed, many of my then-colleagues did well in their subsequent professions: Rennie, Haas, Shand, John McGrath, Ian McKinnon, Tony Hassed, Edna Tait, Geoff Bertram, Ross Jamieson, Rosslyn Noonan, to name a few. We advocated recognition of the People's Republic of China, a cessation of sporting links with South Africa and an end to nuclear testing, and papers such as *Truth* regarded us as dangerous radicals. (I had several nasty exchanges with one reporter, who tricked me into commenting on an issue while he affected to write about another.) But by comparison with those who followed, we were

---

*The Royal Commission set up to inquire into the Godfrey affair at Auckland University had recommended to Government that agents should not be active on campus while enrolled as students. At Victoria, however, a second member of the SIS, who had been at Silverstream with me, was subsequently found to be working there while still a student.

conservative.* The males among us wore short hair, ties and jackets; the women skirts and jumpers; we dressed formally for balls, we were pragmatic issue by issue and we lacked ideologies or wider strategies.

We did *talk* ideologies, however. One of the most stimulating institutions of the period was the annual congress at Curious Cove in the Marlborough Sounds. There students gathered in the summer break for a week of intensive lectures, discussion, partying, swimming and picnics. Speakers in my time included John Rangihau, Jack Shallcrass, Sir Guy Powles, John Marshall, Jim Baxter, Con Bollinger and Austen Mitchell. Twice we organised overseas speakers, William Buckley from the United States and Robin Blackburn from London. Again, the popular press tended to view the whole exercise as a training ground for agitators. But it was a marvellous opportunity to draw back from degree studies and specific issues and examine the world in broader terms, in the company of people who were society's decision-makers or leading critics. The students who honed their wits and enlarged their egos at Curious Cove were among those who made an impact on public affairs subsequently: Geoffrey Palmer, Richard Northey, Helen Sutch, Rosslyn Noonan, Bob Cater, Bill Holt, Brian Easton, and many others.

Of the dozens of lectures I heard there, two stayed in my mind above all others, characterised (it seemed to me) by sanity, reason, and compassionate humour. One was from Jack Shallcrass, a warmly communicative man who has always seemed able to articulate clearly convictions that I have groped towards. In 1965, when he was deputy-principal of Wellington Teachers' College, he spoke on the right to dissent, elaborating on John Stuart Mills' dictum that if all mankind minus one were of one opinion, and only one person of the contrary opinion, mankind would be no more justified in silencing that one than he, if he had the power, would be justified in silencing mankind. Like Shallcrass,

*In fact, it was always difficult to keep a student audience serious during discussion of grave issues. A motion I moved at a general meeting, 'that the French Government be asked not to develop its own nuclear deterrent', emerged mutilated after several amendments as: 'That the French Government be asked to develop its own new clear detergent'.

I have always believed this, though there are times when it is a difficult precept by which to live, especially when one is dealing with the expression of uninformed, foolish or prejudiced opinions. I have more than once created difficulties for myself* by giving others opportunities to voice opinions that are provocative and dangerous. Nonetheless, I believe that the principle of free speech is not divisible, nor does it exist unless it is practised.

'If we treasure our right to be heard,' Shallcrass argued, 'then we must accord that right to every other person. If it is correct for us to deny any person or any section of the community any right, then by change of circumstance he would be correct in denying us. . . . Freedom for the expression of someone's wrong idea secures freedom for the expression of my right idea. Error is essential to the finding of truth. What we know depends equally on knowing what is and is not the case. Hence the futility of enforced orthodoxy — for we can only know if its view is right if we also know other views.'

This is a classic statement of the liberal position by which I have tried to live all my adult life. In the sixties, it was a view that tended to be held by the left and distrusted by the right, and it summed up the raison d'être of Curious Cove. In recent years it has lost ground among radical organisations with whom I might otherwise associate, because of their need to trumpet orthodoxies and silence the voices that would question or test them.

The other theme Shallcrass touched on was 'the political and social irresponsibility of expressing one's own will in the pursuit of one's own ends, without reference to the problems facing the sovereign community'. This phenomenon increased in the late sixties and early seventies, when American gestalt therapy hit New Zealand and inculcated a 'me' and a 'now-centred' philosophy, and political groups based on single issues proliferated. In this context, Shallcrass spoke of the danger of becoming 'trapped in our individualism, unable to communicate with our fellows or to think beyond immediate needs'.

Coincidentally, it was another Curious Cove speaker who impressed me equally and who seemed to point a way through

*See page 180.

some of the difficulties Jack Shallcrass had defined. John Rangihau in the 1960s was a handsome, slightly dissipated man — a kind of Maori Errol Flynn who spoke with striking eloquence in Maori and English, and who made Maori idiom and concepts intelligible to Pakeha listeners. He was then a welfare officer based in Rotorua, though his tribe was Tuhoe and his home the Urewera. At Curious Cove he spoke of Maori obligations to their family, hapu and tribe, and how these superseded other considerations. While Pakeha society lost its extended families and became more individualised, he said, Maoridom was providing blueprints for communal living and resolution of social problems. 'On the marae, Maori can get up and say anything they like to any person at all. But when they go into the meeting house, there must be no harsh words and you must ultimately get unanimity of opinion, no matter how long it takes. By the next morning, you will have lost most of your aggressive tendencies.'

He also raised for the first time (at least in my hearing) the suggestion that New Zealand did not have the good record in race relations that its politicians boasted about to the rest of the world. I had heard the claim frequently — but always made by Pakeha figures in public life, especially the then-Prime Minister, Keith Holyoake. Rangihau told us not to believe it. 'There is a colour bar in New Zealand. I have been refused accommodation in hotels from Auckland to Invercargill, simply because I am a Maori. I have gone around the corner and rung the same place up and given a Pakeha name and they have said yes. Then when I've got there they've said, "Oh, I'm sorry, I thought Mr So-and-So was a Pakeha." This has happened to almost everyone who is Maori. And there are still areas in New Zealand where Maori cannot get work. Insurance companies and banks, for example.'

All this came as a shock to me. I had assumed that the non-racial attitudes I took for granted were general throughout the New Zealand community. But the negative experiences of which he spoke were fully confirmed when I moved subsequently to a district with a large Maori population. And when I became involved in reporting Maori affairs, I was to go back to John Rangihau frequently for perceptive comment and analysis.

The ideals of Curious Cove spilled over into the Tuesday Forum back at Victoria, instituted by Tony Ashendon. Here people literally got onto a soap box (or apple box) at lunchtime and did their best to shout down an audience more interested in interjecting than in listening. Topics ranged from Vietnam to homeopathic cures for carbuncles. I found the experience terrifying but spoke frequently, as I did at the Debating Society, to develop confidence in front of audiences. The only occasion I can remember with total clarity is getting up to face an Open Day crowd, which included parents and would-be students from secondary schools. I hadn't said a word before the hooting started. Someone close to me pointed at my trousers. I looked down and saw my fly was undone. Trying to recover the initiative, I said the first thing that came into my head: 'Well, it is Open Day.' The applause was tumultuous and I stepped down. It was the first time I understood that, whatever one planned to say, it was safer to conclude after a good punch line.

One of the most rewarding jobs I undertook that year was researching the student association's history and helping to arrange a reunion of former executive members. It culminated in a dinner attended by about 150 former student leaders. The oldest, a foundation executive member, died the next day ('but happy,' his daughter informed me, 'happier than he'd been for years'). Toasts were proposed by Tom Seddon, 'King Dick's' son, Sir David Smith and Richard Wild. It was an evening of unexpected hilarity, drenched in nostalgia. I subsequently kept in touch with Tom Seddon and delivered John A. Lee to him the following year when he came to Wellington to address a meeting of the Political Science Society. They had overlapped in Parliament in the 1920s.

This dispersal of attention and energy took its toll. Academically, I had a disastrous third year and had to return for a fourth to complete my BA, majoring in history and English (and still unable to decide which was the more important to me). I married Ros Henry the same year, at 21, and at the end of it headed for Hamilton. There I was able to work part-time with the *Waikato Times* and teach at a Catholic secondary school while I completed an MA. It was a way of both earning a livelihood and postponing decisions about a career. The options now seemed to have narrowed to teaching or journalism, with an inclination towards politics fed by the students' association experience.

CHAPTER FOUR

Into History

AT THE END OF 1968, with further qualifications in history, I chose journalism over teaching. I had in fact been gravitating in this direction for several years with contributions to the student press, a column in the *Evening Post* in 1966, and my involvement with the magazines *Insight* and *Focus*. I wanted to write and I wanted to earn a living from writing. I also wanted an antidote to five years spent among academics and students — to immerse myself in a New Zealand community and learn how it worked at every level, from the operation of voluntary associations to the business of local government. And so I joined the *Waikato Times* as a general reporter, and quickly came to specialise in education, politics and Maori affairs.

The *Times* in Hamilton was a good paper to work for in the late 1960s and early seventies. Its management had been taken over by Philip Harkness, a journalist in his thirties who had succeeded his nonagenarian grandfather. It was unusual for a newspaper proprietor in New Zealand to hold both qualifications (including a degree from Stanford) and experience in journalism. He encouraged the recruitment of graduates, he allowed talented young people their head, and the paper adopted an editorial stance close to that of the *Guardian* in Britain — it was independent of community interests and it was liberal. The then-editor was a former Indian Army major, John Barrett, whose first job had been working on *New Age* for A.R. Orage, publisher of Katherine Mansfield. After a career in the Indian Army, from which he had retired with the rank of major, he had edited a newspaper in Bermuda. He too was civilised and liberal. They were stimulating men to work with.

Once I had joined the newsroom full-time, I took every opportunity to get out of the office and range as far afield as I could in search of stories throughout the paper's large circulation area (from Te Kauwhata in the north, Turangi to the south, Coromandel to the east and Raglan to the west). In particular,

I indulged my love for the bush, fed previously by camping with the family in the hills behind Eketahuna and trips across the Tararuas with my father on holidays from Silverstream. I have always felt an immense exhilaration and sense of equilibrium among forests, just as I have when I am on or near the sea. It's partly an aesthetic satisfaction that comes from walking under huge canopies of totara, rimu and beech, feeling fern brush the ankles, smelling the ground odour of moss, decaying bark and leaves. Psychologically, though, one comes into contact with one's own subconscious in the bush, and one feels integrated because of it:

> In a dark time, the eye begins to see,
> I meet my shadow in the deepening shade;
> I hear my echo in the echoing wood—
> A lord of nature weeping to a tree.
> I live between the heron and the wren . . .

I found no shortage of professional excuses to put myself into such environments frequently. With the Hamon brothers, I scoured the Coromandel ranges for large kauri, and we succeeded in saving a stand in the Manaia Block that the Forest Service had selected for felling. I hunted and found kokako in bush east of Kawhia. I explored caves on Pirongia Mountain and in the hills between Te Kuiti and Marakopa with the Hamilton Tomo Group, and while doing so found extinct bird bones, moa egg shell, and a previously unknown species of land mollusc. I combed Ruapuke Beach south of Raglan for a wreck that a con man claimed to have sighted there. I explored and wrote stories about fortified pa on the banks of the Waikato and Waipa Rivers. And I wrote stories about Taharoa, a coastal community without electricity or shops, that was about to be propelled into the twentieth century by the New Zealand Steel ironsands development.

Because of my interest in Maori affairs, I was assigned that round within weeks of joining the paper. Consequently a large part of my weekends was taken up with attendance at hui and tangi. I was immediately aware of huge gaps in my knowledge and understanding. First, proceedings were conducted entirely in Maori and I couldn't understand a word without someone alongside me to translate. Second, speeches and conversation were sprinkled with references to people and events of which I knew nothing — Tainui, Hoturoa, Tawhao, Whatihua, Turongo, Mahinarangi, Raukawa, Maniapoto; to the fighting chiefs Te Putu, Kiwi, Te Kanawa, Te Wherowhero; to the Kings, from Potatau to Koroki; to the places Kawhia, Whaingaroa, Te Whaanga, Taupiri and, of course, the river, 'Waikato taniwharau, he piko he taniwha, he piko he taniwha'.*

The concentrated dose of all these references, conveyed in a language that was foreign to me, produced something like culture shock. For a couple of months I floundered and wrote stories as best I could. Then I bought a second-hand copy of Leslie Kelly's tribal history *Tainui*, enrolled in continuing education Maori classes, sought out people who could help me, and joined the Waikato Historical and Archaeological Societies.

There was little I could learn about recent Maori history from these latter groups. The historical society did not have a single Maori member and was preoccupied largely with colonial history — Waikato since the coming of the Pakeha. My suggestion at one meeting that Hamilton should revert to its Maori name of Kirikiriroa, for example, was not well received. The archaeologists went to the other extreme. They *were* concerned with Maori history, but largely of the pre-European variety. Although the region was one of the most interesting of the country because of the unusually large number of old habitation sites, and the fact that wooden artifacts were often preserved in the peat swamps, only one Maori, Teremoana Pehimana, belonged to the society. Most Waikato Maori, I subsequently found, regarded archaeology at this time as only one step removed from grave robbing. Indeed, the activities of early ethnographers in the district, such as Andreas Reischek, had given them good cause to view archaeologists with suspicion.**

Some of these feelings became clearer to me once I began

---

*Waikato, river of a hundred bends, and on every one a taniwha.
**Reischek (1845-1902), an Austrian, after receiving warm hospitality from Waikato Maori, had looted burial caves near Kawhia in 1882 and smuggled two Maori bodies to Vienna. One was returned to Waikato in 1985.

consultations with the kaumatua who indicated a willingness to help me. Eventually I abandoned archaeology. Among those elders were Te Uira Manihera, a spokesman for the Maori Queen, who lived close to me in Hamilton and was easily contacted, Piri Poutapu at Turangawaewae Marae, Wetere and Emily Paki at Huntly, Rotohiko and Pei Te Hurinui Jones of Ngati Maniapoto, Winara Samuels of Ngati Haua at Rukumoana, and Eva Rickard at Raglan.

The meeting with Eva was typical of the haphazard manner in which I initially handled the round. The office was told there was a large tangi at Raglan that weekend. I was asked to investigate. I drove to Poihakena, the Tainui Awhiro marae below Te Kopua Hill, and got out of the car nervously. Next to the meeting house was a tent full of old women dressed in black, some of them with green leaves in their hair. While there was no sign of other visitors coming onto the marae, the area was surrounded by dozens of people milling about and talking. I walked up to the marae entrance. 'Haere mai, e Pahau,'* somebody called out in a gravelly voice. It was a woman in black with a large nose and a powerful personality who seemed to be organising things. 'Naumai, naumai,' she said impatiently as I stood there. 'You from the *Waikato Times?*' 'Yes.' 'Well come on in. You got your camera?' 'Yes.' 'Well go and get it.' So I did.

Eva Tuaiwa Rickard hongi'd me vigorously then led me onto the marae. The women in the tent around the coffin began calling out and keening. Still holding my arm, Eva made me pause, bow my head, and wait in front of the mourners. Then we straightened up. 'Right,' she said. 'You go and hongi all those kuia. Then you can take a photo of our Granny Rihitoto.' I did as I was told, all embarrassment gone under Eva's firm patronage. Reluctantly, I even photographed the tupapaku, a centenarian named Rihitoto who had outlived six husbands. She lay in her quilted coffin as if asleep. Her features were Maori but her skin was pale in death. It was only the second time I had seen a corpse. In this context, it was not a frightening experience.

That same day I met Piri Poutapu, who arrived with the party of mourners accompanying the Maori Queen. He patted the seat

---

*I had by this time grown a beard.

beside him on the meeting house porch and invited me to tell him about myself, my job, my ambitions. Then he told me how he had been adopted by Te Puea Herangi at infancy and gone with her to Ngaruawahia to establish Turangawaewae. In the late 1920s, she had sent him to the carving school at Ohinemutu to learn the craft and subsequently supervise its revival in Waikato. Since then he had trained apprentices, carved houses and built canoes. He was a gentle, humble man, already wheezing with the emphysema that was eventually to kill him. His final word to me then was to do nothing at Ngaruawahia without coming to see him first, and to sit beside him at hui there. He said he had been very close to James Cowan and Eric Ramsden*, but that he had barely seen a journalist since.

Wetere and Emily Paki took me under their wing at a hui at Waahi, home of Queen Te Atairangikaahu (who was married to Wetere's son, Whatumoana). First, they said, I must learn Maori, and they corrected my pronunciation and made me practise words in their presence until I got them right. 'Secondly, stick with us and we'll tell you what's going on. Thirdly, if there's anybody Maori you want to meet, we'll take you and speak for you.'

The first person I wanted to meet was Wetere's father, Hori Paki. Leader of Ngati Whawhakia, he was by then over 100 and universally regarded as the patriarch of the Waikato tribes. He had known and worked for the kings Tawhiao, Mahuta (especially Mahuta, from 1894 to 1912), Te Rata and Koroki, and for Princess Te Puea. He was a beautiful-natured old man who believed that aroha and manuhiritanga were the primary Maori virtues and practised them as if they were. To meet him and greet him correctly, I learnt my first mihi, with the help of my Maori language tutors Moana Raureti and Jim Milroy.

I walked with my small family — Ros and Jonty (then an infant) — onto the grass that served as a marae in front of the old man's home at the Rakaumangamanga. He stood to

---

*Eric Ramsden, 1898-1962. A journalist with the *Sun* in Auckland, the Christchurch *Press*, and Wellington's *Evening Post* who specialised in Maori affairs. He was a friend of Te Puea Herangi and wrote copiously about the Kingitanga.

welcome us, leaning on a stick. He was thin, his face skull-like, his skin stretched parchment; but he addressed us all in a firm voice in a mihi he later taught me as a pattern for all subsequent welcomes. Then, breathless with tension, I rose to reply and thank him. 'Tena koe, e pa. Tena koe e taniwha tawhito o te awa o Waikato.' And so on. I relaxed when I saw his approval and his pleasure. Afterwards we ate, drank tea, told stories, and generally enjoyed ourselves. Oddly, he was completely at ease with Jonty. There was 100 years between their ages, and neither understood a word the other said. But they had an instinctive rapport often shared by the very old and the very young, communicating in winks, nudgings, pointings and giggles.

Hori talked most about Te Puea, for whom he had acted as a kaumatua ever since she rose to prominence in 1910 (when he was already in his midfifties). He had shifted an old hall across the river for her to Mangatawhiri, her first community for widows and orphans. He had helped her record Waikato whakapapa and whakatauki in her diaries. He had spoken for her on marae throughout the district. And she had often sent Pakeha scholars to him for advice, such as Johannes Andersen and W.J. Phillipps from the Dominion Museum. One thing in particular intrigued me that first day. Hori said there was another Waikato elder, a kuia, older than he. He didn't know how much older. But she was married with children when he was a boy. Her name was Ngakahikatea, and she lived with a granddaughter up the Mangatea Valley east of Ohinewai.

Again, it was Wetere and Emily Paki who arranged the visit. I have described elsewhere the impact of that first encounter with Nga, on a winter's morning in 1969. Wetere drove me to Matahuru and we stopped outside a small weatherboard house. A mist was rising off the frost-covered paddocks and the sun was just breaking through from a clear sky above the fog. 'There she is,' said Wetere. I rubbed the frosted side window of the car and looked out. An old woman, hunched almost double, was pushing herself with a stick across the grass towards the house. She was draped in blankets and looked very small. With the mist behind her, she seemed to be walking out of the past.

In many ways, she was. Nga dressed nineteenth-century fashion with one tartan blanket for a skirt and another for a shawl. The blue lines of the moko were scarred into her chin. Her memory reached back to the Waikato War and its aftermath, to the time of King Tawhiao. In childhood she had known men and women who were alive when Cook visited New Zealand. In old age she played with children to whom space travel was becoming commonplace. Nobody knew just how old Nga was. There were no records kept at the time of her birth. Estimates ranged from 112 to 120 years. She had outlived four husbands and two years later the last of her sons was to die, an old man. Culturally, she had been stranded and there was nobody living whom she could call a contemporary, not even Hori Paki, whom she referred to as 'he tamaiti' — a child.

When I met her in 1969, Nga sat on the steps of the house, knees drawn up under her chin, her skin wrinkled as screwed-up brown paper. But life rattled inside her like seeds in a dried pod. She stabbed bony fingers as she spoke rapidly in Maori. When she listened, she puffed clouds of smoke from her pipe. By this time she felt her isolation keenly. She told us she had been abandoned by all her old people, even by her children. Consequently, her granddaughter said, the old lady spent hours every day sitting, rocking back and forth, crying, crooning old waiata, and talking to her dead.

I spent as much time as I could with her over the next three years, encouraging her to talk, taping her, and translating with the help of the Pakis and Te Uira Manihera. Once started, she welcomed the opportunity to perform. While her memories of recent years were hazy, those of distant ones were clear. The look of abstraction on her face dissolved as she talked. Her eyes wrinkled in animation and concentration as she bent her mind back. Sometimes she sang to put herself in touch with the past. Then she would speak rapidly for up to an hour. After these bursts she would pause, light her pipe, smoke and rest while we waited. Then she would begin another burst of recollection.

When Nga sang it was almost always waiata tangi. Her voice would seize on a high pitch and hold the notes tremulously but determinedly. The sound alone conjured up a feeling of persistence in spite of loss. Most of the songs were from her childhood, unknown to my interpreters. Although Maori in language and form, many of them suggested contact with Europeans. Here, translated, is one of her favourites:

Why does this wind blow toward me?
It's from the north, where you've gone,
It carries your love back to me.
As you left, you turned and looked at me.
Was the landing place difficult?
Is that why you didn't take me too?
Why have you abandoned me on this wharf,
Tears running down my cheeks?

In spite of such lyrics, Nga insisted she had had little contact with Europeans until her recording sessions with me and the subsequent visits of journalists and film crews. She said she had been a girl just over school age when she saw her first Pakeha, troops garrisoned at Alexandria (now Pirongia) after the Waikato War. This was probably in the late 1860s. Afterwards she insulated herself from the European world by living among the ranks of Maori King supporters at Mercer and Waahi. In the last years she liked to stay with her descendants in remoter districts like Matahuru in the heart of Waikato. She was not comfortable in the presence of Pakeha and she didn't like them.

First and last, Nga regarded herself as a member of the Waikato tribes who had drawn their name, identity and sustenance from the river that scoured out the basin in which they lived. Her reverence for this water was built on 600 years' continuous occupation by her people. It amounted to worship. In every sense, the Waikato had been their source of life: it contained eel, small crayfish, waterfowl and edible plants; it was the swiftest means of transport and communication; its waters held the spirits of the dead. Whenever Waikato people were sick or about to embark on a journey or new venture, the advice of their priests was always the same: 'Haere ki te wai'. Go to the water. And at the water they would sprinkle themselves and recite the names of ancestors. In this way they achieved cleansing, healing and protection.

Nga lived her whole life within the river's reaches, apart from brief visits to family in Auckland, the northern boundary of the tribe, when she was very old. After such visits she had to be taken down to the water so she could kneel before it, pat the surface with her outstretched palm, and call to her parents, grandparents and other kinsfolk beyond life. It was her way of establishing and intensifying her link with the genealogies that were her source of identity.

This ritual was also part of her faith, Pai Marire. She had lived to see Christianity envelop her people who, in their disinheritance, identified strongly with the Hebrews of the Old Testament. But Nga remained loyal to the religion brought to Waikato from Taranaki by King Tawhiao in the nineteenth century. It was a faith that worshipped the old departmental gods as personifications of natural forces, and ancestors as genealogical paths to those gods. Her cosmology was one in which places and buildings had life-forces of their own, and in which the dead, when invoked, clustered around as companions of the living.

Three weeks before she died in 1975, a granddaughter took Nga back to Waahi Pa, old home of Mahuta, the ariki and king who had called on her help most often. At first she was confused by the place and the people who came out to press noses and foreheads with her. Then their greetings began to reach her. Tears ran down her cheeks and she started to call out, fluttering her raised hand as if to fan out the words: first to the meeting house; then to the dead of that marae. She reached out for Tumate Mahuta, senior grandson of her dead king, and fingered his face and spoke to his father, grandfather and great-grandfather Tawhiao as if they were present in him.

The story Nga told most often as she aged was that of her own 'death'. It occurred some time in the early 1960s:

'I became seriously ill for the only time in my life. I became so ill that my spirit actually passed out of my body. My family believed I was dead because my breathing stopped. They took me to the marae, laid out my body and began to call people for the tangi. Meanwhile, in my spirit, I had hovered over my head then left the room and travelled northwards, towards the Tail of the Fish. I passed over the Waikato River, across the Manukau, over Ngati Whatua, Ngapuhi, Te Rarawa and Te

Aupouri, until at last I came to Te Rerenga Wairua, the Leaping-Off Place of Spirits.

'I cleansed myself in the weeping spring and then ascended to a ledge from which hung Te Aka, the pohutukawa root. Here I crouched. Below me was Maurianuku, the entrance to the Underworld, covered by a curtain of seaweed. I began to karanga to let my tupuna know I had come. Then I prepared to grasp the root and slide down to the entrance. But a voice stopped me. It was Mahuta. "Who is it?" he asked. "Ko au," I said. "It is I, Ngakahikatea." "Whom do you seek?" he questioned me further. "My parents. My old people. I have come to be with my tupuna." "They are not here," said Mahuta. "They do not want you yet. Eat nothing and go back where you came from until they are ready. Then I shall send for you. So I did not leap off. I rose and returned to my body and my people in Waikato. I passed over all the places and things I had seen on the way. My family and those who had assembled from Waahi for the tangi were most surprised when I breathed again and sat up. So it is that I live on. Because the spirits of my dead will not claim me. I shall not die until they do.'*

These meetings with Nga sidetracked me for a time down a narrow path of Maori history. Watching her, I realised that it was years since I had seen women with moko. As a boy, I had once crept past a group of them in Rotorua, where we were staying on our way to Northland. They sat huddled together, talking and cackling in their own language. They were as much part of the then unfamiliar landscape as meeting houses and carved gateways. Now the landscape had become more familiar to me, but the moko was gone. In the time I had been attending hui to report Maori affairs, I had not seen one woman with tattoo. Preparing to write about Nga for the *Waikato Times* and the *Weekly News*, I tried to find reference books on Maori tattooing. There was nothing more recent than Robley's *Moko or Maori Tattooing* published in 1896, which noted that it was

---

*Nga eventually died on 1 June 1975. That same day a thick fog rolled off the Waikato River and covered the district for four days until she was buried on Taupiri Mountain.

a dying custom and dealt largely with its application to men.

I decided then to build on what Nga had told me, to search out every woman still alive with moko, and to record their stories. I knew there couldn't be many. The store-keeper at Ruatahuna in the Urewera expressed the general belief when he said, 'There are only twelve in New Zealand, and we've got six of them here.' In fact, travelling back-country North Island roads several weekends a month for nearly three years, I found over seventy of them: twenty-six with chisel moko, forty-five with the later needle tattoo. They lived in dirt-floor whare in bush settlements, in farm cottages, in suburban houses made of Huntly brick, in rest homes, in hospital wards. They lived then in far greater numbers than any of my informers suspected.

They included survivors of Tawhiao's entourages, Kirikino Kohitu of Honikiwi and Nohinohi Heu of Kawhia; Karu Mohiti of Muriwai and Moerangi Ratahi of Whakatane, both companions of Te Kooti Te Turuki Rikirangi in his old age; Rauwha Tamiparea of Parihaka, protégé of Te Whiti O Rongomai and Tohu Kakahi; and Waiarani Ratana of Murupara, former wife of Rua Kenana. Some were centenarians; almost all were over eighty. Many were bed-ridden. It was their great age and their necessarily non-public lives that led other Maori to under-estimate their numbers.

I need to stress now — in view of subsequent Maori sensitivities — that I spoke to these women only when they and their descendants wanted me to. In most instances, they did. Some families were keen that the story of their kuia's moko be recorded and were pleased that I was prepared to do it; some had never even asked about it themselves. When I arranged to have photographs taken — again, only with unequivocal consent — I received large orders for these portraits, which Marti Friedlander supplied free of charge to the kuia and their families.

As I gathered information on tattooing, some experiences etched themselves on my recollection more sharply than others. There was my dawning recognition of how far Maori attitudes to photography differed from European ones, for example. Late in 1969 I took a photograph someone had lent me of a deceased Waikato woman with moko to one of her contemporaries, also with moko, for identification. Makere Hose of Te Kuiti held the framed portrait for a long time, staring at it. She began to cry, silently at first, then aloud. After about ten minutes she leaned the picture against a shelf in her living room and began to talk to the deceased woman in Maori. 'Ah. It's a long time since we've been able to look at each other. It's a long time since we've been able to talk. But you seem just the same. So. You're with your mother and grandmother at last, eh?' And so on.

All this took place in my presence with no sign of self-consciousness on Mrs Hose's part. I had sat down when she began her tangi, but risen to my feet again, because it seemed disrespectful to sit through what was in effect a religious ritual. It was half-an-hour after I had handed her the photograph that she turned to me and said: 'It's Rehara. Rehara Maki. She came from Waharoa, but she attended all our hui. She died over a year ago.'

Being inexperienced, I was perhaps less reticent than I would have been subsequently. I wanted to understand. So I asked intimate questions. I said, 'You treated that photograph as if it were a living person. Why?' 'Ah,' said Mrs Hose. 'It's got her image, you see. And that image is their mauri. Whenever I see a picture of a person I feel that person's mauri, and so long as I can feel the mauri, then it's alive, never mind that the person's dead.' She elaborated when I asked if I could have her photograph taken. 'No,' she said. 'You can look at me, you can look at my moko. But you can't photograph it. Because if you do that you are taking away some of my mauri. And when that happens people lose their spiritual protection. If it goes on too much, they die, like Rehara here. I don't want that to happen to me.'

Shortly afterwards I took a photographer, Allan Baldwin, to a woman with moko who, like Nga, *was* prepared to be photographed. Her name was Kirikino Kohitu and she lived in Honikiwi, a King Country community that had been virtually wiped out by the influenza epidemic of 1918. She was arrestingly beautiful, even though she was then in the last year of her life: a long face that seemed chiselled out of wood, rich brown skin with wrinkles like a wood grain, almond eyes that seemed more Asian than Polynesian, and springy white hair plaited in pigtails. Her moko was a chisel one, done by Anaru Makiwhara of Mercer before the First World War.

On each occasion I visited her, her mind was always elsewhere, in the past. She sat on the step of her whare smoking her pipe, looking towards the ground but into a great distance. It always took time to recall her from that other world. After a while she would look up, puzzled, without recognition. Then a slow smile would begin at her mouth and spread to her cheeks and eyes. 'Aie, tena koe, Maikara, tena koe.' And I would hold her bony hand and we would hongi. Her daughter Inuwai, an old woman herself, loved Kirikino intensely. But she couldn't persuade the old lady to move inside the house. Instead, she went on sleeping in her adjacent whare with dirt floor and unpainted walls covered with pages of the *Weekly News*, some dating back fifty or sixty years. The chimney was corrugated iron. Two black kettles sat on iron bars on the fireplace and there was always a smoked eel hanging from a wire over the ashes. 'She doesn't wake until late in the morning,' Inuwai told me. 'Sometimes I think she's gone and I have to bend down and feel her face to make sure she's still warm.'

Like the other kuia moko, Kirikino talked about far more than her tattoo. She felt abandoned by the community that had predeceased her, and she was hungry to talk about the past, even to me. She had travelled with Tawhiao to Hikurangi and Whatiwhatihoe — vast nineteenth-century settlements of which there is now no trace. She was in Kawhia when Tarawera erupted and thought it was gunfire. And in 1894 she walked nearly forty miles from Kawhia to Parawera for Tawhiao's tangi. The bound tupapaku lay in state there for three weeks. Mourners gathered in their thousands. Kirikino, stripped to the waist and wreathed in koromiko leaves, karanga'd and poroporoaki'd beside the coffin. Then she kept the old king company on his final slow journey through Waikato to Taupiri. At Taupiri, they were greeted by additional mourners from the upper Waikato. As the two groups met a band played a funeral march, rifles fired salutes and dynamite exploded from the mountain graveside (though they later shifted the body). 'There will never be another one like Tawhiao,' Kirikino used to say over and over. 'Never another like him.' On this occasion we photographed her, and I sent back a framed copy to Inuwai.

Less than a year later, after I had shifted to Wellington, I got a short letter from Inuwai. 'Mum never forgot you. She even cried after you left. And I am writing to tell you that the old lady passed away peacefully on November 9.' I went back to Honikiwi that summer. Inuwai was high on a hillside littered with dead logs, collecting huhu grubs with two small grandchildren. It was a desolate place — a rough, tiered surface in a forest left to rot — and a desolate day, with rain clouds blurring the higher ridges. Inuwai didn't see me until I was about ten yards away. She straightened slowly, stared at me, then recognised me and began a long karanga on that lonely hillside. I moved towards her slowly. Then stopped, head bowed, as her grief rose and overflowed. She stood tangi-ing, humming and dabbing her eyes with a white handkerchief. Then she took my hand and nose for a long hongi, saying, 'Michael, Michael,' over and over.

It was later, when we were sitting on a flat stump, that she held one of my arms and told me the most extraordinary story. 'You know that photograph you gave me? The big one of Mum with the pipe in her mouth? Well, we put it at the foot of the coffin so that the manuhiri could see it as they arrived. Do you know, as each one came that picture misted over. All except the nose. You could still see that. The younger ones couldn't understand it and rubbed the mist away. But it kept happening. I knew what it meant. I'd seen it as a girl. The old lady was crying with us and her nose was pressing against the glass, hongi-ing with the people.'

My experiences in the course of the moko project were by no means all like this. At one marae, Manutuke, I approached the kuia there through a daughter who was out of favour with the rest of the family and we were, literally, chased off the marae (this same family later complained to me that their kuia wasn't in my book). On other occasions, though I went with the right introductions and accompanied by local kaumatua, I was politely

98

refused by dignified old women who saw my project, not as information gathering, but as unwarranted intrusion and exploitation.

I remember going to Kawhia with Te Uira Manihera. He was nervous. He had had a dream the night before, and he believed that dreams carried messages. He told me about it as we drove over the range that separates the Waipa Valley from the west coast. 'My wife and I were sleeping,' he said. 'Then all of a sudden we heard voices. Pakeha voices. The next thing she threw off the blankets and exposed her front. I said "Hey, they'll see you." But she left herself uncovered and pretended to be asleep. And then these Pakeha came — one, two, three, four of them — and they looked at her. With lust. It was desecration of something female and something precious. I was most upset. When I woke up I said, "Goodness gracious. What's going on?" I told her about it and she said, "Be careful, drive carefully."'

The dream worried away at him and several times he nearly turned back. We were on our way to see Nohinohi Heu, the last kuia at Kawhia with moko, who had shut herself away from the Pakeha world and consistently refused to have her photograph taken or to even talk about her moko. Te Uira was related to her. An old man himself, he had grown up with her at Taharoa and Kawhia. When he was a boy she was already a kuia. Now he too was anxious to learn more about her history and to help me record it. He thought he could persuade the old lady to speak. But he was unhappy. The message of the previous night had been unsettling.

We turned off the sealed road just short of Kawhia and onto loose metal — the old horse track out to Te Kakara. (Nohinohi had lived there long before cars came to the district.) It wound up a valley alongside an arm of Kawhia Harbour that gradually tapered into a mangrove swamp. Just before the crest of the hill we heard a 'flick-flick-flick' sound from the front of the car and stopped to investigate. The tyre on the right front wheel had an enormous blister. As we looked at it, wondering, the blister burst. The outside skin split from top to bottom. We both just stared. Then Uira said, 'Something's wrong here, very wrong.' And after we'd changed the tyre: 'What's the old witch going to do to us next?' I said nothing, frightened that he would return home.

Then we came over the hill and looked down on Aotea Harbour, calm and bright as glass under the hot sky. Karioi Mountain, source of the iron that blackened the sand right down this coast, rose up behind the water. Nohinohi's cottage stood over the harbour on a small peninsula. It was screened by an impenetrable hawthorn hedge and only the rusted corrugated iron roof and leaves of a cabbage tree could be seen over the top. 'Give me some time with her first, to explain,' Uira said. He waded through the hay paddock and into a hole in the hedge.

I got out of the car to get my gear from the boot — tape recorder, notebook and pen. Above my head a trilling began. A skylark was climbing the sky in slow circles and I left the boot open and lay down in the long grass to watch and listen. The bird rose and hung, rose and hung, and all the while spilled out quavering music. I remembered that the song was said to be a ploy to distract predators, to draw them away from nests.

Uira called to me from the gap in the hedge and I walked over and crossed a stile into Nohinohi's world. It included a garden of jostling vegetables the weatherboard whare, a rectangle of lawn and, by the door, a cabbage tree. Of the surroundings, only the sky was visible. The old lady was sitting on a box by the door. Sitting, but bent with arthritis. Her head alone was held up straight, with an effort, trying to focus on me through hooded eyes. Her jaw was wide and strong and the moko stood out pale blue against the light brown skin. As Uira had told me, there was an alertness about her. She commanded attention. She also had a triangular brooch of old threepenny bits pinned to her cardigan, a sign that she was a follower of Tawhiao's Tariao religion.*

I walked to her between close rows of corn. She said nothing as I shook hands and hongi'd and sat down facing her with my back against the cabbage tree. She just followed me with her eyes. I felt what I was. An intruder. Beside her, Uira began

---

*Tawhiao was a believer in the doctrine of the Trinity and used to explain it by holding up a threepenny bit and saying: 'See? Three pennies in one coin.'

to talk again in Maori. Loudly, because of her deafness. He told her about my project and the other kuia I had interviewed. He said we had come to ask her to share her knowledge with us. He recalled how frightened he had been of her as a youngster, but said he came now with respect, not fear. Nohinohi watched him and waited till he had finished speaking. 'Ka mutu?' she asked. 'Ae,' said Uira. 'Ka mutu.' Then she began to reply in a strained, hoarse voice, brandishing her index finger as though each point was an accusation. I couldn't follow. Uira translated quietly for me as she spoke. 'She says she spends her days more with the dead now than with the living. She can talk to them at any time. Tawhiao was here last night. As she was walking towards him, a tattooed man threw a barbed spear that landed right at her feet. It was the old-time challenge. "Will you dare to sell your tribe?" Tawhiao asked her. "After your tribe, what next?"'

Nohinohi's face was getting redder as she spoke and her voice was choking as if she was being strangled. 'Nowadays many Pakeha come to her wanting her picture or to record her voice. But she says they can't have them. They can't have the Maoritanga that has been entrusted to her. It was different in the days when she was young. Then everybody had Maoritanga. Now there is only her. Her moko is her mauri, her life force. It is as much an emblem of her tapu and mana as that blossom is a sign of life in the tree.' She pointed to the cluster of white flowers spilling out of the cabbage tree's head.

'She says she belongs to the past, to Tawhiao and to her parents, and she can't come forward into the present. She says I should know that,' said Uira. Nohinohi paused, worked up, gasping for breath. Uira took her hand and tried to quiet her. 'Taihoa, taihoa,' he shouted into her ear. But she pushed his hand away and went on. Uira quoted her directly. 'No reira. I can find only one thing to say. You tell your Pakeha friend. When the time comes, I want to go to my kainga with my moko unseen and my voice unheard. No one will take them from me.' She stopped talking, flushed and panting. Uira waved me away. I got up without saying anything and crossed back over the stile. I felt as separate from her as it was possible to be from another person.

When I looked back at them they were still talking, more quietly now, heads together. Uira's arm was round the old lady's shoulders, reassuring her. Back at the car I heard the skylark, still singing. But even as I looked up for it the music stopped. Seconds later I saw it, floating down slowly. Feeling safe, it disappeared behind the hedge and the tree.

To my surprise, I did see Nohinohi once more, on a moving and public occasion. Just before I left the *Waikato Times* in 1971, Queen Te Atairangikaahu put on a farewell tea for me in Mahinarangi meeting house at Turangawaewae, with the elders with whom I had worked most closely: Piri Poutapu, Te Uira, Tumokai Katipa, Wi Huata, Paraire Herewini, and several others. I found it a slightly uncomfortable occasion, because we didn't share the same view of what was happening. Piri said to me, only half in jest: 'We didn't give you permission to leave Waikato. You've no right to go.' They were farewelling me as an ally, a brother, a Waikato. This was emphasised by Uira's speech: 'Michael, greetings, and also farewell. We hope that in the years to come, you will remain part of Waikato and her people. From those who will be sorry to see you leave, we bid you fond farewell. Haere ra, Michael.' For my part, my professional loyalty had always been to my occupation. If people were satisfied with the news and feature writing I had done, it wasn't because I was favouring them; it was because (in my mind) I was representing their activities and their views fairly and proportionately, something I tried to do subsequently in the field of Maori history.

For that day at least, however, I was a favourite son. Te Atairangikaahu asked me if I had any ideas as to how the marae might appropriately celebrate its fiftieth jubilee the following year. The answer came to me in the proverbial flash. 'Moko,' I said. 'Make it a day for the moko ladies. There aren't many of them left and I've got all their names and addresses. They'll probably never be seen together again as a group.' Later, I set out the proposal more coherently in a letter and sent her the names and addresses.

The result was that in August 1971, some sixteen kuia with moko came to Turangawaewae Marae as guests of honour. They were led by Nohinohi Heu as senior elder of Ngati Mahuta, Te Atairangikaahu's own tribe. The tangata whenua women called them on and Nohinohi was the first to appear up the narrow path and onto the marae proper. She was bent double and had to use two sticks to walk, one in each hand. But she held her head up proudly and fiercely, and looked from side to side as she edged across the marae she hadn't set foot on since Te Puea died twenty years before. With her were Ngakahikatea, Tiraha Cooper, Makere Hose, Rangi Ruri, Hari Salmon, Pare Hapimana, and a host of women who had become my friends and surrogate grandmothers.

Later, inside Mahinarangi, the queen welcomed the kuia and told them how they had come to be brought together. Tiraha Cooper stood and mihi'd in reply, and thanked me for my contribution. I was like her, she said: a trustworthy Pakeha (she had been brought up Maori, given a moko and spoke little English; but she did not have a fraction of Maori blood). Then the more lively ladies rose and entertained us with song and dances for another hour. Pirihita Pateriki of Matata made poi out of her long white handkerchiefs and showed us how she had led the Arawa welcome for the Duke and Duchess of York in 1927. It was a happy day. Within a year, half the women present were dead.

Several factors combined in 1971 to cause me to appraise what I was doing. At work I had been promoted to leader writer and acting news editor. There was no increase in salary, and I now spent my days behind a desk, organising the other reporters' assignments and writing editorials that few people read, however carefully one crafted them. (And however liberal they seemed: we were the first daily paper in the country to oppose New Zealand involvement in Vietnam and sporting contacts with South Africa; this had come about at least in part because of my vigorous arguments at editorial conferences.) Some of my colleagues began to make it obvious that they felt I was devoting rather too much attention to race relations issues. Editorially, I had agreed wholly with Nga Tamatoa protests against the Waitangi celebrations ('What cause do Maori have to celebrate the Treaty?'); I emphasised in everything I wrote about race relations that integration in New Zealand had been — up to that time — a one-way path that only Maori had trodden; and I questioned the ability of New Zealand institutions, based on British and Western models and cultural assumptions, to deal fairly with those whose values and lifestyle were not Pakeha.

I had predicted major disruptions in New Zealand life if adjustments were not made to recognise that the Maori were now an urban people, to meet legitimate Maori needs and aspirations, and to include Maori at all levels in decision-making on public policy. I persuaded the paper to give strong editorial support to the establishment of a Maori Research Centre at the University of Waikato, to provide 'action-oriented' research into areas of actual and potential race relations conflict. Reactions to these views were mixed. Some of my colleagues — especially those who had strongly supported the All Black tour of South Africa in 1970 — believed that Maori-Pakeha relations would be fine if people like me stopped writing provocative articles and stirring up resentment where none had existed previously.* Others such as Richard Long, Phyllis Gant, Warwick Roger and Judy McGregor, were supportive.

I had also come under strong attack from the Minister of Finance, R.D. Muldoon, for the paper's sponsorship of the Maori Research Centre. After he had disparaged the need for the centre and claimed that the University Grants Committee had not supported the idea, I wrote an editorial criticising his and the Government's short-sightedness in this matter. This produced a phone call from the minister who abused me, accused me of distortion, and insisted that the decision not to proceed with the centre had been made by the grants committee. I checked this allegation. Both Alan Danks, chairman of the UGC, and Don Llewellyn, vice-chancellor of the university, confirmed that I was correct: the grants committee had approved the application for the centre and it was the Government which had decided

---

*'New Zealanders take pride in their tradition of racial equality,' I had written as early as January 1968. 'But this tradition has never been tested under the kinds of conditions that are now developing [Maori urbanisation], nor those which have inflamed racial tension overseas.'

not to proceed with it. Muldoon came back fighting. He replied that he had not known the UGC had approved the proposal in 1966, 'before I became a member of Cabinet. A cabinet minister can't be expected to know all the details of all portfolios.' I was able to respond that, in that case, a cabinet minister should not speak as if he did know all details of all portfolios. We had won that round, and the centre was eventually established. But, again, I was made to feel that I had pushed the issue too vigorously for a journalist who ought to be displaying a kind of neutered detachment.

The other matter on which I was aware of conflict — this time more personal than professional — was religion. Whatever one does or believes subsequently, the cultural conditioning of Catholicism, especially Irish Catholicism, has a certain indelibility. It is like being Jewish or Polish. 'You can leave the Faith, but does the Faith leave you?' I felt during those years in Hamilton that the Faith was leaving me. Perhaps it was a consequence of being in the most conservative diocese in the country (possibly in the world, outside Italy and Ireland), ruled rather than presided over by the most Reverend James Michael Liston.

Jimmy Liston was approaching ninety at that time. He had ignored the Pope's request that bishops retire at seventy-five. He had refused to set up a senate of priests as directed by the Vatican Council (and as established in other New Zealand dioceses). He banned the use of folk music at Masses for the young on the very weekend that Archbishop McKeefrey attended one in Wellington. And he suspended two priests — one of whom I knew well — for taking part in a demonstration against the Vietnam War; the previous month he himself had marched to protest against the Warsaw Pact invasion of Czechoslovakia. While he was a man of great personal sanctity, Archbishop Liston was obviously out of touch with the mood of his church. As the earlier closure of *Insight* magazine had demonstrated, he was not diverted from his course by the Vatican Council's call for a free, communicative search for truth and its affirmation of the supremacy of the individual human conscience. He saw himself as the guardian of the minds and morals of his flock, who knew better than they what was good for them.

The problem for me was not so much being Catholic as being Catholic in New Zealand. If one read international Catholic literature — as I did at this time — then the Church seemed to be in a healthy state of ferment. European and American theologians were stressing involvement in human problems rather than insulation from a hostile world, a recognition that man's perception of truth changes and that the mysteries of the universe could not necessarily be contained in a single philosophical or theological system. They also emphasised a concept of the Church as the people of God rather than as a bureaucratic hierarchy. Issues being debated more openly overseas — birth control, clerical celibacy, divorce — were beyond discussion in New Zealand at that time. It seemed that, having been forced to switch the liturgy from Latin to English, the New Zealand bishops were fearful that further change might bring disintegration.

On several occasions I came into conflict with the conservative backlash. Twice I tried to discuss some of the issues with Archbishop Liston by telephone, in my role as a journalist; on both occasions he simply hung up. He declined to make appointments for interviews. I didn't bother him further. Then I reported the views of a visiting Dutch priest, Father Jacques Vink, on theological trends in Holland and Germany. Father Vink was a quiet and saintly man, who lived in a mixed religious community in Amsterdam. He had talked largely about the Church's commitment to the poor and the underprivileged in his city; and about the extent to which concepts such as the Incarnation, the Virgin Birth and the Resurrection could be regarded as mythology rather than historical events. Poor Father Vink. He did not realise how different the climate was in New Zealand from that in Holland. He was subsequently condemned by several New Zealand bishops, including Archbishop Liston, in letters to the secular and religious press. His views, they stressed, did not represent those of the Church in New Zealand (he had not said they did).

Another cause for disappointment was the Church's attitude towards social issues. The New Zealand bishops at that time seemed equivocal about war and peace. It was axiomatic to me, for example, that nuclear weapons could never be justified because of the inability of those using them to distinguish between combatants and non-combatants. There was official silence on this question. And the hierarchy appeared to be in support of the American position in Vietnam. Indeed, when I interviewed Archbishop (later Cardinal) McKeefrey on the question, he said the war was simply part of a Chinese plan to extend hegemony over the whole of South-East Asia. 'Where would Australia and New Zealand be in such a situation?' On purely local issues the Church seemed slow to help those who needed help and who — in the message of the Gospels — ought to have been the first candidates for Christian attention. I knew from Catholic Maori that Archbishop Liston refused to take their problems seriously, regarding them — in the words of one — as 'erring children'. And Jim Baxter was getting little support from his fellow Catholics for his work with the growing number of drug addicts in Auckland and his campaign against the kinds of treatment practised in Oakley Hospital; the major opponent of his view that addicts were sick people rather than criminals or scum was a senior Auckland Catholic policeman.

All these factors combined to strengthen my impression that, in the Auckland diocese at least, reform within the church was going to be a long time coming; and that in New Zealand the values of the secular middle-class were determining those of religion rather than the other way round. The hounding of Lloyd Geering by a large section of the Presbyterian Church seemed to reinforce the latter view. Oddly, the few reforms in the Catholic Church that had taken place seemed to me to be the wrong ones: *Aggiornamento* had resulted in the beauty and suggestive mystery of the Latin rite being replaced by a simplified litany in English that seemed prosaic and flat, utterly lacking in the feel of antiquity, continuity, mystery and divine reverberation that I had experienced at school. The sense of awe had been replaced by that of the commonplace, and to me the whole process felt like one of impoverishment, subtraction rather than addition. Later, when I read the views of Evelyn Waugh on this aspect of Catholicism, I concurred completely: 'He believed that in its long history the Church had developed a liturgy which enabled an ordinary sensual man (as opposed to the saint who is outside generalisation) to approach God and be aware of sanctity and the divine. To abolish all this for the sake of up-to-datedness seemed to him not only silly but dangerous. . . .'

I would not say I ceased to be Catholic — the mark of Catholicism, as I have suggested, seems indelible. And in the company of Catholics with a social conscience, and those undismayed by open-mindedness, I continued to feel at home. But I no longer felt that the Catholic community as a whole shared or even valued these qualities. The feeling was heightened when I spoke to the Catholic Women's League in Hamilton on human rights, and emphasised New Zealand's poor record in race relations (disguised only by Maori forbearance). It was apparent that not one person in the room agreed with me or had encountered the experiences to which I referred.* In 1971, therefore, I felt ready to move on; ready especially to return to a city in which I might find a wider community of interest and feeling. Three further events accelerated this inclination. My daughter Rachael was born. My Irish grandmother died; and I was interviewed for a journalism teaching position when I was in Wellington for her funeral. I was offered the job and I accepted.

---

*I had a similar experience in 1981, when I spoke to the Waikato Founders' Society on historical differences between the Springbok tours of New Zealand in 1956 and 1981; only on this latter occasion, about one-fifth of the audience did seem to agree. The majority that did not expressed their feelings emphatically.

CHAPTER FIVE

Tangata Whenua

IN 1971 I returned to Paremata, this time with my own family. I began teaching at Wellington Polytechnic and commuted daily to the city. I was delighted that my children could, for a time, experience the environment in which I had grown up so happily. I loved being able to row, fish and walk again around the harbour I still knew better than any other place on earth. Later, we moved into Wellington and lived communally with a group of families in Karori.

The journalism course, organised with flair by Christine Cole, was an immensely stimulating environment in which to work. We were able to call in at short notice other journalists, social critics and public figures, from the Prime Minister and the president of the Federation of Labour to Jim Baxter, and we did our best to simulate the conditions and pressures of a newsroom.

After Hamilton's conservatism, it was a relief to have access again to a community of like-minded people. I joined the Catholic Peace Fellowship and Amnesty International. I spoke at seminars on the media and on protest; and Ros joined the National Organisation for Women, which was beginning to set up consciousness-raising groups in Wellington. I remained involved in journalism on a freelance basis, writing for the *Listener* and keeping a watching brief on race relations, and I completed my book on Maori tattooing.*

The moko project had improved my Maori language and my rudimentary knowledge of Maori etiquette. It had prepared me for rejection as much as for acceptance. It made me aware for the first time of the considerable regional and tribal variations in Maori language and kawa. It brought me into contact with a range of authorities on Maori history and art, many of whom

---

Moko — Maori Tattooing in the Twentieth Century, 1972, Alister Taylor; photographs by Marti Friedlander.

remained friends subsequently: the old ladies themselves, especially Herepo Rongo, Rangi Ruri, Makere Hose and Hari Salmon; the Pakis, Te Uira Manihera, Piri Poutapu, Pine Taiapa, Winara Samuels, John Rangihau, Mohi Wharepouri, Harry Dansey, Sally Marshall-Tuwhangai, Ngeungeu Zister, Koro Dewes and others. It offered me a tantalising glimpse into the vast body of Maori oral literature and an awareness of its diminution every time an elderly person died. And it gave me a subsequent entrée into Maori communities the length of the North Island. Moko was to prove a beginning rather than an end in itself. But this was not apparent to me until the year after it was published.

Shortly after I arrived in Wellington, I was selected to attend Te Huihuinga Tamariki, the 1971 National Youth Congress (definitions of youth being flexible — I was by then 25). This conference added momentum to my interest in Maori experience and strengthened my conviction that it had been shamefully downplayed in the country's national historical equation. The 'angry young men' of the congress, held at Otaki, were members of Nga urban-based groups of young Maori radicals which had originally grown out of the Auckland University Maori Club. Its most forceful leaders were Syd and Hana Jackson and Taura Eruera. At the congress, Nga Tamatoa was represented by Poata Eruera and Val Irwin from Auckland and Eruera Nia from Wellington.

One of the discussion groups into which I was drawn was the race relations council. And it was in that forum, not surprisingly, that the Maori contingent exerted most influence. They began by arguing that integration in New Zealand had always been tantamount to assimilation; and they insisted that New Zealand history books 'be immediately rewritten to incorporate Maori history and points of view'. This last proposal provoked most argument. The whole group — Maori and Pakeha members — was in favour of the concept of multi-culturalism (then a novel term). But rewriting other people's books, Keith Sinclair's *A History of New Zealand*, for example, posed problems. What about copyright and authorship? 'What you need to do is write new books concentrating on Maori history and viewpoints,' I argued. 'You're a writer,' Poata Eruera shot back at me. 'What have *you* done to spread an awareness of Maori history?' 'Something, but not much,' I had to reply.

In spite of the naivety of the motion — and it was passed as originally framed — I was impressed by the force of feeling behind it. The Tamatoa members had confirmed the conclusion I had been close to reaching from another direction. Maori elders were ready to talk about tribal traditions and history. Pakeha historians had no further excuse for not seeking them out. It was time a serious effort was made to record them on a national scale, to communicate their views to a Maori and Pakeha audience and redress a glaring imbalance in the historical record. I was also keen to be involved in such work, should the opportunity arise. But perhaps the opportunity would have to be created. I could never make much progress as an unpaid weekend historian. Books took a long time to research and write and generated little income. Meanwhile bills had to be paid.

In the wake of the conference, Guy Salmon and I made submissions to the Statutes Revision Committee on the Race Relations Bill then before Parliament.'* It was an intimidating experience. The chairman, Sir Leslie Munro, and members of the committee seemed unsympathetic, and they fired questions back at us like lawyers (which many of them were) cross-examining witnesses in court. For those unaccustomed to it, the atmosphere was not conducive to quick and clear thinking. Looking back at our submissions, they seemed excessively moderate by the standards of the 1980s. We began:

> We reject both the concepts of assimilation (implying an absorption of minority cultures by the majority one) and integration (implying a combination of the values and institutions of two or more cultures). We prefer the concept of multi-culturalism, whereby cultures are encouraged to exist alongside one another, retaining their differences and respecting one another. We see this concept as an inclusive rather than exclusive one, allowing voluntary movement among cultures. In the New Zealand context, this means in

*It resulted in the setting up of the office of the Race Relations Conciliator.

particular movement between Maori and Pakeha cultures.

The group feels this policy is desirable because of its sensitivity to minority groups, its prospects for harmonious social relations within the groups, and because it would offer individuals the widest possible range of human experiences. To quote Martin Luther King, we believe New Zealand should come to see multi-culturalism not as a problem, but as 'an opportunity to participate in the beauty of diversity'. Among the consequences of the multi-cultural concept are the need to build up the base of minority cultures (especially Maoritanga) and to reduce an overbearing influence on the part of the majority culture.

All this was ahead of its time, however. The committee seemed obsessed with the idea that integration was a workable and working goal that ought not to be questioned. And Guy made a serious tactical error by suggesting to one member, Dr Gerald Wall, that as a Pakeha he had no understanding of what integration meant. Dr Wall was the only person present married to a Maori.

If the experience did little else, it confirmed another impression: that most Pakeha New Zealanders were woefully (though perhaps not wilfully) ignorant about Maori views and values. How could one convey to them the kinds of encounters that I had had in Maori communities and homes? How could one express in words alone the information and emotional charge that accompanied the karanga, the tangi, the whaikorero? Images and body language were such an integral part of Maori culture. At about the same time I had become one of the *Listener*'s fortnightly television reviewers. This heightened my awareness that the then NZBC was doing nothing for its Maori audience, nor anything to educate its Pakeha audience about that other Maori New Zealand. And yet, the more I thought about it, the more film and television seemed potentially the most arresting, affecting and practical way of conveying the kinds of experiences I had in mind.

I began to think about specific situations that would lend themselves to exposition on television. There was Herepo Rongo in Raglan, for example, one of the kuia moko we had taken to Turangawaewae for the anniversary hui. I had met her at

Nohinohi Heu of Kawhia, with her threepenny badge inspired by Tawhiao.
(Waikato Times)

Celebrating the fiftieth anniversary of Turangawaewae Marae inside Turongo House. The kuia moko performing are Ramariki Rangawhenua Kerei and Pirihita Pateriki.
(Joy Stevens)

Re-established at Paremata, with the children and my mother.

Filming on Raglan Harbour with (from left) Te Uira Manihera, Herepo and Eva Rickard (obscured). Cameraman Keith Hawke, soundman Craig McLeod. (Pacific Films)

Preparing to shoot an interview with Piri Poutapu and Te Uira Manihera, Turangawaewae Marae. Barry Barclay is at right. (Pacific Films)

With Ngoi at Tokomaru Bay.

Planning a shoot with Barry Barclay.

The Parihaka aunts in Te Niho-o-te-Atiawa: (from left) Sally Karena, Ina Okeroa, Neta Wharehoka.

that first tangi I had attended at Poihakena Marae in Raglan in 1968. Like Kirikino Epiha, she was a beautiful and large-hearted woman. But the course of her life had given her every cause for anger, and for distrust of Pakeha officialdom. In microcosm, her life mirrored the history of many Maori people and communities over eighty years.

She had been born, she told me, at Horea, site of an old Methodist Mission Station on the northern head of Raglan Harbour, which she always referred to by its old name, Whaingaroa. Later, she had lived on family land (ownership of which eventually passed to her) high on the coast between Raglan and Whale Bay. Later still, during the Depression, she joined her husband on her father-in-law's property at Patikirau on the northern side of the harbour. She bore nine children — and buried six of them under the pine tree that was the family burial plot there. Then came further troubles. A Native Land Court agent, Tony Ormsby of Ngati Maniapoto, persuaded her father-in-law, Mokomoko, to put his mark on a piece of paper, explaining that it would provide him with a pension. The old man couldn't read, but duly marked the document. In fact it was a deed transferring ownership of the land to Ormsby, who resold it to a Pakeha farmer. The whole family, angry but ignorant about how to seek redress, were forced to leave their homes.

They settled again on the Raglan side of the harbour, at the Tainui Awhiro community around Miria Te Kakara meeting house and marae. Here they were disturbed again. With the approach of World War Two, the Department of Civil Aviation was establishing emergency landing strips down the coast and the Raglan County Council offered the land around Miria Te Kakara. The whole community was paid compensation and shifted though Herepo refused to accept any of the Government's money ('black pennies' she called it: tainted money). The only consolation was that Civil Aviation promised to return the land to Tainui Awhiro once it was no longer required for the war effort.

The end of the war brought further duplicity, however. The land was given to the Raglan Aero Club, who leased it to the Raglan Golf Club. Not only did Herepo not get her home and marae back, she was confronted by the sight of Maori and Pakeha golfers (but mainly Pakeha) hitting golf balls over the community's urupa. Not only had the living been insulted but the dead were now being desecrated. When she tried to move back onto the land she had inherited on the coast she found that the Maori trustee had transferred her shares to a nephew. She had no legal right to live there any more. (She had been notified of the application for this transfer by. letter, but she couldn't read.) Finally, she acquired a house below Eva Rickard's on the hill at Te Kopua, overlooking the golf course that distressed her so much.

As I noted, she had every reason to be bitter. But she was not, except when she talked about particular examples of Maori or Pakeha dishonesty. At other times she treated Pakeha with as much aroha as she displayed towards her own family. And she was utterly without self-consciousness. Once she was talking or singing in her own language, she did so fluently and movingly whether the audience was Maori or Pakeha. She seemed to me to be the 'ideal subject for a television documentary. Apart from her qualities as a performer, her world would open up those very themes and values of which it seemed to me Pakeha New Zealanders were most ignorant.

I tried to interest Maori in broadcasting in such a programme — people such as Bill Kerekere and Selwyn Muru — but they were too tied to their existing responsibilities in radio. Also, I sensed, they were constrained by Maori implications of which I was not aware, and which they did not discuss with me. Then, at James McNeish's suggestion, I went directly to Michael Scott-Smith in television documentaries, and he put me in touch with John O'Shea and Barry Barclay of Pacific Films. That year, 1972, happened to fall within the period in which the NZBC was most receptive to commissioning programmes from private companies. Barclay and O'Shea were enthusiastic about the idea. Barry and I visited Raglan, ascertained that Herepo and Eva Rickard were willing to work with us, and jointly prepared a script. Scott-Smith formally commissioned the film on behalf of the NZBC. John O'Shea meanwhile negotiated the possibility of a series of films on Maori themes if our first one was successful. Thus began one of my most interesting eighteen months.

Barry, who directed the films and wrote the scripts with me, is a Ngati Apa whose Maori antecedents came from the Manawatu. I had been sent to him, not because of his Maoriness (he had been brought up without contact with his Maori side) but because of his skills as a film maker. With Tony Williams, he was one of John O'Shea's bright young men and had already made some outstanding documentaries, including one which James McNeish had scripted on Opononi and Opo the dolphin (*The Town That Lost A Miracle*). We got on well, personally and professionally. We shared a Catholic background (he had trained for the priesthood), an interest in Maori things, and intuitions about how films should work. In particular, we were determined that we would not make programmes about subjects; we would try instead to persuade people to make programmes about themselves — about their values, their preoccupations, their insights, the things that impelled them to call themselves 'Maori' rather than 'New Zealanders'. Our role, we agreed, would be that of facilitators: we would encourage them to talk, and we would listen and record accurately. There would be no commentary from outside 'experts', no learned intermediaries, Maori or Pakeha, analysing what was said.

The first programme, *The Spirits And The Times Will Teach*, was shot during my August vacation from Wellington Polytechnic. It was relatively straightforward, making use of associations I had formed while writing the book on moko. It began with a conversation about the past with Ngakahikatea, to evoke a feeling of antiquity and a view of life that had originated in the nineteenth century. It went on to a discussion with kuia moko and kaumatua about the significance of tattooing. It concluded with the main section: a look at the past and present life of one old woman with moko, Herepo Rongo, and her place in Raglan. By showing how Herepo lived and how her community related to her, it touched in a brief but integrated way on all the elements that would emerge in subsequent programmes — death, tapu, mana, land, and so on.

Because I knew the participants, the people interviewed and filmed were relaxed and articulate. The very qualities that made them effective communicators in an oral culture made them superb performers for film and television. We shot in English and Maori, and subsequently used voiceover translations for the Maori sections. Our policy was that people should speak in the language in which they were most comfortable. Herepo, of course, was the star. We filmed her on the Raglan golf course, berating the Government for not returning it to the Tainui Awhiro people and admonishing those who were playing golf on the cemetery section.* On the water at Patikirau, she burst into a poroporoaki for her dead children, completely unconscious of the presence of cameras. At Poihakena Marae, she rose again and called unselfconsciously: to the house, to the land, and to her dead ancestors. And in a moving climax to the programme, we filmed her resealing and reimposing the tapu on a desecrated tomb. We were immensely pleased with the result. And so, to our relief, were Herepo, Eva Rickard and the Raglan Maori community.

With one programme literally in the can, I took a year's leave of absence from Wellington Polytechnic. Barry and I travelled the North Island seeking locations for the five other hour-long films we wanted to make under the general title *Tangata Whenua***, discussing them with the communities we visited, and screening *The Spirits* as an indication of our approach and treatment. The reception we received varied enormously. Some kaumatua, deeply suspicious of both Pakeha and television, wanted nothing to do with us. Others, such as the leaders at Ratana Pa, listened to what we had to say and quietly declined to become involved. Still others debated the proposal with us, rejected us, and then changed their minds. We finished up with ten major locations for the remainder of the films: Waikato, Auckland, Mataura Bay, Te Teko, the East Coast, Hokianga, Porirua East, Ruatahuna, Parihaka and Waituhi.

Waikato presented the major surprise of the series, and taught me at least one valuable lesson. We wanted to base an entire

*The screening of this programme was the beginning of the Tainui Awhiro campaign to have the golf course returned to Maori ownership. It was eventually handed back in 1984.
**'People of the land'; but with connotations of 'those who were here first' and 'host people'.

programme on Maori organisation there, using the Kingitanga to demonstrate how a large federation of tribes achieved cohesion when most others were having to fight disintegration. I hoped to be able to explore the history and growth of the Maori King movement through the recollections of its elders. I also hoped they would speak about the phenomena of the spiritual world (taniwha, matakite and so on) that confirmed their view of life. Individual kaumatua I already knew — Piri Poutapu, Te Uira Manihera, Whitiora Cooper, Tumokai Katipa, even Dame Te Atairangikaahu herself — were enthusiastic about the idea. But, wanting to observe correct protocol, I wrote formally to the queen's Tekaumarua or council of advisers for permission to proceed. They turned us down.

This was a surprise and a disappointment. I had carefully set out in my letter what we proposed to do, and stressed that we wanted a Waikato Maori view of the Kingitanga, not our own. At Dame Te Ata's suggestion, Barry and I met with her council one night at Turongo House to discuss the matter. The first thing that became clear to me was that most of the council had not read my letter — or, if they had, they had not registered its contents. I would now make a distinction between people who are literate and those who are 'aliterate' (who can read, but who trust and absorb information conveyed by oral discussion rather than by correspondence). 'A face seen, Koro Dewes had warned me, 'is an argument understood'; a letter is simply a piece of paper. The second thing that became apparent was that the council had divided along lines that had determined its previous groupings and decisions — the very fact that certain kaumatua supported us meant that others opposed our project.

There were also substantial arguments against our proposal, mainly from Henare Tuwhangai, the council tumuaki: the fear that something tapu would be commercialised ('who will you sell this to?')*; the fear that Waikato could be seen to be promoting itself boastfully over other tribes; the feeling (based on previous

---

*Strangely, after the series had been screened on television, the only groups who wanted to use the films to raise money (albeit for community purposes) were Maori. We declined every request, because that was one of the undertakings we had given to our subjects from the outset.

experience) that no publicity was better than bad publicity. After lengthy discussion failed to produce a consensus, I was prepared to abandon the programme. But Dame Te Ata asked if she could see us in our Hamilton motel the following day.

What she proposed as a compromise was that we make the programme; but that rather than work with Waikato as a whole we interview only those kaumatua who had expressed support for us. She would let it be known that she was in favour. And she would find a marae to work closely with us (we wanted to film a community that supported the Kingitanga and show its members preparing for a poukai or annual loyalty hui). For the latter she suggested Tauranganui, a Ngati Tipa pa near the mouth of the Waikato River. We accepted this advice and everything fell into place. We interviewed Poutapu, Manihera, Katipa and Cooper, and we were warmly embraced by Waka Kukutai and the people of Tauranganui, whose poukai provided a visual and emotional climax to the film. The sight of the queen's party coming onto that marae alongside the river, led by calling kuia dressed in black and a brass band playing, rain falling lightly, was one of the most riveting spectacles we recorded. It caught all the excitement — the build-up and the release of tension — that accompanies Maori rituals of encounter. And the *Waikato* film as a whole was probably the most integrated and popular programme of the series.

More typical of our approach to setting up films, however, was the manner in which we approached the Ringatu segment of the *Two Prophets* programme. After informal discussion with members of the Ngati Awa, Whakatohea, East Coast and Tuhoe sections of the Hahi Ringatu, we decided to approach Tuhoe for permission to film their religious activities. Just as the Kingitanga is a unifying force for the Tainui tribes, so Ringatu provides a calendar of ritual that binds the hapu of Tuhoe and continually renews their sense of identity and commitment to one another. Tuhoe also appealed to us as a people who had kept their Maoriness intact more intensely than other tribes, largely because of the relative remoteness of their communities in the Urewera from European influence. And Te Whai-a-te-Motu meeting house at Ruatahuna, built for Te Kooti, was both the cradle of Tuhoe culture and one of Ringatu's major shrines.

John Rangihau, then working as a district welfare officer for the Department of Maori Affairs in Rotorua, took Barry and me to Ruatoki for a Tuhoe tekaumarua — a twenty-four-hour cycle of Ringatu services held over the twelfth day of each month. The marae was long established, with a late nineteenth-century meeting house and a mauri that was palpable as we were called on. John was exactly the kind of intermediary we sought to have with us at each of the places in which we wanted to film. If he disapproves of a project, he does nothing; if he approves, he opens doors, points you in the right direction, then leaves you to it. In this instance, after the Ruatoki elders had welcomed us with karakia, mihi and waiata, he pointed to the marae and said to me: 'Speak.'

I was wretchedly nervous. In spite of my (by this time) four years of sporadic lessons in Maori, I had never stood and spoken on a marae, in Maori and in front of an accomplished and critical Maori audience. On this occasion, however, as I rose from my seat and stood between the manuhiri and tangata whenua on that cold winter evening, the mist coming off the valley floor as the sun went down into the Ureweras, I felt enclosed by a flow of sympathy from the kaumatua on the meeting house porch. I mihi'd to them and then to the dead. I explained why we were there, what we wanted to discuss with them. Then, as I sang the Waikato waiata tangi *E Pa To Hau*, the local people crossed the marae and joined me and took it over with a Tuhoe tune for the same song.

We still had a long way to go. We spent a large part of the next twenty-four hours, in between services, debating in the meeting house what we wanted to do, dealing with objections similar to those raised by the queen's council in Waikato. And we had an additional problem: after seeing our film about Herepo, some of the locals felt that the tomb-resealing sequence was a warning that filming would attract grave robbers to their district, which had previously been free from such Pakeha scourges. In the end we were asked to come to the next tekaumarua, at Te Tira Hou, the Tuhoe meeting house in Auckland. And there, after further debate, we were at last invited to return and film interviews and services at Te Whai-a-te-Motu at Ruatahuna, the focal point for Tuhoe activities. It would be the first time that Ringatu ritual had been filmed.

Surprisingly, it was older people, tohunga such as Ira Manihera and Hikawera Te Kurapa, who were most persuasive on our behalf. In an argument we heard again and again on other marae, they lamented the loss of their young people to urban communities and concluded that one of the few ways to reach out and touch them and influence them, was television. And when these elders and others such as the tattooed kuia Te One Whero spoke about the history of Tuhoe and Ringatu on camera, they were doing so more for the benefit of their own young people than for a Pakeha audience.

The Maori urban migration was a more explicit theme of our programme on land, which we called *Turangawaewae — A Place to Stand*. We shot this at Tokomaru Bay, Porirua East, and Waima on the Hokianga. In Tokomaru Bay we focused on the decay of rural communities, the effect on those places of the loss of adults in the working age-group, and the desire of many young Maori to return to rural districts where they had personal roots and a sense of history.

The dominant figure in the programme was Ngoi Pewhairangi,* the kind of character around whom legends accumulate. Although she valued and practised humility above all other qualities (she always entered her marae, Pakirikiri, through the back entrance), no individual on the East Coast since Apirana Ngata had attracted more mana. She organised her own community with quiet authority, and her people would have done literally anything for her. She was the greatest composer of modern Maori music, having inherited this mantle from her aunt, Tuini Ngawai. She was an exceptionally gifted teacher of Maori language and culture. She was wise and articulate when she spoke of serious matters — people often had to strain to hear what she said; but strain they did. She was devastating in repartee and a superb raconteur.

Dozens of images of Ngoi spring to mind. I mention only

---

*Later known to a wider Pakeha public for her composition of the hit tunes 'E Ipo' and 'Poi E'.

two. Greeting a busload of inebriated and sleepy rugby supporters, including her husband Ben, returning from Gisborne: 'Hello, here comes my wet dream.' And describing how their truck was stripped of its wheels one night when she and Ben — unknown to the robbers — were huddled in the cab, at first asleep, and then paralysed with fear when they realised what was happening. When Ngoi finally sat up and shouted at them, the hardened criminals got such a fright they not only abandoned the scene of the crime, they left a considerable cache of tools behind.

In matters of gravity, however, Ngoi was grave and eloquent. I interviewed her, for example, on her view of the laws of tapu: 'When you learn anything Maori, it has to be taken seriously . . . genealogies, history, traditional knowledge, carving, preparing flax, in fact, nature itself. Tapu is something that teaches you how to respect the whole of nature, because Maori things involve the whole of nature. . . . Nowadays, people raise the question about whether these things involving tapu should be taught in schools. Well, it's difficult. I wouldn't teach them. You see the way things are done in the classroom, teaching can become mechanical. And there are dangers. Take flax, for example. There are a lot of restrictions involved in flaxwork. The reason why old people hesitate to teach the young ones about this sort of work is because of the restrictions and tapu connected with it. If anyone learning breaks the rules connected with dyeing of flax, someone will have to suffer the consequences. . . .

'I'll give you an example. We were preparing kiekie and we had an old lady here teaching us how to do it. She even went into the bush with us to show the men how to cut the kiekie and strip them and bring them back. This was my first experience of the tapu placed on this type of work. We went through the whole process of boiling the kiekie and that wasn't so tapu. But the dyeing was. It was placed in the mud for about two weeks and that old lady herself went on a trip to collect it. They brought the kiekie back here and found the dye hadn't gone through. The first words she uttered were that something had gone wrong or that somebody had done wrong. "There's nothing we can do about it. Someone will have to suffer the consequences," she said. "Someone will die because the dye hasn't been done properly and whoever placed it in the mud must have broken the law of tapu." Two days after, the old lady died. This is the first time I'd ever known that tapu really had this effect. I believe in it now. . . . It's especially hard to communicate this sort of thing to Pakeha, unless it's to one who lives on the marae and is brought up in this environment to see the values of Maori culture and the tapu placed on things. He's got to see it and see how Maori suffer through the breaking of tapu connected with all the culture. Then he'll realise there's some value in tapu. But you can't teach it. It's something that has to come from within.'

Subsequently, Barry and I agreed that — although we were recipients of lavish hospitality and extensive co-operation almost everywhere we filmed — nowhere were we made to feel more at home than on Ngoi's marae and among her people. When we left Pakirikiri, Ngoi and her band of women workers sat up half the previous night to compose a waiata that commemorated our having been there and wished us well. It was a characteristic gesture on her part.

The other section of *Turangawaewae* centred on the life of the Davis family. From their home and jobs in Porirua East, where they were working to build Maraeroa, an urban marae, we followed them back to their ancestral marae in Northland: Karetu in the case of Ted, and Waima for Meretiana. Waima was a community typical of Hokianga. Like dozens of others, it had been swamped by the wave of Europeanisation that swept through the district in the nineteenth century. When it had passed, the land and culture had been ravaged, the kauri timber had gone to build cities in the south, the gum was torn from the ground. The Maori communities remained, but their inhabitants had European features (and, in many cases, European names) and they were poorer. They suffered from bad health, and from the malaise that follows the undermining of traditional social supports and cultural controls.

In the charged moments of life, however (and this was what we wanted to capture above all else on film), at times of birth, marriage and death, Waima responded in characteristically Maori ways. It also retained its role as a spiritual and cultural source for hundreds of former inhabitants and their descendants who had scattered all over the country. Fortuitously, while we were filming the Davis family replenishing themselves there, the community's oldest kuia died in Auckland and was brought home for burial. Could we, we wondered, film part of the tangi to illustrate how Waima came back to life in such circumstances?

The situation was volatile. We had permission to film with Meretiana Davis and her relatives and elders at Waima. We had had no contact with the family of the deceased woman, Karani Moetu. The thing to do, kaumatua Whiti Bedggood advised us, was to go to the tangi at Taheke, the neighbouring settlement, and make our request to the people there. We did so, and our proposal produced one of the longest and strangest nights I can remember.

Whiti Bedggood, a Te Mahurehure tohunga, was blind and confined by a stroke to a wheelchair. When we arrived at the Taheke Hall in the dark we had to carry his chair up the steps. Then I wheeled him through the doors and into the light. As the women began to karanga and keen, he poroporoaki'd to them, a spine-tingling performance that I had never seen before from a man. All the way to the back of the hall, to the coffin and the immediate mourners, he sang out his greetings and farewells to the dead. When he reached the principal mourners they rose and hongi'd with him, and he identified them. He not only seemed in no way handicapped by blindness, he appeared to know and see more because of the concentration of other senses.

Replying to the mihi, I explained why we were there: not so much to farewell an old woman we had never known (though we did honour her and grieve with the bereaved); but to witness a community, renewing its bonds among the living through its rituals for the dead. I asked if we could film this process, noting that it would in fact become a tribute to Karani Moetu, by showing nationally the aroha and respect in which her people held her. The debate that followed was confused and confusing and at times acrimonious. Before we arrived, those present had been discussing who would act as guardian for the tribal taonga for which Karani Moetu had been caretaker. After my contribution, a section of her family gained the impression that I was making a bid to seize the relics and put them in a museum. Another woman mourner was convinced our intention was to put her grandmother's face on a biscuit tin. All these misunderstandings arose from memories of things that had happened in the past, revived in strongly emotional circumstances. Discussion continued for the whole night. There had been no argument over where the old lady was to be buried; so in a sense the argument over whether or not the burial should be filmed was a substitute for that ritual discussion, and did her honour by emphasising that she was a person of importance.

At dawn, the family and the community had reached consensus: we *could* film, but we would have to respect the ritual of the burial and submit to the process of whakanoa like the rest of the mourners (in practice this meant having our cameras, tape recorder and clapper board sprinkled with water from a stream as we left the cemetery). Even then, the matter was not resolved. As the funeral procession was about to move into the cemetery, a carload of relatives who had not been present at the whaikorero arrived and wanted to know what we were doing. And the issues had to be canvassed all over again. Eventually we filmed and the service, among the wooden memorials characteristic of Hokianga cemeteries, was among the most affecting in the series.

We shot elsewhere with many other people: in Te Teko with Eruera Manuera and Wi Tarei; in Auckland with Eruera and Amiria Stirling; on the East Coast with the Stirlings, Kawhia Milner, Whaia McClutchey, Api Mahuika, Koro Dewes, Tom Te Maro, Sid Haig, Tamati and Tilly Reedy; at Porirua with Te Oenuku Rene and Rongopai Davis; and with Syd and Hana Jackson and other members of Nga Tamatoa who had come to Tokomaru Bay. Once actual filming was under way, our schedule was punishing. On one weekend alone we shot in Hamilton for the opening of a Maori language seminar, at Panmure for the opening of the Tuhoe meeting house, at Herne Bay with the Stirlings for the leadership programme, back to Hamilton for a teaching session at the seminar, back to the Stirlings in Queen Street and then on to the Ringatu services at Panmure. At the same time Ngoi Pewhairangi was disappointed that we couldn't fit in her hui at Tokomaru Bay. In the course of this rushing from one corner of the North Island to the other, I kept a journal (as I have done intermittently at other times). My intention was to write a report for the NZBC on what we had learned, positively and negatively, in the course of making Maori programmes. I believed such advice might be helpful for future projects.*

Extracts indicate the kind of issues with which we were preoccupied daily:

It would be impossible to do this kind of work adequately without some knowledge of spoken Maori: to introduce oneself in acceptable, comprehensible terms; to reply appropriately to formal welcomes; to explain one's purpose fully; and (in some key cases) to interview non-English speakers. More than any other factor it has been the one that has made the difference between a positive and negative community response to our overtures. It's also seen as a symptom of sincerity of interest. Doors have been closed in the past because of a literal lack of understanding about people's purpose, or because of an assumed lack of caring deduced from ignorance of basic Maori ('How can they expect us to believe that they really want to record something of our Maoritanga when they don't even care enough to learn the language?' says Eva. 'Would they send a camera crew to France without someone who could speak French?' The answer, of course, is 'Yes').

The crew, unwillingly, are learning the conventions: don't touch an old person's head or pass things over it (they will tolerate these things, coming from ignorant Pakeha, but not make much effort to co-operate); don't sit on a food table; don't wash your hands in the dishes' sink; don't talk about tapu things over food or cigarettes; stand to reply to a welcome and, if it's inside a meeting house, don't move about while you talk; leave a koha; sing when asked to, especially if the

---

*In the event, nobody in the organisation showed any sign of wanting such a report, or — at least in the short term — of wanting to make further Maori programmes; this was possibly because the organisation became wholly preoccupied with the reorganisation that produced Television One and Television Two.

host has sung first; avoid beginning new projects on a Friday. Little things. Cumulatively, however, they add up to acceptance or rejection.

We have discarded concepts such as time and relevance. It's partly because of a rural mode of communication, partly a Maori one. There is a strong suspicion and dislike of the city hustler who breezes in with pre-conceived ideas and tries to mould people. The tempo that works is a bit like the one you adopt for a tolls operator: 'transfer charge, person to person, number calling, person calling, number charged to, number calling from, who's calling' — if you break the sequence or accelerate the pace you destroy the rhythm and communication collapses. Within the right tempo, you have to approach the subject of conversation in slow concentric circles, deal with it, and back out gradually the way you came in. Interrogative interviewing too is out for old people. You have to nominate the subject and let the interviewee talk without interruption, whaikorero-style. It's slow, but it's worth it. Given time to think at their own pace, people are more likely to be satisfyingly articulate. Or, if you want short answers, set up a group conversation making clear what you want. If it is not clear, be reconciled to a little shooting and a lot of editing.

The groaning table (euphemistically called a 'cup of tea' but embracing sponges, trifles, fruit salad, and cream) has to be dealt with, in spite of work or diets. Eating with people, especially those who don't speak English easily, is a major way of cementing relationships. It gives hosts confidence and makes them far happier about discussing more consequential things, later. More important, though, eating is part of the whakanoa or decontamination process that visitors must go through in a Maori situation, to rid themselves of alien tapu. Pakeha who refuse the cup of tea and piece of cake not only give offence, they may be thought to be endangering the well-being of their hosts.

Living communally also requires total dedication. It's not easy if you're not used to it: at Tokomaru Bay, if you escape from the marae for a walk along the beach and some precious moments in your own company, one of the locals will spot you, catch you, apologise for neglect and think of things for you to do — like taking you back to the kitchen or down to the pub. If you are 'of the people' you have to be 'with the people', very much in the plural and very often.

For the crew — all Pakeha but Barry — the oddest single feature of the series was that whenever we filmed around a topic that our informants regarded as especially tapu, accidents seemed to occur. Twice while we were recording interviews on sensitive matters fires broke out close to us — apparently as a result of spontaneous combustion (one at Raglan and one at Takapuwahia). The first we had to put out ourselves with wet sacks, because there was nobody else about at the time. At Mataura Bay, two farmers disregarded Te Kani Poata's instructions and went and scraped around under a pohutukawa tree that had formerly been a burial place. The following day our filming was constantly interrupted by an Orion aircraft combing the coast for the bodies of a man and his son who had been swept out to sea while fishing off the rocks. After we had filmed Karani Moetu's burial at Waima, a child dashed across the road from the cemetery, was hit by a car, and needed hospital treatment. When we tried to shoot the singing of the first hymn at the Ringatu service at Ruatahuna, the electricity failed. Immediately we had interviewed the tohunga Hikawera Te Kurapa about the significance of Ringatu ritual, one of our light stands toppled and shattered the glass filters and the bulb.

Commenting on the last of these incidents, John Rangihau voiced what had been in the minds of many of our informants throughout the series. 'You have just finished something that has never been done before. You have filmed the ritual of the church of our ancestors. Now, to remind you of the gravity of these things, your light has been put out. You can be thankful that the price was not a human life.'

The business of film-making was not unrelieved seriousness, however. We were frequently caught up in the exuberance and sense of fun displayed by our succession of hosts; and the post-filming parties that on some occasions lasted until dawn were rich experiences, crammed with laughing, crying, singing and hugging. They bonded us even closer to the people with whom we had worked. At times the very cultural differences that separated us were sources of most hilarity and subsequent rapport. I'll never forget the look on Craig McLeod's face when the party at Ruatahuna decided to polish off his case of imported Chilean cabernet because they didn't want to exhaust our supplies of beer ('Save you fullas' beer. We'll get rid of the plonk first'). On another occasion, when Craig asked for one minute's silence for the atmosphere track on his tape, Te One Whero asked if they should close their eyes and bow their heads too. And Mohi Wharepouri provided us with the best unusable interview of the series. 'There's no prejudice at Parihaka,' he assured us. 'None at all. Everybody's welcome here. Chinks, niggers, wogs — the lot.'

It was Parihaka that presented us the greatest challenge. And the resulting programme on the pa and its history (actually half a programme, part of *The Two Prophets*) was the only one I regard as an unmitigated failure. Everyone we spoke to outside Taranaki, Maori and Pakeha, warned us about Parihaka. 'You'll never be able to make a film there,' they said. 'The community is too divided: by historical factors and by personality clashes. Too much has happened. You're more likely to provoke further argument than consensus.' We ought to have taken these warnings more seriously than we did. Less than a year before, an NZBC proposal to make a documentary there based on a script by Peter Coates had been rejected by the Parihaka people. But Barry and I were confident about the value of what we were proposing to do, and about our own integrity. We had handled potentially difficult situations with the Kingitanga, the Hahi Ringatu and individual communities; we could do it again. The worst that could happen we believed, was that Parihaka could turn us down, as the Ratana Church had. If so we would have lost nothing by trying. In fact the outcome of our approach was far more complex than we could have imagined.

Parihaka has two marae based on the followings of its two nineteenth-century prophets, Te Whiti O Rongomai and Tohu Kakahi. At the end of their lives (the early 1900s) the followers of these men had become rivals rather than partners and the rivalry had persisted among their descendants. Barry and I began our negotiations by approaching individual elders from both sides: Mohi Wharepouri and Jim Tonganui from the Tohu followers; Ina Okeroa, Sally Karena, Neta Wharehoka and Marj Rau from the Te Whiti group. All except Jim Tonganui offered the same advice: call a meeting of the people at the pa and put the proposal to them. Jim Tonganui, by contrast, said he wanted nothing to do with us and we were not to call on him again. So we wrote formally to the trustees of the pa, who included representatives of both marae, and asked them to convene a meeting. They did so and the resulting hui was held at Te Niho, the house of Te Whiti's followers, attended by about eighty people.

It was a difficult meeting for me to get to on that particular weekend because of family commitments. So I brought the family with me. I remember doing my mihi with Rachael clinging to my leg, and wondering if that was tikanga. The discussion that resulted was a long one, and raised issues with which Barry and I were now intimately familiar. I explained the series and why we wanted Parihaka to be included in it, then we both answered questions about it. We stressed that Te Whiti and Tohu were figures of national consequence, whose struggle at Parihaka had provided a spiritual uplift for the Maori people at a crucial and dangerous time. We also emphasised what we believed to be the international importance of their programme of passive resistance, worked out decades before Gandhi's and nearly a century before Martin Luther King's. New Zealanders, Maori New Zealanders at Parihaka, had led the world in this aspect of human development.

The major reservations expressed to us were a fear that we would — as some people had previously — highlight the role of Te Whiti and ignore Tohu; and that by filming ritual and spiritual activities at the pa we would commercialise the sacred things that Parihaka held in trust (Te Whiti himself had specifically condemned such commercialisation and photography). We answered as best we could. We simply wanted to give the people of Parihaka the opportunity to tell their own story in their own words; the purpose was educational; it seemed to us unthinkable to have a series about Maori history and culture that excluded Parihaka; and the only money involved would be the presentation of a koha while we stayed at the pa and the payment of wages to the crew while they were filming — they were professional people working for their livelihood and could not be expected to do so for nothing.

The weight of argument against us left us pessimistic. To our astonishment however, the hui agreed that we should return to the pa with a film crew for the ceremonies that would take place on 6 November, the day that commemorated Parihaka's deliverance from John Bryce's forces in 1881. We would be permitted to film ritual on the day and to interview participants. There were no dissenters from this final decision. I was asked to write a letter to the trustees to formalise the arrangement. It seemed too good to be true. It was.

We returned to Parihaka on 5 November as planned, having spent the previous weeks filming in the far north. The day we arrived a letter reached me, forwarded from Wellington. It was from the secretary of the trustees, Neta Wharehoka, and said we were most welcome to stay at the pa as agreed previously. But no filming would be allowed on 6 November, the day of the ceremonies. What had happened, we found out later, was that at the subsequent meeting of trustees, those who objected to our proposal and who had boycotted the hui had argued against our coming. And they had raised objections to our films — particularly about their allegedly commercial nature — that we were unable to answer, because we were not there. The invitation to stay at the pa on the understanding that we did not film on 6 November was a compromise arrived at by two factions on the committee of trustees. Faced for the first time with knowledge of these restrictions the day we arrived, Barry and I had to make a snap decision: either we stayed and filmed what we could on 5 and 7 November, making the situation that had developed part of the programme; or we abandoned the idea of including Parihaka in *The Two Prophets* and went home. We had the crew with us. Whatever we decided they had to be paid, because they had withdrawn from other work to be there. So we decided to stay. It was a mistake.

All manner of things went wrong. We interviewed the Te Niho elders who had agreed to speak with us and they dried up with fear and self-consciousness once the cameras were rolling, something that had never happened in previous films; we interviewed another kuia, regarded by some as the spiritual successor to Te Whiti, and she talked incoherently (by the time we had edited the film to try to make sense of it there was barely anything left); when we tried to interview the Rangikapuia elder who had agreed to speak to us, we discovered that his followers had got him so intoxicated that we couldn't put him in front of the camera; when we went across to Rangikapuia for the hakari on 6 November (without our cameras), we and some other visitors (Maori) were abused by the elder performing the mihi to the visitors and accused of an intention to 'sell' Parihaka to the highest bidder.

We finished the three days there with very little film. Again, we had to make a decision whether to scrap the project and write off what we had been able to film to that point; or to proceed and try to assemble something coherent from it. Again, I believe now, we made the wrong decision. We continued. We continued because we had been authorised to be there, regardless of what had happened subsequently; and because I felt a responsibility to those who teere supporting us and relying on us to tell the Parihaka story. So we used whatever footage we had as best we could, and we intercut it with historical photographs of the pa and an interview with the historian Dick Scott, who had worked previously at Parihaka with the full co-operation of the Te Niho people. The result was an honest effort, but a sad account of the effects of continuing division within the community. To end on a positive note, we filmed young people building a whare at the pa from traditional materials, and said (without fully believing it) that there was hope that the feuds of the past would be resolved by the generation upcoming.

Nobody was satisfied with the programme. Neither Barry nor I, as film-makers; nor the Te Whiti people who supported us so strongly; nor the Tohu followers who had decided that they hadn't wanted the film shot at all; nor the people who had appeared on the programme.* In retrospect I accepted that we had been wrong to proceed and I deeply regretted that we had.

*This outcome was not, as some people suggested subsequently, a Maori-Pakeha misunderstanding. It was a Maori-Maori one. The all-Maori Koha television crew was having identical problems a decade later, including one incident in which a Bay of Plenty marae threatened to sue the programme for $1 million on the ground that they had 'breached the principles of Maoridom and made a mockery of the traditional treasures of the people. . . .'

It was some time before I was able to communicate again with the Parihaka 'aunts', who had offered us warm hospitality and encouragement, and who were deeply hurt by the consequences of the programme.*

Tangata Whenua went to air in November and December 1974. While we were acutely aware that it was not unflawed, Barry and I felt that we had produced the series as well as we could, given our previous lack of experience and the total absence of precedents in this area of television. For the period it was screening it came third in national ratings and was watched by about one million viewers. We waited in trepidation for audience and critical reaction, especially for Maori reaction. When it came, to our immense relief, it was largely favourable. The *Sunday Times* critic, Marlow, not known for his sympathy towards things Maori, voiced the general verdict. Under the heading 'Ta, Mike, and Well Done' he wrote:

> Strange isn't it, how long it takes people to see what is right in front of their eyes? Here we've had all that marvellously photogenic Maoridom, all those deep-etched faces, so full of history as well as suffering, and we've done nothing about it. Until now, Michael King and company deserve everybody's thanks, as well as our warmest praise for the *Tangata Whenua* series. It will be a milestone in the development of New Zealand television. And who knows? It may even answer Michael King's prayers and become milestones in the development of better understanding between the races in New Zealand.

Even more reassuringly, Maori reviewer Harry Dansey wrote in the *Auckland Star*:

> For this emotive and disturbing weekend, *Tangata Whenua* was the very guide I needed to point me to the fact that present tensions are, all in all, transitory things and we all in the end, like Herepo's children, will lie quietly beneath a pine tree, or, like her ancestors, uneasily under the sward

---

*Ten years later I was involved in what could have been a re-run of this experience: see chapter eight.

of a golf course. I have no idea what the moving efforts of Michael King and Barry Barclay had on others. All I know is that last night when I needed it, they showed me the soil from which I sprang and the past that explains at least in part the emotions of the present. They did well, so very well.

These comments were typical of North Island reaction to the series. There were dissenters, however. As I expected, the Parihaka segment of *The Two Prophets* produced an anguished reaction from Parihaka people because it dwelt on divisions within the pa and because some of the interviews had had to be dropped because they would have discredited the speakers. Some Pakeha too were overtly hostile to the series because it highlighted Maori preoccupations and showed aspects of Maori lifestyle that differed from those of non-Maori. Robert Gilmore wrote in the *Auckland Star*:

> If a newcomer to New Zealand were to have watched *Tangata Whenua* last night what would he have learnt? He would have assumed that Maoris live in the past, cultivate backward-looking, indulge in anti-Pakeha talk when their profitless crimes against property are detected, cannot cope with modern life in the way poor immigrants from China and India can, that they let roofs rust and let weeds thrive in dairy pasture. Admirable though the intention, handsome though the production of *Tangata Whenua*, it surely projects to Pakehas (with NZBC imprimatur) yet another dollop of the legend of hori no-hopery.

The further south reviewers lived, the less importance they seemed to attach to the series. The *Dunedin Star* commented:

> Nobody can say the Maori people are not getting a fair trot on television. Indeed, series follows series on Maori culture and legend these days, to such an extent that one cannot help wondering just what Maori audience the programmes command. If the Maori people are getting tired of a steady diet of their own culture, how are the Pakehas feeling? It is hard to escape the notion that the NZBC, like most media, has become guiltily besotted with the idea that Maori culture

is a 'must' — which could represent another dubious triumph for the small band of 'stirrers' who are using alleged neglect of the Maori people as their platform for consistent and often quite unjustifiable drum-beating.*

Barry and I did not respond to criticism. Happily, we did not need to. Viewers did so on our behalf, and in large numbers. Their comments appeared to confirm the success of our intentions. Keith Sinclair, for example, replied to Robert Gilmore in the *Auckland Star*:

> Pride in Maori tradition is precisely what the programme is about and succeeds extraordinarily well in expressing. It portrays a real New Zealand which most of us do not know and do not understand and if Mr Gilmore's remarks about 'whinging' and 'no-hopery' are any guide, do not wish to understand. It shows us a noble, exciting, earlier and alternative New Zealand. There are taniwha in the Wanganui; ancestral spirits on the shores of Waikato. There is room for poetry as well as for Mr Gilmore's 'profitable farmers'. I regard this programme as the best New Zealand television series I have ever seen.

Eleven years on, I don't regard *Tangata Whenua* with the same sense of satisfaction I did in 1974. In the climate of the 1980s it seems a presumptuous and even patronising undertaking, and I cringe at my mistakes, mispronunciations and errors of judgement (particularly in regard to the Parihaka segment). The context of the early 1970s generated a different perspective, however. Apart from action song programmes such as *Pupuri Ra* and *Te Rangatahi*, television had until that time done little to reflect Maori preoccupations and lifestyle. As I wrote in the *Listener* in 1972, if television continues 'to concentrate exclusively on aspects of New Zealand society that are culturally derived from Britain and the United States, then we are viewing a distorted picture. Further, our audiences are being deprived of participation

---

*This comment was, of course, nonsense. Up to 1974, after fourteen years of television in New Zealand, there had been a grand total of six Maori programmes, almost all of them made up of singing and action songs.

in ways of life that are open to them here, but of whose existence they may be completely ignorant.

Tangata Whenua broke this early monocultural mould of New Zealand television. It gave Maori an opportunity to speak for themselves about their lives. It went some way towards informing Pakeha New Zealanders about Maori attitudes and values, it whetted a Maori audience's appetite for more documentaries reflecting Maori viewpoints, and it opened the way for later programmes, such as *Koha* and *Te Karere*, produced by Maori. In secondary schools, the *Tangata Whenua* films also provided audio-visual material for Maori studies at a time when nothing else was available. For all these reasons, making *Tangata Whenua* in 1974 was justifiable, even necessary. Although it was understandably self-congratulatory, I hoped that the NZBC's final annual report (in 1975) was largely correct in its assessment that the series had 'possibly done more towards helping the European understand the Maori people, their traditions and way of life, than anything else previously shown on television'.

CHAPTER SIX

Te Puea

A LATE-NIGHT ENCOUNTER in 1974 was decisive in determining what I wanted to do beyond *Tangata Whenua*. I was to meet Barry Barclay in Auckland for a final filming session. As I boarded the Silver Star in Wellington, I saw Pei Te Hurinui Jones, then chairman of the New Zealand Maori Council. He had been one of my most helpful contacts when I worked for the *Waikato Times*. We agreed to meet later in the evening for a meal.

I had mixed feelings about Koro Pei. While I admired his Maori scholarship without reservation — his knowledge of Tainui genealogies and traditions, his book on King Potatau, his editorial work on Williams's Maori Dictionary, his completion of Apirana Ngata's volumes on tribal songs, *Nga Moteatea* — he was a cold, cautious and conservative man. He was a strong supporter of (and sometime office-holder in) the National Party, in spite of that organisation's conspicuous lack of expertise in Maori policy; he was a vigorous supporter of New Zealand's rugby contact with South Africa; and he mistrusted Nga Tamatoa and its campaigns for the promotion of Maori language and the cessation of the Treaty of Waitangi celebrations. We had often argued. In personal and professional matters, I was much closer to his older brother, Rotohiko, long-time secretary to successive ministers of Maori Affairs.

Pei had always helped me, however, always given advice when I asked for it. And he had even complimented me on my earlier work ('You displayed a fine touch of sensitivity and understanding of things Maori,' he wrote to me after one of my articles on Ngakahikatea in the *Listener*). By 1974 he was not as influential in the Kingitanga as he had been in the time of King Koroki and Te Puea — his advisory role had been supplanted by younger men, considered more 'progressive' in the eyes of the movement's leadership. But he was at the height of his influence on national Maori affairs.

We joined each other in the dining-car and ordered a bottle

of wine with our meal. He was more relaxed and more expansive than on previous occasions when we had talked, possibly because I was not reporting him, and I eventually raised the subject of Te Puea Herangi. I told him that knowledge of Te Puea's charisma and achievement was the strongest impression I retained from my time in Waikato; and that the impression was not diluted by the fact that, outside Waikato Maori circles, few people remembered her or had even heard of her. There were few references to her in general books on New Zealand. And yet, as John Pocock had remarked in *The Maori and New Zealand Politics*, she was probably the most influential woman in our political history. Surely what was needed was a major biography of the woman, and surely it ought to be written while those who knew her best were still alive (she had died in 1952, and by 1974, her protégés ranged in age from their sixties to their eighties). Surely Pei himself was the man to write the book, I suggested, because of his unequalled knowledge of Te Puea and his literary capacity, rare in Maori ranks.

Pei laughed, shook his head and then was quiet for a long time. At last he said, 'You have no idea how difficult it would be.' I didn't say anything. 'Firstly, I know too much about her — so much that I would find it difficult to make judgements. She was an immensely complex woman. Let me tell you what happened when John Thomson died.* Hera, Te Puea's sister, brought the body through to Turangawaewae. Te Puea announced that he would be buried on Taupiri, a rare honour for someone who was Ngati Maniapoto rather than Waikato.

'But Ngati Matakore had other plans. Thomson's family wanted him buried in the family plot at Kihikihi. They looked to me, as senior tribesman present, to put their case at the tangi, which I did. We debated all night, and Te Puea was not pleased with me. The Thomsons even threatened to call in the police. Finally, next morning, Haunui** arrived from Waahi. As he came on to Turangawaewae with his supporters, he chanted: "Haere, haere,

---

*A Ngati Matakore relative of Pei's from Kihikihi, and a stalwart of the Kingitanga. He died in June 1937.
**One of King Tawhiao's last surviving sons, and regarded as senior member of the kahui ariki.

haere. Haere e hoki ki to ukaipo" [farewell and proceed homeward to the place where your midnight cries were soothed at your mother's breast].

'Te Puea had to accept the result of this intervention, and I went over to shake hands with her. But she wouldn't have anything to do with me. "So you've got Haunui on your side, have you?" was all she said. Then she refused to communicate with me for months — no letters, no telephone calls. If we had anything we had to say to each other, we did it through a third party. It was a long time before I was reconciled to her, and then only because of a peculiar circumstance.* Now what could one make of incidents like this in a biography, without hurting her reputation? And there are other things I know about her, personal things, which if I said the people would never forgive me. And yet not to say them would be to seriously misrepresent the woman.'

He was quiet for a few more minutes and I didn't say anything. 'Anyway,' he said at last, 'I'm over-committed already, with Maori Council business, and with land matters. A book like that would be several years' work, fulltime. I could never do it.'

'What about somebody else?' I said. 'A Pakeha?' he laughed again. 'Nobody, Maori or Pakeha, could understand her diary. Besides, they would never let you.' (By 'they' he meant the kahui ariki at Waahi.) 'What about Tumokai?' I asked. Te Puea's husband had been seventeen years younger than her. By 1974 he was in his mid-seventies and, with Pei, was a trustee of Te Puea's estate. 'Oh, Tumokai wouldn't mind,' said Pei, 'but he didn't know everything that went on. And he wouldn't be allowed to make the decision.'

Pei ordered another bottle of wine and went off on a different tack. He said that Te Puea used to refer to his brother and himself as 'those bloody Hurai (Jews)'. Their father, Daniel Lewis, was Jewish. He had married their mother, Paretekorae, in the King Country, then taken the family to the Coromandel where he worked felling kauri, at first at Wharekawa and later at Kennedy's Bay, where Pei was born. When the South African War broke out he enlisted with his brothers and his Maori family

*See *Te Puea*, p.166.

never saw him again. Rotohiko and Pei were eventually adopted by David Jones, their mother's subsequent husband.

The story had an extraordinary sequel. In 1968, when Pei was awarded an honorary doctorate by the University of Waikato, a member of the Lewis family read in the paper that his father was Daniel Lewis. Daniel Lewis was, by this time, long dead. But one of his brothers, Sam Lewis, Pei's uncle was alive and still practising law in Cambridge in his nineties. So Pei and Rotohiko, by now in their seventies, met their uncle and other Lewis relatives for the first time. They were both deeply moved by the experience.*

I went back to my sleeper and made notes of our conversation. Then I put the question of Te Puea to the back of my mind. We still had *Tangata Whenua* to complete. And I had already set in motion another Maori volume — *Te Ao Hunhuri* — a collection of essays by Maori authors on aspects of Maori culture. I had commissioned and edited the contributions as a result of the same conviction that had motivated *Tangata Whenua*: that Maori were forcefully and comprehensively articulate about things that affected Maori, and that the role of the electronic and print media ought to be one of carrying their views to a wider audience, to stimulate debate among Maori and to educate Pakeha about Maori values and preoccupations. My own role again was that of facilitator and co-ordinator, the person who ensured that publication took place.

I wrote in the introduction to *Te Ao Hurihuri* that its major purpose was 'to convey information and feeling about the way in which Maoris — as distinct from other ethnic groups in New Zealand — relate to one another and to the places in which they live and meet.' Other intentions were to emphasise 'that Maori things could and should be written about by Maori participants rather than by Pakeha observers'; and that 'Maoritanga is not something homogeneous. . . . Regional and tribal variations in history, kawa and dialect are considerable and should be preserved.' And I concluded by noting that 'the material in this book is not to be treated lightly. In Maori terms,

---

*Sam Lewis had also served in the Boer War. In 1974 he was elected president of the dwindling South African War Veterans' Association.

it is deserving of respect, and should not be divulged in breadth and depth to those who have not served an apprenticeship of sincerity and gradual accomplishment.'

It seemed at the time necessary to say all those things. There had been considerable evidence in 1974 of a Pakeha backlash against the bicultural policies of the Kirk Labour Government. The *New Zealand Herald* had voiced 'uneasiness about the direction in which Maori affairs are being steered' and suggested that changes in policy were preserving and reinforcing feelings of apartness instead of hastening the day when New Zealanders were simply New Zealanders. Even the supposedly liberal *Listener* had questioned whether there was 'a Maori life pattern sufficient to sustain a sense of identity distinct from European culture'.

I had no doubts about these issues. The experience of making *Tangata Whenua* had confirmed what I had known before, that most Maori did not want to become simply 'New Zealanders'. They wanted to be allowed to be Maori first — and Maori who lived and behaved as Maori — and New Zealanders second. I also had no doubt that there *was* a Maori life pattern sufficient to sustain a sense of Maori identity. The fact that major New Zealand publications could even raise such queries meant they were out of touch with existing Maori culture and aspirations; and certainly that they were not listening to Maori voices. Hence *Tangata Whenua*; hence *Te Ao Hurihuri*.

After the screening of *Tangata Whenua* late in 1974, the general critical acclaim and my securing a Feltex award for the scripts, I assumed that I would find further work in television. In fact, the success of the series led to further books. The people I approached in television, including the controllers of programmes for the two new channels, were not enthusiastic about further Maori documentaries. 'We've done Maoris,' was the attitude. 'Come up with other ideas.' At the same time several publishers wrote to me, said how impressed they had been by the films, and asked if I had any ideas for Maori books. I did, of course. I decided to make a bid for a Te Puea biography while her lieutenants were still in a position to help me.

The major problem was that I could not be commissioned

to write such a book — nor seek funding to work on it full-time — until I had permission from the kahui ariki and acceptance from Waikato as a whole. Unlike a non-Maori subject for biography, Te Puea was regarded as family and tribal property. It was unthinkable to proceed with the book without the approval and full co-operation of the people who acted as guardians of her reputation (and of her diaries and personal letters).

Towards the end of 1974, therefore, I wrote to Dame Te Atairangikaahu and told her what I would like to do. I asked her to discuss the proposal with Tumokai Katipa and members of her family, and for permission to begin work on a biography if all those people agreed. Dame Te Ata summoned me to Turangawaewae for a meeting with herself, Charlie Mahuta (her senior uncle), Alex McKay (a Pakeha, formerly Te Puea's secretary) and several other kaumatua.

I was excessively nervous about the meeting, even though I knew everyone who was going to attend. A great deal seemed to be at stake. I had by this time thought about the prospective book and investigated the Ramsden papers in the Turnbull Library. From being a good idea, it had become something I really wanted to do, and I had given notice of my intention to resign from Wellington Polytechnic so as to be able to work on the book single mindedly. I was also influenced by the fact that my marriage had ended. While I was involved with *Tangata Whenua*, Ros had decided to live with (and eventually to marry) somebody else. We had separated amicably. I no longer had a family based in Wellington, although I wanted to see as much of the children as possible. The prospect of a project that was more than a job — that would absorb my attention completely for a time and turn my mind from unsettling recollections — appealed strongly. But before anything further could happen, I needed Waikato support.

The afternoon meeting at Turongo House, Turangawaewae, seemed a harsh one. I was fed and made welcome, but nobody gave any indication that they supported my request. Dame Te Ata asked me to explain again what I proposed to do and why. Alex McKay asked me why a non-Waikato Pakeha should write the book. I said I believed that I was not entirely 'non-Waikato'

— I had a background of four years' moving among Maori in the district, and I already knew and had a communicative relationship with the people who would be the major sources for the book. As for being Pakeha, I felt that had advantages in addition to disadvantages: I was a writer by profession; I would not be subject to some of the obligations and complications that would affect Maori working on such a book (I remembered when Koro Dewes from Ngati Porou had wanted to write his thesis on Waikato poukai; the idea had been rejected by local people on the ground that he was a Maori from another tribe; conversely, I had seen how ambivalent people were about Robert Mahuta, Dame Te Ata's adopted brother, working on academic projects within Waikato; in that case the problem seemed to be that they felt they knew him *too* well).

Finally, Alex McKay said to me, 'How do you propose to deal with the human side of Te Puea?' I asked him what he meant. 'The human side,' said Alex, looking uncomfortable. 'Her relationships with other people.' 'Do you mean her sexual relationships?' I asked. He nodded, looking displeased at my directness. 'The same way I would deal with everything else,' I said. 'Where something is relevant or essential to an understanding of Te Puea's character — or to an understanding of the major events in which she was involved — then I would include it. Where it wasn't, I wouldn't. Nothing would go into the book for prurient reasons.' Alex nodded again. He didn't look satisfied. 'That woman is like a mother to me,' he said finally, warningly.

No decision was conveyed to me that afternoon. Dame Te Ata asked if I could remain in Waikato and come to a function at Turangawaewae the following Saturday. I said I could, and I would, and until Saturday I lived anxiously, spending part of the time with Tumokai (who, as Pei Jones had predicted, was not consulted about the proposal) and Piri Poutapu. I was not optimistic. The feel of the meeting had not been positive. When I walked into Kimiora hall at Turangawaewae the following Saturday night, Dame Te Ata took me aside for a private conversation. 'That's all right,' she said. 'What is?' I asked, puzzled. I had prepared myself mentally and emotionally for rejection.

'The book,' she said. 'You can do it. Go and see Alex tomorrow about what we want you to do.' And that was it. I was ecstatic. I spent the remainder of the evening in a state of euphoria, though I didn't drink, and I drove back to Hamilton feeling confident and optimistic about the immediate future.

There was still much to be arranged before I could begin work, however. Alex McKay informed me that I could not have unrestricted access to Te Puea's diary and letters held at Turangawaewae. There was too much in them, he said, of a private and family nature. However, he would help me all he could, and when I wanted factual information or chronology checked from the diary, he would do that. Other papers there, including photographs, were open to me. I could talk to anyone I liked, and all the kaumatua and kuia concerned would be urged by Dame Te Atairangikaahu to co-operate with me.

The next step was to arrange funding and cheap accommodation, because my salary from Wellington Polytechnic would cease within the month. The publishers Hodder and Stoughton agreed to commission the book. I applied to the Literary Fund, the Arts Council and the Maori Purposes Fund Board for grants, with supporting letters from Alex McKay on behalf of Dame Te Atairangikaahu and Waikato. While all this was in motion, I received a shock. I heard that the Turnbull Library had commissioned historian Graham Butterworth to edit Eric Ramsden's papers on Te Puea, and to produce a biography from that material. This was a blow. In the two decades since her death, nobody had shown any interest in writing about her. Now, two books were to be in preparation simultaneously. In a country the size of New Zealand, there wasn't room for two biographies about the same person appearing at the same time; one would inevitably undercut the other.

For a time, my project was in the balance, and my publishers considered withdrawing their commission. Eventually, to both my relief (for myself) and regret (for Graham Butterworth) the matter was resolved. In the light of my far more extensive project, and my official imprimatur from Waikato, Butterworth's commission was the one that was withdrawn. Some Maori critics subsequently questioned whether I should have written the biography, and I had to point out to them that the alternative was not that a Maori would have written it or even that nobody would have written it; it would have been written from Wellington by a Pakeha without Waikato associations.

I also received some of the money I applied for: $2000 from the Arts Council, $750 from the Literary Fund, and $500 from the Maori Purposes Fund Board. I need to stress, in view of allegations made a decade later, that these were the only grants I ever received for a Maori project. And they were necessary at the time because I was going from a full-time job with an annual salary in the vicinity of $10,000 to full-time insecurity, with the prospect of about one-quarter of that amount in the following year. I made a down-payment on a second-hand Holden, because I was going to have to travel as much as I had in the course of *Tangata Whenua*, but this time at my own expense; and I returned to Paremata to rent a cottage from Bob Munro, a retired professor of chemistry and patron of writers and artists.

Paremata was an ideal base from which to work. I was there for most of the next five years, researching *Te Puea* and writing a doctoral thesis. I had a quiet location under macrocarpas, well away from the sight and sound of other human activity. I looked down to the harbour, and found that the sight of the sea was as healing as it had always been. I kept a dinghy anchored there, and supplemented what for a while was a meagre diet with kahawai and trevally. The children came to stay weekends and school holidays in surroundings we all enjoyed, and the congenial neighbours included writers Sam Hunt and Jack Lasenby.

From Paremata I made trips into town for long research sessions at the Turnbull and General Assembly Libraries and National Archives. I alternated these with even longer trips to Waikato, to interview those who had known Te Puea well. My major informants were Tumokai, Piri Poutapu, Alex McKay, Te Uira Manihera, Winara Samuels, Bob Mahuta, the Jones brothers, and Heeni Wharemaru. I also spent many months pursuing dozens of other people who had known her less well or for only limited periods of her life. The interviewing was, of course, the most enjoyable part of the project; the typing of transcripts the most time-consuming and tedious. One hour's taping generated about six hours' processing.

The most important and moving times were those I spent with Tumokai Katipa. Tumokai, known as Dave, was an industrious and warm-hearted man. He was seventeen years younger than Te Puea and only twenty-one when they married in 1922. He was chosen for this partnership because of his energy, his strength and his reliability. It was not an equal match: he was in awe of his wife-to-be. 'We looked up to the old lady as more of a God than anything else. . . .' But in time Te Puea came to confide in him completely — not to seek advice which he might not be competent to give, but to use him as a sounding board on whom she could clarify her thoughts and relieve her frustrations. He was the one person with whom she could be completely herself, and the one who knew everything about her life.

In 1975, twenty-three years after Te Puea's death, he was still living in the house they had shared on the Turangawaewae Estate and working off the mortgage on the farm they had bought in 1940.* I spent lengthy nights with Tumokai, sitting at his kitchen table by the wet-back stove that left a sound like a bongo-drum on my tape-recorder. We wouldn't speak of Te Puea until food and drinks were cleared away. He was slow to warm up mentally after a full day's work on the property. At first he would find events and personalities difficult to recall. But then, as the evenings advanced, the mists would lift and the past come back to him with extraordinary clarity. By one or two o'clock in the morning he was unstoppable, carried away by recollection and nostalgia. It was always I who had to call a halt, worried about his capacity to work the next day. There were whole passages of interviews with him that I was able to quote verbatim, because his ingenuous reportage and communication of feeling needed no elaboration. One was his description of the night that Te Puea revived the Pai Marire religion at Mercer, when Waikato men were being imprisoned for their refusal to fight in World War One. The whole community was gathered inside the meeting house at Te Paina for the evening whaikorero.

---

*It was finally paid off in 1977, when Tumokai was at last persuaded to retire at the age of 76.

'It was getting dark in there. We only had two kerosene lamps hanging from the roof in the centre so that the light flickered on some people's faces and others were in deep shadow. We were all uncertain, frightened, not knowing what was going to happen to us. Then Te Puea stood by the door and said it was time to begin. "But first," she said, "we must karakia. Is there somebody here who will lead?" She expected a parson to stand up. But do you know there wasn't. There was absolute silence. All the Christian churches had deserted us then because they thought we were breaking the law. They didn't want to get caught with us or go to prison with us.

'And then this old kaumatua from Manukorihi in Taranaki stood up. He was there with some of his people who also didn't want to fight because their land had been taken. And he reminded Te Puea of the saying of Tawhiao: "I have taken my faith from the base of the mountain, and I have laid it back there. In time of difficulty you will find it there." Now Tawhiao had said that before he died. He was referring to his bringing Pai Marire from Taranaki, from Te Ua Haumene. He did it because the Pakeha churches had fought with the soldiers in the war. But once he said he'd laid it back there, that was it. The people stopped doing that karakia. They hadn't done it since. And Mahuta had allowed the Christian churches to come back in. But now this kaumatua was saying, "Here is your time of difficulty, now is the time to take this faith up again from the base of the mountain." And Te Puea said, "Yes, you're right." And at that moment two Waikato elders, Hoani Taurea and Te Hira, stood and started up their chant, one leading and the other answering. "Rire rire pai marire." And there was a roar all round the hall as the older people from Tawhiao's time joined in. And they all remembered Tawhiao and those days with him, and the tears were rolling down their cheeks as they chanted. I didn't know what was happening. I looked at my mother and she was crying too, crying and chanting. So I asked her what was going on. And she just whacked me to keep me quiet till it was over. But later on she explained to me.'

Tumokai frequently cried as he told these stories. We'd pause while he dabbed his eyes and sniffed, reliving the past, remembering the host of people he had known who were now dead. I often felt an intruder at these sessions. I was encouraged only by the conviction that such knowledge, such feeling, should not die with the man who had experienced these things. I was consoled too by the fact that he loved to talk and at that time, apart from the sessions with me, had few opportunities to do so. He lived for my visits and seemed bereft and uncomprehending when they had to become less frequent. I was writing a book; he was conducting an intense relationship.

My second most important source was Piri Poutapu. Poutapu, originally from Cambridge, had been adopted by Te Puea as a small boy. She had been everything to him: mother, father, mentor, sister. He gave me an affecting picture of what it was like to grow up as one of her 'orphans':

'We had to eat exactly what was put in front of us: soup, bones, puha, bread, eel. If anybody left anything — crusts or fat — then crack over the head with a stick; and there was nothing for that person next time round. But we loved her like a mother. We knew there was always a reason for this sort of treatment. Because she was looking after us. She had a big load on her shoulders and she had to share it round. It was all part of our teaching. That's how we learned to survive. She was always thinking of what individuals could do for the people as a whole, and making us think that way too.

'There were times we'd get very close to her. At the pa or out on tour, she'd sometimes gather us all round her and tell us stories. Often the history of our people, jokes about things that had happened to us, the work ahead of her, her plans for each one of us. That's how I learned that I was to do building and carving, Dave was to do the cropping, Rangitaua to look after singing and the marae, and so on. It was all planned. In the evenings, when we were together like this, she'd teach us songs and haka doing all the actions herself. She could really be fun — flashing her eyes and rolling them. We'd all laugh. We loved her in those moments too.'

Poutapu was one of the loyal workers who had gone with Te Puea to Ngaruawahia in 1921 to build Turangawaewae Marae on a blackberry-covered riverbank. Later, she had sent him to the carving school at Ohinemutu, so that he could return to Waikato and revive the craft there. He was a man of complete integrity and honesty. When Te Puea had proposed leaving a two-third interest for life in the Turangawaewae Estate to Tumokai, Poutapu was the one person who resisted her, on the ground that she would be violating her own principle that everything they did was 'for the people. I reminded her that this was what she had instilled into me all my life. And now she was saying that one person was to inherit the benefit of something we had all worked for. I told her it was wrong.' This was tantamount to a cardinal accusing a Pope of heresy. Te Puea, who found the disagreement intolerable, banished Poutapu from Turangawaewae for the last nine years of her life. He was able to return only after her death when he became principal kaumatua there.

The whole year I worked with Piri on this project, his emphysema became progressively worse. But he was determined to tell me everything he knew. On one occasion, when he had spent an hour discussing Te Puea's early love life, we discovered that the tape recorder had not been recording. Although he was gasping for breath and his daughter Tete and I urged him to stop and rest, he insisted on telling me again, at once. 'I mightn't be here next time you come.' On my last visit he was slumped in bed and very weak. We talked, but without taping. He said he had told me everything I needed to know. Previously, he had tried to persuade me to accept a carving, a tekoteko figure he had done some years earlier. I told him I could not, that it ought to remain at the pa. On this final occasion, after I had hongi'd him and was taking my leave, he reached under the bed and pulled out a large and ornate kete. 'This is for you,' he said. 'I had it done especially. You can't refuse it.' I took it. As Tete escorted me to the door she said: 'You've got a huge responsibility, Michael. He trusts you completely. He trusts you more than he trusts any of his family.' A fortnight later he was dead.

Alex McKay, a Pakeha who had himself been 'adopted' by Te Puea in 1919, was a good-humoured man and a superb raconteur. He had observed the Kingitanga and its leaders at close quarters for over fifty years, and he was one of the organisation's major links with the news media and with the Pakeha world. He was also the keeper of Te Puea's diary and principal guardian of her reputation. He was not always pleased with some of the things Tumokai, Poutapu and others told me, but he never tried to censor my work. And I showed him everything I wrote before publication. Frequently we argued amicably over whether or not certain events had taken place. He denied, for example, that he had wired on Te Puea's behalf acceptance of a CBE in 1937, against her wishes. But I was able to show him a copy of a letter he had written to Eric Ramsden the same year saying he had done precisely that. He also contested vigorously my account of Te Puea's tangi and burial — until I, again, showed him my written source, a contemporary letter from Te Kani Te Ua. It was all a salutary lesson on how perishable the unaided human memory can be.

One of my most interesting relationships was with the Jones brothers. As mentioned previously, I got on well with Rotohiko ('Mick'), the older brother. He too was a natural and unhurried story-teller and his recollections covered not only his lifetime association with the Kingitanga, but also his thirty years in government working alongside ministers of Native and Maori Affairs. I stayed for days at a time at his home at Otewa, near Otorohanga, and was looked after superbly by his wife Kahu. In addition to what he was able to remember, Mick also produced a sizeable quantity of Maori Affairs correspondence and reports, which he had removed from the office when he retired in 1963. I was able to arrange to have these deposited with National Archives.

Mick had become a strong Labour Party man in the course of his years in Peter Fraser's office. His brother Pei had been an equally strong National supporter. In the 1930s and early 1940s, Pei had been closer to Te Puea than his older brother. In the last years, that balance was reversed. Pei, for a variety of reasons, was at first unwilling to help me with the biography, in spite of having been the one to sow the idea that I might write it. He seemed peeved that I had consulted Mick before

I came to him (but Mick was, as I told him, the tuakana or senior member of the family). He was also hurt that the decision to entrust me with the project had been made at Turangawaewae without reference to him. He was, as he kept reminding me, executor of Te Puea's estate. On my first two visits to him at Taumarunui, he met me formally in his office in the Puketapu Incorporation and told me nothing.

Only late in 1975, after I had explained that everything about him in the book would represent other people's views of his role in the Kingitanga, did he agree to talk. We subsequently had several lengthy sessions at his house, and he wrote me long letters. But he, alone among everybody I interviewed, would not allow me to tape him. And he disagreed with my description of him as 'Te Puea's protégé'. He considered that his genealogical ties actually made him senior to Te Puea; others, including Rotohiko, disagreed. Pei too died in 1976, while I was still working on the book.

I wanted as far as possible to make the biography a reflection of Waikato views of Te Puea. Hence my interviews with those who had known her were not simply embellishments, as one academic reviewer alleged.* They were crucial to directions that the book would take. In many instances, I found consensus among those views; in some cases I did not, and had either to draw my own conclusions from evidence or to point to conflicting or dissenting views. I ended up relying more heavily than I had intended on documentary evidence: partly because there was more of it than I had anticipated (especially in Eric Ramsden's papers and among those at Turangawaewae), and partly because the recollection of eye witnesses recorded on paper at the time something happened frequently solved disagreements and confusions that arose decades later in people's minds.

I worked on *Te Puea* for nearly three years, spending part of that time writing it at Pawarenga, north of Hokianga; and in Menton, France, on the Katherine Mansfield Fellowship. While Menton may have seemed an incongruous place to complete a

---

*William Worger referred in the *New Zealand Journal of History* to the book's 'colourful oral material' and a 'tendency to lapse into anecdotal narrative'.

New Zealand book, especially a Maori book, it brought several advantages. Once I was there I had — of necessity — to abandon research. Had I remained in New Zealand I could have gone on interviewing people and chasing documents for a further two or three years. Secondly, I found it easier to form perspectives about New Zealand and Maori affairs from a country that was 12,000 miles away. And thirdly, for the first time in my life, I was able to work uninterrupted on a major project — to simply write, without the continual distraction of telephone calls, visitors, and the need to earn a living.

The book was published at a function at Turangawaewae in October 1977, on the twenty-fifth anniversary of Te Puea's death. About 1000 people, mainly Maori, attended. Mick Jones, now frail and slow but warmly humorous as ever, launched the volume and told his story about first seeing Te Puea at Mercer when he was nineteen:

'I had visions of a fairytale princess dressed in courtly robes and was very anxious to see her. We went to the meeting house first and my uncle said, "Where's Kiri?" and they said, "In the dining room." So we went there, but they said, "Oh no, she's out the back, cooking." I was surprised at that, to find a princess in the kitchen. Out there we found a circle of women sitting on an earth floor peeling potatoes and Te Puea was among them, wearing a sack-cloth apron. That was my first sight of her. That night, after Te Rata's party had arrived, they were given a big reception, in what was then the Mercer Town Hall, by the Mayor and the Pakeha citizens. Straight after there was a ball. Te Puea insisted I go in her party and even provided me with a young lady. This time, as we paraded through the hall, she was in a full-length dark red dress made of velvet, and had a kerchief tied around her brow. She looked every inch the princess I'd imagined her to be.'

Keith Sinclair spoke also, saying complimentary things about the book and emphasising Te Puea's importance in the context of wider New Zealand history. And, finally, I thanked Waikato in general and my informants in particular for their generosity to me. I presented copies of the book to Dame Te Ata, Tumokai, and others who had worked most closely with me. I mourned the absence of Piri Poutapu and Pei. The remnants of the TPM, Te Puea's old concert party, punctuated the speeches with waiata and performed action songs. It was a nostalgic, moving and satisfying occasion.

Within a matter of two years, Mick Jones, Alex McKay, Winara Samuels and Te Uira Manihera were also dead, emphasising that if the book had not been written when it was, it could not have been written; or, at least, it would not have been written with the benefit of the recollections and views of those who had known Te Puea best. A decade later, only Tumokai (who had by this time lost his memory) and Heeni Wharemaru survived from her close associates.

Reaction to the book was overwhelmingly positive, from Maori and Pakeha sources. The *Dominion* called it 'probably the best biography yet written by a New Zealander'. And Jock Phillips in the *Listener* said that the author had 'once more enriched our national culture and added to our canon of heroes'. To an almost embarrassing degree, reviews by Maori writers were even more enthusiastic. George Marsden of Ngapuhi, then senior lecturer in Maori Studies at Hamilton Teachers' College, wrote: 'I rejoice with the rest of Waikato, for the warmth, sincerity and diplomacy with which Michael King has applied himself to his sacred task. He has earned a place of honour among the kahui ariki of New Zealand literary greats, and in Maori idiom, "E Tama, e hara koe i te tangata! He taniwha, he taniwha, he taniwha!"'

My Maori correspondence too was heavily congratulatory. From Dame Te Atairangikaahu: '[the book] brought tears to my eyes. It brings to life the woman she was. Thank you for a job well done and congratulations.' Heeni Wharemaru wrote: 'Tears streamed down my cheeks . . . yet at the same time I felt strong feelings of arohanui for you. After years of silence, Te Puea is again upon everybody's lips. Tena koe Michael, e te Rangatira, for your tremendous work.' And Frances Winiata: 'Her personality is right there . . . she steps straight out of the pages as we knew her.'

There were reservations, however. Te Puea strode through life with determined and gigantic footsteps, and sometimes she crushed people in her path. The descendants of some of her 'victims' were hurt by the book. I had examined the basis for Te Puea's feud with the Kaihau family, for example. This was crucial for an understanding of why she had helped elect Maui Pomare — a non-Waikato — to the Western Maori seat in 1911. It was also the cause of her buying the farm at Ngaruawahia in 1940, when the Kaihaus would not allow her and Tumokai to remain on the property they had developed over the previous eleven years. No direct communication reached me from the Kaihaus themselves, but Elsie Locke wrote to me from Christchurch:

'The Kaihau family have been deeply wounded by the way they come out in this book. Even small children have been humiliated, and older ones thrown into despair. . . . In dealing with Maori things we have to remember that nga mahi o nga tupuna have a place in contemporary life . . . you can't make the separation of generations . . . you must consider the effect on the living.'

I mention this reaction, alongside the others, to show how different factors can be in Maori and non-Maori biographies. In a non-Maori book, it is enough to reveal information about the past if it is true, and if it sheds crucial light on the motivation and behaviour of the central character. In a Maori book, this rule of thumb can cause other complications. As Elsie Locke reminded me, the doings of ancestors have a bearing on the lives of their descendants; mana (or its absence) is an hereditary quality. In this instance I could only apologise to the Kaihaus and explain why I had written as I had. This kind of problem, though, remains for Maori or Pakeha writers of Maori history. And I am by no means sure that simply censoring the events of the past because of their effect on the living is an acceptable solution; nor are the Maori authors and would-be authors with whom I have discussed the matter.*

---

*The same consideration arose again in 1982, when I was writing a booklet on Sir Apirana Ngata for the Department of Education. One member of the Ngata family insisted that I expunge any reference to Ngatapa, where in 1869 Ngata's great-uncle, Ropata Wahawaha, had 100 Maori prisoners stripped, shot and pushed over a cliff. Further reference to this incident, I was told, would embarrass the Ngata family.

One consequence of the Te Puea biography was that I saw far more of Sally Marshall-Tuwhangai, a Waikato kuia who lived in Porirua East. I had met her when I moved to Wellington from Waikato: she, with Apa Watene, was the strongest support for the Waikato Ki Roto Poneke group. I already knew her mother, Kore Crown, an even older kuia who had for years cooked at the Terawhiti Station near Makara, and astonished residents of the very Pakeha suburb of Karori by shopping in her black dress, with sharks' teeth and black ribbons hanging from her ears.

Sally, in her early sixties when I met her, was all heart. She had a large number of adopted children in addition to her natural ones and a nephew living with her permanently. She took under her wing and taught anyone who was interested — Maori or Pakeha — in Maori language, waiata, and patere. Her only condition was that those students be wholly committed to such learning and approach it seriously. One of her former pupils was Tungia Baker of Ngati Raukawa-Ngati Toa. In Wellington, Sally made herself available to me for advice on all Maori matters, but especially for assistance with Waikato dialect and history. I eventually developed a routine of visiting her weekly from Paremata, having a meal with her, then talking late into the night. At her insistence, I resumed lessons in Maori language.

There was one particular project we discussed, and which she then kept pressing me to begin. She had read and enjoyed all my books, and lent them (and lost them) constantly to relatives and friends. But the biggest gap she saw in Maori literature, and the one she wanted me to fill, was a general Maori history. 'With lots of pictures, Maikara,' she kept saying. 'Lots of pictures. Our people respect them more than the written word.' We talked about what ought to be in such a book, and it began to take shape in my head. But it stayed there for a further five years.

Another consequence of *Te Puea* was that it brought me into contact with a South Island Maori friend, who wrote: 'I feel that I understand something of you. You occupy a unique place as Pakeha chronicler for the Maori, you have our trust, in exactly the way my father did.' This friendship put me in touch with South Island Maori activities for the first time, and I stayed on several occasions at Rapaki on Banks Peninsula.

154

When Barry Barclay and I had been carrying out initial research for *Tangata Whenua*, a Maori advisor had told me to ignore the South Island. 'There are very few Maori there,' he said, 'and they're not especially Maori. They've been assimilated by Pakeha.' To my discredit, I had believed this. It was far from true. The Ngai Tahu and Ngati Mamoe of the South Island had intermarried and intermingled with Pakeha earlier than most of their North Island compatriots; in many instances their physical features did not seem Polynesian; and there were far fewer meeting houses dotted about the South Island landscape. But the heart of Maori communities there (Tuahiwi, Rapaki, Temuka, Otakou) was strongly Maori. The rites of passage were pure Maori. Crises were dealt with in distinctively Maori ways. The Maori language (with dialect) had survived there and was undergoing revival. Hui, tangi and tribal trust board and runanga meetings were held there as frequently as in the north. At the time I began to visit there, in fact, the South Island Maori profile had never been stronger: the country had a South Island Minister of Maori Affairs (Ben Couch), a South Island president of the Maori Women's Welfare League (Elizabeth Murchie) and a South Island chairman of Parliament's select committee on Maori Affairs (Rex Austin). And the acknowledged ariki of the south, Riki Taiaroa-Ellison, whom I met at a family gathering, was a man respected nationally for his knowledge, his wisdom and his sheer goodness.

In 1979, Ros and the children shifted to Auckland. I followed, took up a post-doctoral fellowship at Auckland University, and remained in that city. My sister Louise and her family were already there. My brother and his wife and children joined us several years later. My parents, now retired, were only a four-hour drive away in the Bay of Plenty. After being a Wellington family for most of our lives, we were (suddenly, it seemed) an Auckland clan. It was from there that I completed a succession of other books, none of them Maori, and began work on a biography of war-time Labour Prime Minister, Peter Fraser.

From Auckland, I remained in close touch with Sally Marshall-Tuwhangai. She was as disappointed as I that my move meant an end to my Maori lessons and to the weekly conversational contact we both enjoyed so much. I called on her whenever I was in Wellington, and wrote regularly when I went overseas briefly in 1981. While I was abroad I received no letters from her, which was unusual. But I didn't worry. I returned in time to attend the launching of *New Zealanders at War* at the Army Museum at Waiouru.

Halfway through this night function, on the eve of Anzac Day, an Army officer I didn't know asked me if I could spare a moment to speak to somebody. I said of course. He led me through the crowd to the back of the reception area. There a large group parted as I approached and revealed Sally in a wheelchair, emaciated and breathing with difficulty. I rushed to her, and we hongi'd for a long time. She said, 'I *had* to come, Maikara. I wasn't going to let you down.' Hazel Mahu took me aside and said what I could see for myself. Sally had cancer and hadn't long to live. She was in intensive care in the hospital at Tokoroa (where her daughter June Ormsby lived), and she had insisted on being brought to Waiouru for the book launching. The Mahus had driven her, and would deliver her back to hospital that night.

I left the function and took Sally to a quieter part of the museum where we sat and talked. I was unspeakably moved to see her in that state, and by the fact that she had fought to be with me that night. Later my mother joined us, and Sally was able to meet the rest of my family for the first and last time. Just before she was wheeled out, she hongi'd, kissed me and said, 'Remember our book. I want to know that you'll finish that one too.' I said of course I would, and promised to visit her in Tokoroa the following week.

When I arrived at the Ormsby home exactly seven days later, the house was surrounded by cars. As I walked through the kitchen door John Ormsby said, 'You're too late, Michael. Mum tried to hang on for you, but couldn't wait' — as if she had just gone visiting. She had died only ten minutes earlier and was still warm when I kissed her. I couldn't believe that, if I shouted loud enough, I wouldn't be able to wake her. I had lost a good friend and an influential Maori ally.

CHAPTER SEVEN
Home Thoughts From Abroad

UNLIKE MANY OF my contemporaries, I possessed no powerful urge to travel outside New Zealand. Certainly none to do the Grand Tour of Europe and the United Kingdom. It wasn't that I felt no pull towards Europe; just that my interests in New Zealand were stronger. I was born in New Zealand, I belonged to that country, there was so much I didn't know about it and *wanted* to know, and this process seemed to me to be life-long. In spite of the family's origins in England, Scotland and Ireland, and my strong interest in them, I did not regard any of those places as 'Home'. In fact I discouraged and actively resisted such a notion. I felt none of that 'great gloom [that] stands in a land of settlers with never a soul at home' articulated by Allen Curnow and others of his generation of New Zealand writers. For most of my generation, New Zealand *was* home; and I experienced great satisfaction living there.

And yet, and yet . . . there were intimations of other ties, of other voices that seemed to call from other places. I loved Irish literature, for example: Yeats, Joyce, Donleavy, Edna O'Brien. These writers spoke to me. The places and people they described stirred race memories. The streets and pubs of Dublin and the bogs of Connemara did not seem unfamiliar. Then there were the other novels — those of Jane Austen, George Eliot, Dickens, Robert Louis Stevenson, Thomas Hardy — the books in which my education had immersed me — that evoked the landscape and towns of England and Scotland.

And there were the buried recollections that went straight back to my English-Irish grandmother, who had died in 1971. These were activated one day in 1975, when I was driving on an unsealed road between Te Awamutu and Wharepuhunga, blackberry and pig-fern piled on either side and coated with dust. I was on my way to an interview for the *Te Puea* book. I switched on the car radio and picked up the National Programme broadcasting a brass band backing a group of North Country

157

singers. The old '78' record sounded muted and resonant, as though played inside an oil drum. I recognised the tune immediately, but at first could not remember why. Then I began to make out the words. It was a Tyneside song, one of the first I ever heard, that my grandparents used to sing in the cottage at Ngaio before I went to school. At that age, I thought it was 'The Bleedin' Races', because that was how they said it. Now I heard, when the record finished, it was 'The Blaydon Races', composed by Geordie Ridley and regarded as a district anthem in Northumberland.

The sound of the music and the dialect I had begun to forget had a curious effect. They left a feeling akin to homesickness, an appetite to visit the places to which I was connected but had never seen; especially Hexham and Glasgow. Coincidentally, I had the opportunity to do so within a matter of months. I was awarded the Katherine Mansfield Fellowship to work in Menton, France; and I was able to visit England and Scotland en route. I was by then thirty years old.

I saw nothing of Europe on that first flight in. The Continent was blanketed in cloud, from Italy to England. The first glimpse we had of land was when the plane came out of mist over Beacon Hill on its approach to Heathrow. And there, suddenly, was England; and equally suddenly, a sense of excitement. Subdued light, spacious parks, rivers with punts, hedgerows, and then row upon row of terraced houses; each aspect known to me from film, television, books, or hearsay, and yet each revealed with the full freshness of first sighting. In spite of all my preconceptions, my stern patriotism, the feeling was one of déjà vu. The friends who met me intensified it by taking me at once on a tour of London landmarks: the Tower, Tower Bridge, Buckingham Palace, Westminster Cathedral, the Houses of Parliament, Picadilly Circus, Trafalgar Square, Marble Arch, Hyde Park and Speakers' Corner. It was odd to be in a foreign country in which so much was already known to me. Added to that was the poetry of placenames — Peckham Rye, Putney, Chelsea, Barnes Hay. They played on my ear like a familiar tune.

In the North, of course, I *was* in a sense going home. En

route for Newcastle, where my grandmother's surviving brother lived, I visited Durham, site of her favourite cathedral. But even her descriptions had not prepared me for the startling manner in which the modern town is dwarfed by the Norman church and castle. Both rear off the peninsula formed by the River Wear. The town is lilliputian at their feet. Durham was my second European cathedral after Westminster. Only those who have entered them can comprehend the massively uplifting effect of soaring stone arches, stained glass, cold light and contained silence; and all this accompanied by an awareness of great antiquity, of mammoth labour, of assured permanence, like a suggestion of eternity. The spectator begins to understand at least part of Christianity's former ability to sustain awe.

I wandered through the nave, the choir, the aisles and the transept. I stood at the great slab of Cuthbert's tomb. I discovered the mighty instrument known as 'Father Smith's Great Organ'. And, finally, I knelt in the soft light of the Galilee Chapel. Here the effect was different, more protective. The columns and arches were closer, the ceiling lower. The walls were decorated by faint thirteenth-century paintings, including one of the local saints Cuthbert and Oswald. To the right was Bede's tomb with its simple inscription: 'Hac sunt in fossa Bedae venerabilis ossa'.

As I knelt I thought about the dead, my dead: the Catholics of Ireland and Northumbria; the monks of Lindisfarne who, before bringing their relics here, had carried Christianity to most of Northern Europe; the monks of Jarrow, Bede's community; the invading Danes and Normans who had set in motion the events that raised the cathedral; and the victims of the Reformation who, after five centuries of worship, were driven from this place. I gathered these dead about me and was comforted by a sense of their presence and companionship. Had I been Maori, I would have poroporoaki'd and keened with them. Instead, I nursed lines of Eliot: 'We are born with the dead: See, they return and bring us with them.' Never had I felt more aware of the past in the present, nor more secured by it.

Newcastle was a short train ride away. Great-uncle George, now eighty-three (he had been the youngest in the family), lived with his three unmarried sons at Scotswood, one of the earliest housing estates in the city. The taxi-driver who drove me there was unwilling to abandon me on the street. 'D'ye want me to wait and see y're all right?' he asked. 'No,' I said. 'They're relatives.' 'I don't know,' he said. 'Where did y'say y're from?' 'New Zealand.' He shook his head bleakly. 'Aye. Well a lass from Lancashire was killed here last month.' The street *did* look menacing. Faded bricks, slate roofs, grills ripped off drains, streetlights smashed; and, staggering on the corner, the remains of a telephone box. I went through a gate in a fence topped with barbed wire and up to a house with bars on the window. I knocked at the open door. A stooped elderly man shuffled up the hall in slippers, and I knew at once it was Uncle George. He had my grandmother's dark eyes and jowly cheeks.

'Aye?' he said. 'Uncle George.' I stretched out a hand across sixty-five years of family history, profoundly moved to meet this tough old miner who had spent his whole working life in the pits. I clasped his hand. 'I'm Michael,' I said. 'How *are* you?' His face clouded, and he removed his hand to clutch his abdomen. 'Eee, I've got the most terrible pains,' he said (he pronounced it 'tirrible peens'). And so we spent the first five minutes of the historic family reunion discussing great-uncle's digestion. While we were talking, another short man with glasses appeared at Uncle George's shoulder. He looked not unlike me. 'Come in, Man, come in,' he said. 'If the vandals don't get ye, the communists will.' (It was like a line out of 'Sixteen Tons', I thought. Perhaps miners the world over spoke the same language?)

Inside, Sunday dinner was cooking and the table set for dominoes. Throughout the morning the extended family drifted in to meet me — George's married sons, daughters-in-law, grandchildren, great-grandchildren. I was enveloped in North Country warmth and mannerisms, a reminder of my grandmother's home. Uncle George introduced me as 'Our Michael', sentences began with 'Eee . . .' and the men drank 'jars' and had a 'gargle'. Our 'gargle' was alternate mouthfuls of Newcastle Brown, and sherry and whisky (mixed), which cousin Brian called *aperitif de la maison*. At the same time we all played dominoes, knocking when we couldn't put one down and laying a penny in the kitty.

Then we ate a dinner of roast chicken, beef and yorkshire pudding and vegetables. The leeks were the work of 'Young George' (then sixty-five) who grew them competitively and had won cups.

In the afternoon Brian walked me down to the river. It was a sad sight for the bright-eyed pilgrim. The 'Waters of Tyne' of which my grandmother had sung so sweetly were now turgid and clogged with industrial pollution. And the banks from which Uncle George and the boys had caught salmon in earlier years were lined with munitions factories and stank. We walked through Blaydon: a vandalised railway station and three gigantic factory stacks on the site of the race course. Again, the contrast with the past. The Mecca of the north, the subject of 'Blaydon Races', 'Blaydon Keelman' and other prideful ballads, was now entirely industrialised. Not only was there no sign of 'spice stalls, and monkey shows, and old wives selling cider'; there were not even houses or people.

That evening the unmarried cousins took me on a round of pubs and workingmen's clubs. I was glad to be surrounded by three of them in their heavy shoes as we strode through the streets of Newcastle, ignoring threats and brawls. It was no surprise to me that they had been mistaken for Russians on their annual holidays to Ostend and Majorca — they had a reassuring gruffness and stockiness. Conversation in the clubs was difficult. It was partly the accents, which at times did indeed sound Russian; and partly the topics. I had imagined, for example, that one of the few subjects a New Zealander could talk about in England was race relations. But it came up in this fashion: 'Ah. New Zealand. What d'ye do with your darkies back home?' 'Oh,' I said vaguely, 'there's not much prejudice.' 'Eee, there's no prejudice here, either,' said the man I'd been introduced to. 'There's nothing in the rules to stop darkies applying to the club for membership.' 'No,' said another. 'Mind you they'd never be accepted. They cause too many fights.'

Back home, after a late supper of cold pies and sausage rolls, the family sang. My grandmother used to speak of the musical evenings with which, in the days before gramophones, radio and television, they entertained themselves. What was surprising was that the English family *still* sang; and not only sang, but did so like angels. They gave me 'Blaydon Races' in three-part harmony, 'Cushy Butterfield', 'Keep Your Feet Still Geordie Hinny'. And just before we went to bed, Uncle George sang 'Bonnie Tyneside' in an accent and voice that could have been those of my grandmother.

The following day I headed for Hexham with yet another cousin. That too was a moving experience. Hexham is a market town surrounded by countryside, little changed by the twentieth century except for an industrial zone down by the river. We found most of the places that had been important to my grandmother and which I knew from photographs taken nearly seventy years before: Tyne Green, the Sele, the Meeting of the Waters. We had lunch at the last of these and I was relieved to see trout fishermen thigh-deep in the Tyne. Here at least the water still ran clear over the boulders and under the willows and could not have been too different from my grandmother's time.

After lunch we found the Spital, the manor house where my great-grandfather had worked, now preserved as the local golf club. St Mary's Church, where my grandmother had been baptised and married, was locked and we couldn't find anybody to open it; nor could we find family headstones in the overgrown graveyard. On top of Hexham hill we found the Abbey, though, unchanged and imposing. But inside it felt stripped, empty, as though the soul was gone. I was reminded of my grandmother's belief that this was the fate of all post-Reformation churches that had abolished the eucharistic presence and the sanctuary lamp that signalled it. Certainly the Abbey contained no ethos, none of the sense of life and history that pervaded Durham Cathedral.

Finally we began to look for Chareway Cottage, the old family home, a climax we had deliberately postponed. After half-an-hour we did come upon it, but with a mounting sense of horror. It was in the area taken over by the kinds of minor industry that create noise, vibration and smoke. Close by, the Tyne bank was clogged with a caravan settlement that could have been mistaken for a rubbish tip. Surrounding cottages had been replaced by small factories and workshops. Chareway Lane, down which my great-grandfather had walked home from the Spital at night, was asphalt-sealed and lined with terraced houses. And three-quarters of Chareway Cottage had been demolished to allow buses in the terminus alongside room to turn.

There was a fragment of the old house standing, sealed with concrete blocks. Underneath, one cell survived from the former house of correction. Somehow, this visible mutilation seemed more painful than clean annihilation. We learnt later that the demolition had been an error, carried out in the face of National Trust protection. This only served to heighten the pain. We managed to force our way inside, but there was no vestige of the family's occupation, which had ended with my great-grandmother's death in 1924.

In Glasgow I had no relatives to seek — at least none I knew about. My paternal grandmother's brothers and sisters there had died without issue. Instead, I looked for the suburbs in which my father's family had lived, Maryhill, St George's Cross, the Gorbals. Compared with Hexham, they were grim places and the need my Scottish grandmother had felt to emigrate in 1919 became far more comprehensible to me than in the case of my other grandparents. The family homes had been apartments in great sandstone blocks built in the mid-nineteenth century. A film of dirt seemed to cover everything — streets, footpaths, shops and apartments. The dominant colours were black and grey. The populace seemed pasty and pimply. Unemployment was still widespread (thirty-six percent of the working age-group), families lived in only one or two rooms without basic amenities, and the major social problems were truancy, vandalism and alcoholism. The shops were not well-stocked, except for the off-licence liquor stores, and they had to have grills over the counters. ('We get people trying to break in with axes,' one assistant told me.)

By an extraordinary coincidence, I found my grandmother's birthplace, 5 St Clair Street, when it was within days of demolition under the slum clearance programme. The sandstone building alongside had come down, Gran's was to be next to go. It was a deserted block, doors covered with corrugated iron, curtain tatters flapping through broken glass. I was able to photograph the window of the room in which she had been born, above the remains of Grindlay's Store. The only shop still open in the street was a fishmonger's, with a long queue outside for cheap fillets. Unlike Hexham, Glasgow did not feel like home. I felt no wish to return there, especially after I had seen Edinburgh and the Highlands, with their high hills, clear air and clean lochs.

I didn't visit Ireland. I had neither the time nor the money to see it properly, nor the knowledge to find the villages from which ancestors on both sides of the family had emigrated. When I did go there, I wanted it to be a proper pilgrimage — researched, planned, well-funded. Otherwise I would have been getting no more than a taste of the country from which I wanted a deep draught, and that would have been profoundly unsatisfying. I promised myself that Ireland and Ireland alone would be the object of a subsequent trip.

To reach Menton and the Katherine Mansfield Fellowship I made my way by car down the eastern side of France — through the Somme, Amiens, Ardennes, Reims, Verdun, the great battlefields of the First World War. It was an awesome experience: miles of graves (one of them my paternal grandfather's), new towns built on the sites of ancient ones entirely laid waste, medieval buildings left mutilated, local museums filled with photographs and medals and mud-caked relics of war dug up on their doorsteps. Witnessing the scale of destruction and loss of life, and feeling the still palpable sense of death that pervades that part of the country, it was easier to understand why some Frenchmen chose to capitulate in World War Two.

I descended through Dijon, Lyon, the Rhone Valley, and burst finally into Provence, a stark and beautiful landscape: tree-crowded towns, Roman ruins, medieval villages. And everywhere the smell of lavender, thyme and Provencal cooking. Menton itself, on the French-Italian border, was a joy. It had an old town on the hill, dating from the thirteenth century and dominated by a baroque cathedral, St Michel. It had been the original home of the Grimaldis of Monte Carlo. Surrounding the old quarter was the new resort, sprawling along the shore of the Mediterranean.

Katherine Mansfield is New Zealand's major link with Menton and with France. She worked there in 1920, staying mainly at the villa Isola Bella with her companion Ida Baker. There she completed 'Daughters of the Late Colonel', 'The Young Girl', 'The Stranger', 'The Lady's Maid', and 'Poison', and she began a number of other stories. It was to commemorate this association that the Katherine Mansfield Fellowship was established in 1969. Garavan, where Isola Bella and the Katherine Mansfield fellow's writing room stand among stately homes and lush vegetation, is right on the Italian border, a mile east of Menton's old town. The Romans called Garavan the Bay of Peace and it still deserves that description. It is sheltered from prevailing winds and basks in sunshine for most of the year. It is a benign place in which to live and work.

I found the French (or at least the Mentonnais) polite and helpful, once they found that I was making serious efforts to speak their language and that I was the Boursier Katherine Mansfield. Some of their attitudes were in marked contrast to those back home. The words they used with most respect in conversation, for example, were écrivain, artiste, musicien — these were invested with the same reverence that New Zealanders reserve for 'doctor', 'lawyer', and 'accountant'. Specific highlights of the year were the music festival (which featured Richter and Michelangeli) and the town's art exhibition. The gardener in the villa at which I stayed had left school at the age of eleven; but in old age he recited poetry for hours at a time as he worked.

The district reeked of antiquity. It was there in the hard, shaped stone, in buildings that had contained human activity for centuries, in land that had been cultivated for millenia. The Via Aurelia, built by Julius Caesar to march his troops to Gaul and Britain, ran alongside the Katherine Mansfield Room; Roman monuments lie scattered along the coast, most of them in better condition than those in Italy. And internationalism is unavoidable. On one memorable day I had breakfast in France, lunch in Monte Carlo, and dinner in Italy — all without travelling more than five miles. All this impresses the sensitive colonial and triggers sometimes conflicting emotions.

It was helpful, though, to establish that one was not English.

The antecedents of the English community in Menton go back to Queen Victoria (for whom the railway station next to the Katherine Mansfield Room was especially built) and to William Webb Ellis, the founder of rugby football, who is buried there close to Aubrey Beardsley. Both had gone there to recover from illness. The contemporary Menton-English lived like characters out of Somerset Maugham (who, after all, had lived only a few miles along the coast at Cap Ferrat). They had the exaggerated national characteristics of expatriates. Their lives were dominated by bacon and egg breakfasts, elevenses, gins and tonic, and a widespread unwillingness to speak French. They tolerated France, they told me, because of the climate and the absence of taxation. They were also the most snobbish and bitchy people I have encountered. Most defined themselves by whom they were related to or descended from (the *sister* of Michael Redgrave, the *mother* of Simon Gray); and in conversation they ran one another down ('He's put it around that she's been presented at Court. But my dear, she *hasn't*. She only met the Queen at a public function').

Aware of all this, I tended to exaggerate my non-English background. Once when I was buying liver, then changed my mind because of the price, the exasperated woman serving me threw up her arms and said, 'Ooo! Les Anglais!' 'Madame!' I said firmly. 'Je ne suis pas Anglais. Je suis Néo-Zélandais.' That didn't seem sufficient, so I continued. 'Mon grand-père est mort en France pendant la Grande Guerre. Pour votre patrie.' I didn't say that he had come from Scotland to die, not New Zealand. But the effect was startling. The woman put down the liver and wiped her fingers. She shook hands with me vigorously then went out the back to fetch her husband and three sons, who also shook hands with me. All the while the woman was saying, 'Son grand-père. Mort pour nous. . . .'

Given the freedom to go to a desk every day and simply write, without the need to earn supporting income, I finished the biography of Te Puea at Menton and began that of Andreas Reischek, the Austrian naturalist. I wrote more intensively than at any other time, before or since. And when the time came to leave, there were two climaxes that made the end of my stay as memorable as my arrival.

On my last night, I cleaned the floor of the Katherine Mansfield Room and left a present and a note for the incoming fellow, Barry Mitcalfe. Then I took a fond and final look and turned to leave. The door, however, would not open; the bolt had become detached from the handle. I opened the windows and experimented with easing myself through the bars on the outside. But I would have had to have been a three-stone midget to succeed. So I did something I had never had to do before in France: I called for help. 'Au secours, au secours!' It sounded oddly pedantic, not the least urgent; indeed, all I succeeded in doing was setting off a chain of barking dogs. Nobody came. Only once in the next two hours did a man walk past the room. I bellowed at him, but his passage coincided with that of the only goods train to go past, a long one, and he didn't hear a thing. In the end I had to attack the lock with a knife, a bottle opener and the heavy door handle, which I had managed to unscrew. I wrecked it completely and in the process got it off the door. And then I was able to escape. It was as if, as Anton Vogt told me romantically, the spirit of Mansfield was trying to detain me. If so, it was the only time she had made her presence known to me.

The finale was Corsica. Once a year Corsica shows itself to Menton, rising out of the sea like the Kaikouras from Island Bay. Only more jagged, more wild-looking — an untamed land facing a tamed one. The island was there the morning I left and it seemed auspicious: a rare occurrence to end a rare experience, like some kind of blessing. As I flew out of Nice on a mid-December afternoon, people were swimming. I found to my surprise that I was looking forward to London's crispness, its cold and snow. I had enjoyed six months of almost unrelieved sunshine and bright light. But, at the end, the Midi seemed characterised by a blandness I did not want to perpetuate. Mankind, Auden said, needs a gap. I certainly needed a gap. I was ready to return to the real world of seasons.

In the course of time in England, France, Germany and Austria, I had several opportunities to meet other writers. Some were immensely supportive: the New Zealand expatriates Dan Davin in Oxford, Kevin Ireland in London, and Anton Vogt in Menton, for example; Patrick White (who turned up in France as a tourist), Iris Murdoch, Arthur Koestler, Stephen Spender, Robert Lowell, John Betjeman and Nigel Nicolson.

I had heard of Anton Vogt — poet, teacher, performer — long before I left New Zealand. But I had never met him. He had emigrated in the early 1960s, releasing a stream of invective against the country's xenophobia, welfare-state mentality and inability (then) to tolerate diversity and eccentricity; especially its inability to tolerate Anton Vogt, who was colourful, clever and exuberant. I saw him first on Bastille Day 1976 on the balcony of a crowded restaurant on the French-Italian border. I watched in astonishment as an enthusiastic man got to his feet and entertained uncomprehending patrons with Rex Fairburn's parody of Michael Joseph Savage, *The Sky is a Limpet*. He had a fine voice for recitation, basso profundo, and was unperturbed by the confusion of his audience. The New Zealanders at his table were helpless with laughter, however, and I soon joined them. He encored with telling imitations of James K. Baxter and Denis Glover.

In the long friendship that followed, Vogt reminded me constantly that the eighteenth-century definition of patriotism had been that of a discontented man. A patriot, he said, is one who criticises his country unmercifully at home and defends it with equal intensity abroad. And this was precisely how he lived. In 1951, during Parliamentary Select Committee hearings on the Police Offences Act, the chairman, Clifton Webb, asked coldly: 'Mr Vogt, you're not a New Zealander, are you?' (Vogt had been born in Norway.) 'Mr Chairman,' Vogt replied, 'I am the only person in this room who is a New Zealander by choice.' And so he was.

Dan Davin, by contrast, was a donnish character who seemed to exemplify the dangers of leaving home too early, before establishing roots of one's own (as many of my own contemporaries had done). Son of a Southland railway worker, he went to Oxford on a Rhodes' Scholarship in 1935 and stayed there, completing an impressive career by becoming Academic Publisher for Oxford University Press. 'I am not a strong nationalist of any sort,' he told me. 'An expatriate by definition is an expatriate wherever he is. It doesn't matter where you live. You can't escape your dreadful self. And you'll always remember some other damned place that seems better than the one you're in.' Both Davin and Vogt, like Kevin Ireland, were generous and hospitable men who provided homes abroad for New Zealanders, emotional filling stations where travellers could re-charge themselves before moving on.

Of the other writers, my favourite was Iris Murdoch. She too had a New Zealand connection (her father was born there). At the PEN Congress in London, she showed a remarkable capacity to reduce complex matters to proportions that could be coped with in motions and resolutions. In conversation she exhibited a sense of mischievousness that seemed surprising in the light of the Gothic character of so many of her novels. She denied that, as her friend Davin alleged, her characters were unreal. 'Nonsense, she said. 'People in life are all far more odd and sinister than they are in my fiction. But we often don't know this, because they are also secretive and cunning.'

It was confidence-building to meet people whom — from New Zealand — one could only admire at a distance; to talk with them, and to discover that they were human and in many cases displayed areas of ignorance and prejudice as large as those of anybody else. In general, though, the English delegates to the PEN Congress were patronising and distant, feeling no fellowship with writers of whom they had not already heard. And the Europeans acted like a closed club for their own amusement. Whereas the Americans there had huge appetites for encounters with new people and told their own life stories within five minutes. I can remember thinking it was a pity there could not be some kind of compromise among English reticence, Continental snobbishness, and American energy.

The year I went to Europe, I also taught journalism for a term at the University of Papua New Guinea in Port Moresby. That experience produced several traumas. The first was the shock of finding oneself part of a white minority among a vast black majority, something every European should experience. It makes one far more understanding of the emotional and psychological state of people in the converse situation. The second was that, after only days in such a place, one's aesthetic perceptions change. I had believed previously, for example, that all Highland Papuans — men and women — looked the same, and that they were not a handsome people like Polynesians or Micronesians. In a short time this feeling disappeared. Highlanders became individuals in my eyes (as did Tolais, Bougainvillians, Manus Islanders, and others), they took on as wide a range of features as any people with whom I was familiar, and concepts such as beauty or ugliness ceased to have any meaning.

I taught a class of twenty-four, with the help of another New Zealander, Ross Stevens. Members were drawn from all over that large and complex nation, and we also had two Solomon Islanders. As students, they were paragons of virtue compared with their New Zealand counterparts. They were anxious to learn. They were embarrassingly attentive in class and felt deprived if they were not given homework. Learning for them, of course, was a key to opportunity — an escape from village society (literally a stone age one in most cases) into newspapers, radio and the public service. Some finished up in the Prime Minister's department, another became a diplomat in Washington. Their heads were full of the Western dream. They wanted to own a house and a car and all the other accessories and status symbols that a professional salary would bring. It was in vain that I tried to persuade them to question such goals; there are cycles that people have to live through themselves, without short-cuts. At the time I taught these young men and women, they simply wanted, as far as possible, to achieve identical lives to those of the European expatriates who had formerly governed their country.

Apart from the sweltering heat and crime in Port Moresby, I loved Papua New Guinea: the idyllic beaches, the rich wildlife, the material and spiritual culture visible outside the towns. I managed to visit the Trobriand Islands, and I spent a fortnight walking and driving through the Highlands, from Mt Hagen to Goroka. In Hagen the contrasts in a country hurtling from a neolithic past to modernity were sharply apparent: locals

170

in arse-grass (to use the pidgin term) shopping in super-markets; the New Zealand nurses I stayed with spending their evenings drinking Earl Grey tea, listening to Nina Simone, and sleeping on water-beds, and their days extracting arrowheads out of fighting tribesmen. The whole experience was in contrast to that of living in Europe, and in many ways an antidote. It reminded me that the problems of the Third World are more fundamental — feeding large populations, creating expectations with education, matching the values of traditional communities against those of industrialised societies — and that they affect a far larger proportion of humanity, than those of the so-called First World.

The effect of my travels in that year and the one following was unexpected. I felt more, not less, a New Zealander. I became more deeply conscious of my roots in my own country because I had experienced their absence. I missed physical things, like empty land and seascapes, driftwood fires, bush, New Zealand bird-song. And I missed common perspectives with Maori and Pakeha New Zealanders: the short-cuts to communication that people from the same cultures share in accepted reference points, recognised allusions, a similar sense of comparison, contrast and incongruity, a peculiar sense of humour. I had resented being ignored by some Europeans and patronised by others, diminished in their eyes simply because of the place in which I was born (a feeling analogous to being the target of racial prejudice); being made to feel that the centre of the universe was *there*, and that what happened on the periphery, where I came from, was of little consequence.

All this contributed to a conviction that New Zealanders, for all their faults, had virtues that were precious: an unwillingness to be intimidated by the new, the formidable, or class systems; trust in situations where there would otherwise be none; compassion for the underdog; a sense of responsibility for people in difficulty; not undertaking to do something without seeing it through — what Davin called 'a kind of power behind the scrum that one felt was lacking in one's sometimes more fastidious English colleagues'; a lesser degree of racial prejudice (though not an absence) than that apparent in many other parts of the world.* With the perspective of distance, New Zealanders seemed to have gone much further towards developing cultural traits than they had at home, where one was far more conscious of variety and disagreement. I also became more conscious of the value of my Maori associations; of what New Zealand would lose by way of its modest sense of antiquity, ritual, poetry, grace and humour if it were left solely with its Anglo-Saxon heritage.

It is difficult to enumerate all the ingredients of a feeling of belonging; but for me they lie almost exclusively in New Zealand. Other people and other cultures have contributed to them, but the mixture and emphases are our own, and they are valuable. They have to be guarded against those who would pollute them, whether they be bullying and insensitive figures in public life; or those who would seek to swamp our fragile culture and sense of identity with the mass-produced and therefore cheaper products of North American, European and Australian cultural assembly-lines (television programmes, books, records). If we want to remain New Zealanders, to feel like New Zealanders, to act like New Zealanders, to present ourselves to the wider world as New Zealanders — then we must be able to listen to our own voices and trace our own footsteps; we must have our own heroes and heroines to inspire us, our own epics to uplift us; we must persist in building our own culture with our own ingredients to hand, and not import those ingredients ready-made from abroad. We can never shut out the rest of the world, but we must try to greet it as an equal partner — not as a land culturally bereft and waiting to be colonised and exploited a second time.

I have turned down one job offer outside New Zealand. And I have chosen not to pursue others that might have materialised. The reason is that I feel content as a Pakeha New Zealander (though never, I trust, complacent). The professional opportunities that interest and challenge me here are sufficient to occupy a lifetime. My place is in New Zealand, New Zealand is my place. Those who suggested in the early 1980s that Pakeha should

---

*I was angered by numerous incidents of prejudice in England. On one occasion, I sat in a railway bar while a Midlands soccer team kept summoning the Indian steward by calling out, 'Hey Sooty.'

abandon New Zealand and return to their countries of origin, are talking nonsense. Which countries (most of us, including Maori, have more than one)? Even if we wanted to, those countries have no room for us, would not welcome us back en masse as long-lost sons and daughters, any more than Savai'i in Samoa would welcome back the entire Maori population of New Zealand if that island turned out to be (as seems likely) the original homeland of the Polynesian people.

All of us born here — Maori and Pakeha — belong here if we feel out roots here. If our egalitarian myths are not yet realised — and they most emphatically are not — then that constitutes a challenge to bring them closer to fulfilment, not an excuse to reject them or to banish whichever section of the population seems most blameworthy.

CHAPTER EIGHT
The Climate Changes

BY THE MID-1980S, the climate in Maori affairs had altered drastically from that which I had encountered more than a decade earlier. In 1971 the Maori radicals were arguing that Pakeha historians had neglected Maori history and ought not to; that they had been writing about the history and culture of Aotearoa as if the Maori ingredient did not exist. I was one who accepted wholly the force of this argument and set out to redress the imbalance. In 1983, however, a year I published two further Maori books, the argument of some radicals had shifted ground. As a consequence of the rise of mana Maori, the argument was no longer that Pakeha historians *should* write about Maori history; it was that they should not.

There had been hints of the shift in opinion as early as 1978. After publication of *Te Puea*, Sid Jackson wrote a scathing attack on elders who 'had fallen over themselves to tell Pakehas at least part of what they want to know.' It was, he said, 'a crazy unforgivable blunder by Waikato people which allowed [King] to be the person to write this biography. . . . There are many Waikato, and even more Maoris from other areas, who could have been and should have been entrusted with the privilege of writing this book.' Who they were, he didn't say; nor did he say why they had previously stood by and watched Te Puea's closest colleagues die one by one without any effort to record their recollections.

The same year, Professor Sidney Mead complained in the *Listener* that 'the Pakeha are reaching into Maori culture and pulling out features with which they can identify, taking hold of quite generous portions which they then try to fit into a Pakeha cultural world.' Later, reviewing the second collection of Maori essays I had compiled and edited, Professor Mead wrote with an edge: 'In essence, *Tihe Mauri Ora* represents a new sort of do-gooding. Its editor has salved his conscience by making it possible for Maori writers to say what they like on anything

of their choice through the missionary-like zeal of Michael King.' Missionaries were no longer wanted, even if they now promoted Maori rather than Western ideology.

One Maori publishing proposal actually came to grief because of my (Pakeha) involvement. In 1978, on the strength of the two Maori books I had edited previously, the publisher Methuen approached me for assistance in compiling a Maori tribal history of New Zealand. I believed it was an excellent idea, and that it would fill the major gap in the country's historical literature, especially for the period archaeologists call (misleadingly and unfairly) 'prehistory'. The idea was to divide New Zealand into twelve major tribal districts, find Maori writers who belonged to each region, and commission them to write about the history of their own people — the canoe traditions of their arrival in Aotearoa, their expansion and settlement stories, an account of the leaders, politics and battles of the pre-European period, and finally a Maori analysis of Maori-Pakeha relations in their area. The whole would provide, for the first time, a national Maori view of New Zealand history. I was strongly in favour of the proposal, and suggested calling the resulting book something like *Nga Iwi O Te Motu: One Thousand Years of Maori History*. I believed it would not only make Maori historical experience and an analysis of that experience available to a wide Maori and Pakeha audience for the first time; it would also have a consciousness-raising effect on Maori, particularly young Maori, who had been brought up to believe that New Zealand history began with the explorations of James Cook or the signing of the Treaty of Waitangi.

I was realistic, however. I told Methuen it would not be an easy project to float and complete. I suggested that they set up a Maori advisory committee representative of all tribal areas to test the waters and select contributing writers, and that they try to find a Maori editor. To the publishers' credit, they followed these suggestions, although they created a procedure far more complex than that which they had originally envisaged (which had simply involved me commissioning twelve writers and bullying them through to the completion of their texts). Professor Bruce Biggs of Auckland University agreed to act as chairman,

and we sought advice widely on who the tribal representatives should be.

The committee worked well together in three meetings and achieved general agreement on how to proceed and on the appointment of writers. The project collapsed, however, when several problems proved insoluble. No Maori writer or academic would agree to act as editor (the candidates either turned the offer down on the basis of over-commitment, or remained steadfastly uncommunicative, a response we were all able to interpret). When it was proposed that I should be editor, in a 'facilitator role' rather than in one which would control content, some members of the advisory committee thought that my name would have to be omitted from the cover and the title page. I was happy to accept this. Tamati Reedy, Ngati Porou representative, announced after consultation with his kaumatua and people that they preferred to compile their own tribal history before being part of a national publication. And Tuhoe wanted nothing to do with the project if I, a Pakeha, was editor. And that was the end of the proposal, in spite of the fact that the ten other regions agreed to participate and nominated their Maori authors. It was a close decision; but it was unthinkable to publish such a work without Tuhoe and Ngati Porou participation, or with authors for those regions who did not have the blessings of the tribes concerned.

In 1983, after five years in which I had written no specifically Maori books, I completed the volume I had planned with Sally Marshall-Tuwhangai *Maori — A Photographic and Social History*. Later the same year my biography of Dame Whina Cooper was published. The coincidence of both events uncovered a wider and deeper Maori resistance to Pakeha writing Maori history than I had encountered previously. Reviewing *Maori* in the *Listener* Keri Kaa wrote: 'We have kept quiet for too long about how we truly feel about what is written about us by people from another culture. For years we have provided academic ethnic fodder for research and researchers. Perhaps it is time we set things straight by getting down to the enormous task of writing about ourselves.' Witi Ihimaera wrote that *Maori* 'should be avoided at all costs . . . best wait until somebody else, preferably

Jonty and Rachael King with Paremata kahawai.

The beach below the cottage – a clutter of rocks, boats and children's toys.

Interviewing Tumokai Katipa at Turangawaewae Marae.
(Brian Latham)

My hideaway at the mouth of Wangape Harbour, Pawarenga.
A splendid place in which to think and write.

Great-uncle George Tierney with three of his sons at Scotswood, Newcastle, 1975.

Cousin Brian shows me the Blaydon Station and (where the stacks stand) the site of the old Blaydon race course.

Menton and the cathedral of St Michel.

Below: *Outside the Villa Isola Bella and the Katherine Mansfield room with Patrick White.*

Camping with the children on the Northland coast and in the Urewera: the New Zealand I missed most while abroad.

Interviewing Whina Cooper at Panguru for her biography.
(NZ Woman's Weekly)

Intensive course for Maori journalists, Rotorua, 1985. (Kerry Grant)

Interviewing Ben Symonds, last surviving New Zealand veteran of the South African War. (Colin Simpson)

With the children in Auckland.

With Maria Jungowska,
Opoutere, 1985.
(Robert Cross)

Lewis King (left), Auckland Museum, Dawn Parade, Anzac Day 1985.
(New Zealand Herald)

Maori, does it better.'

Nobody would answer what seemed to me to be the most relevant question: would anything be different in the book (apart from the selection of photographs) if it had been written by a Maori? I doubted it. I had concentrated on reflecting Maori views All but one of the examples Keri Kaa gave of alleged Pakeha insensitivity or misjudgement were actually Maori judgements that I was quoting from Maori authorities and opinion leaders (Pine Taiapa's belief, for example, that needle tattoos did not have the same mana and tapu as chisel moko applied with full traditional ritual).

A similar reaction became apparent when *Whina* was published. Whereas most Pakeha reviewers analysed the book as the biography it was (Is it faithful to the evidence? Does it shed light on Whina Cooper's character and motivation? Does it set her in the context of her times? Is it well written?), some Maori writers used the occasion of publication only to explore the question of whose property Maori cultural material was, and who should have access to it. The reviewer in *Broadsheet* went so far as to propose a Maori editorial committee to 'screen' all future books on Maori topics.

Such Maori views were by no means universal, however. Other Maori critics (Ranginui Walker, Kara Puketapu, Bill Parker, for example) praised both *Maori* and *Whina*. And *Maori* won that year's Wattie Book of the Year Award. But the message I was now hearing with increasing frequency and clarity was this: Maori are in the process of taking control of Maori affairs away from the Pakeha gate-keepers; one area among many in which they want to exercise self-determination is writing about Maori history and culture; and the ultimate consequence of this pendulum swing is that Pakeha must vacate the field in favour of Maori researchers and writers.

Broadly, this view was one with which I was in sympathy. It represented an end point towards which my work had been aimed. In journalism and in history, I had always regarded myself as a kawe korero in the Maori field — someone who tried to carry aspects of the Maori view of the world to those who were not Maori and might otherwise be ignorant of such views. If all this had an ultimate objective, it was to make the Pakeha majority aware of Maori preoccupations, sensitive to Maori values, and responsive to Maori needs. If there *was* a problem for me, it was that I had always been unwilling to relinquish this work entirely while the Pakeha majority still had much to learn and Maori writers were still to emerge in my field (as they had done by this time in anthropology, fiction and poetry, and some areas of journalism). Like Nelly Melba, I was constantly being urged to make a series of positively last appearances.

By 1984, there were still no Maori historians (in the sense of people who wrote and published history for a Maori and Pakeha audience).* There was an ample sufficiency of Maori *oral* historians; but they had always been there. The problem of co-ordinating their views and transmitting them to a wider audience through publications, of making oral literature literate, remained. Some Maori, such as Professor Sidney Mead of Ngati Awa, Joe Pere of Rongowhakaata, Ruka Broughton of Taranaki, Ngahuia Te Awekotuku of Te Arawa and Sidney Melbourne of Tuhoe, had carried out historical research in their own tribal territories. But they were not yet publishing. And they were encountering in turn problems of a specifically Maori kind, which those who had sought simply to drive Pakeha out of the field had not anticipated. Sid Mead, for example, wrote to me: 'My work on Eruera Manuera has run into problems with his children, my aunties and uncles, and it does illustrate one of the ironies of the whole situation, namely that Pakeha academics seem to have more advantages than disadvantages in taking on a project such as biography of a Maori. We who are Maori have to put up with our relations getting in the way. So my biography is dragging. . . .'

Meanwhile it was Pakeha writers still who were carrying Maori history to Maori and Pakeha readers: Anne Salmond, Judith Binney, Ann Parsonson, Margaret Orbell and others. By 1984

---

*Although Donna Awatere's *Maori Sovereignty* that year proposed a Maori ideology which could be seen as a perspective for the viewing of past and future writing about Maori and about race relations in New Zealand in general; and another Maori, Piritihana Mikaere, was writing a book on the South Island prophet Te Maiharoa, eventually published in 1988.

this continuing phenomenon was antagonising some Maori (by no means the majority; but a significant proportion of opinion leaders). The depth of antagonism was revealed in an article in the Auckland magazine *Metro*, which had its origin as a profile of me as a full-time writer. After I had talked at some length to the journalist about why I had directed so much time towards Maori history, he asked if I would recommend Maori spokespeople who would give him a perspective that contrasted with my own. I said certainly. I was pleased at the prospect of the issue being debated. I suggested he interview Albie Tahana, the able and articulate chairman of Mana Motuhake; and trade unionist Atareta Poananga, who had accosted me at the launching of the Whina Cooper biography and said she hoped I would write no further Maori books. The reporter spoke to them both, and quoted them at length.

While Tahana's views did not surprise me (they were close to my own), Poananga's did — or, rather, the depth and bitterness with which she voiced them. Some of her opinions also seemed to be off-target, aimed at people other than myself. She accused me of being an 'academic raider' (though I am not an academic and have no ambitions in that direction), of exploiting the goodwill of those who had helped me (though I continued to receive warm letters and visits from such people), of giving the Maori I had written about false mana (the mana of Te Puea, Whina Cooper and James Henare were established in the Maori world long before I wrote about them), and of lacking an ideological framework (social anthropology) to write about Maori-Pakeha relations. She suggested that Pakeha writers should restrict themselves to confronting racism in their own society, though how this could be done without writing about Maori-Pakeha relations, she didn't say.

This onslaught had an unforeseen consequence. It brought me an avalanche of messages and telephone calls from other Maori stressing how strongly they disagreed with Poananga. One, Makere Schroeder of Te Ati Awa, wrote back to *Metro*: 'The ultra extreme views expressed by Atareta Poananga do more damage to Maori people than anything Michael King could ever write or say. . . . To verbally assault him is to verbally assault the kaumatua who entrusted their knowledge to him. One has to earn their trust and respect before they will part with such wealth. . . . Over the years King's work would have made more Pakeha aware of their inbuilt racism than any of the negativeness of Atareta Poananga, and at the same time would have given many Maori people an insight into their heritage which may have been lost to them.'

Others, figures as ideologically separated as Sir James Henare and Dun Mihaka, expressed their support to me privately. And the requests from Maori for me to take up further Maori projects continued to flow in. Some critics had spoken as if I rushed about the country looking for Maori subjects on which to write. In fact the only Maori book I initiated was *Te Puea*; the others were either commissioned by publishers or written at the request of Maori subjects. I have always been asked to write about more Maori topics than I was willing or able to handle, and almost all such requests have had to be refused. That situation has continued. In the period I was writing this memoir, for example, I was approached by the trustees of a marae to write its history, by a kaumatua to write the history of Tainui in Tamakimakaurau, and by the family of a Maori carver to write his biography. In each case I suggested that the people who approached me find a Maori writer. None was able to do so.

In 1985 I ran into further flak from some Parihaka people. Four years earlier I had been commissioned by the Department of Education to write booklets for secondary school Social Studies on four Maori leaders. After checking with the tribal areas concerned, I agreed to do so. One was to be on Te Whiti O Rongomai, whom I admired above all other nineteenth-century leaders, and I was especially careful about sounding out the elders of Parihaka, particularly those who were Te Whiti followers. I spent a night in the meeting house of Te Niho O Te Ati Awa, discussing the project with them, and then referred the draft of the booklet back and forth between Taranaki and the Department of Education for much of the next two years. As the text evolved, the in-put was that of the people of Parihaka rather than my own.

I was astonished, therefore, to hear on the Maori news in

1985 that a deputation of Parihaka people had gone to Wellington to seek withdrawal from schools of the Parihaka film in the *Tangata Whenua* series, and to ask that the Te Whiti booklet be referred to the trustees of the pa prior to publication. Both these things had already been done: the film had been taken out of schools, with my full support, in 1982; and the process of consultation over the booklet had been continuous. The previous occasion that the text had been sent up to Taranaki for a meeting of the trustees, it had not been picked up by them from the bus station. I never found out whether the broadcasting of these items represented a mistake on the part of a journalist, or a misunderstanding by a member of the Parihaka delegation. Whatever the explanation, the incident illustrated again how charged circumstances became when Pakeha were writing Maori history, and I decided to accept no further commissions of this kind.

What I continued to do, however, was participate in training Maori writers to take over many of the functions previously carried out by Pakeha alone. From the time I was at Wellington Polytechnic, I worked hard to recruit Maori journalists. It seemed to me then (and does still) that the continuing gap between Maori and Pakeha views of experience, and the continuing ignorance on the part of most Pakeha of Maori perspectives, will not be bridged until Maori are represented in journalism in at least the same proportion as they are in the general population. Newspapers, radio and television provide the major raw material for a nation's view of and evaluation of itself. If Maori activities and preoccupations are not clearly and emphatically reflected there, what chance is there of communicative understanding between Maori and Pakeha?

My feelings as to why there *ought* to be such an understanding remain the same as they were when I undertook *Tangata Whenua*. Maori are the country's indigenous people. They therefore have prior rights to existence in New Zealand. This means physical *and* cultural existence. But the culture will survive only if the institutions of the majority culture respect, understand, incorporate and promote Maori values and attitudes. And that will only come about if the majority culture knows what those

181

values and attitudes are. The negative grounds for urgency are that — with the faster growth of the Maori population, its enlarging presence in New Zealand cities, and the rise of mana Maori — a failure on the part of Pakeha to accommodate Maori needs and aspirations will result ultimately in civil disorder. By 1985 the validity of these considerations was unchanged; the urgency for improved cross-cultural communication was even greater, a process Race Relations Conciliator Hiwi Tauroa correctly identified as a race against time.

It was difficult to recruit Maori into newspapers, radio and television in the early 1970s. Journalism was not an option recommended to Maori graduates and school leavers; and there were few Maori faces in the industry to encourage others to join (in those days the only two I was aware of were George Koea and Harry Dansey). Associated with this, the Maori journalism students I did manage to recruit had a high drop-out rate after they entered the industry — in part, I am sure, because their taha Maori received little recognition or support from their colleagues, and often provoked active disparagement. There was a widespread feeling among professional journalists that to have a Maori perspective on news was to display prejudice; and yet the same accusation was never levelled at Pakeha perspectives. Indeed, throughout this period New Zealand radio and newspapers placed correspondents in other parts of the world specifically to provide a New Zealand perspective on overseas news.

In spite of these handicaps, some of my protégés from those days survived and performed well: Philip Whaanga, Paul Ransey, Lesley Boyles. Others opted out of journalism in favour of other occupations. By the early 1980s there were more Maoris in journalism — and some outstanding figures such as Derek Fox and Chris Winitana — but they still represented only about two percent of the profession. With Gary Wilson of the Journalism Training Board, and the strong support of Race Relations Conciliator Hiwi Tauroa, I embarked on a new initiative: an intensive attempt to attract Maori school-leavers into existing journalism training courses; and an effort to train more mature Maori from other occupations and place them immediately in the industry. Parallel with these efforts, we ran hui for Pakeha journalists on marae in the main centres — to bring them together with Maori opinion leaders in their communities, to discuss ways in which the news media were failing their potential Maori audience and methods of rectifying this. I also wrote a handbook for the training board, for distribution to all journalists reporting Maori affairs.*

The effect of these combined measures was not fully apparent by 1985. Some newspapers, particularly the Auckland and Wellington dailies, had improved the breadth and depth of their Maori coverage considerably. Most graduates from the intensive courses found jobs in the industry. Most journalists too, it seemed, were sympathetic to this affirmative action programme. But some were not; and some newspapers were at best non-cooperative and at worst actively resistant to the whole idea.

Over the same period I had also tried to recruit Maori into my various workshops in history and professional writing. I had had less success here than in journalism, although two of my earliest students, Bub Bridger and Bruce Stewart, produced some outstanding fiction. Bub was and is a unique phenomenon in New Zealand writing — a genuine primitive, a kind of literary Grandma Moses. When she joined my class she was nearly fifty, with no previous experience in writing. She was of Ngati Kahungunu descent, through a grandparent not acknowledged by the rest of her family. For most of her life she had been regarded by Pakeha as Maori; but by Maori as Pakeha, because she could not establish her whakapapa or hapu connections. She brought up four children on her own in trying circumstances and did not begin to write until they were adults. When she enrolled in my workshops, she exhibited an eye for psychological significance and a lyrical facility with words that were entirely uninfluenced by education or literature. The first story she wrote was accepted by the *Listener*, and from that point (1973) she was published and anthologised. Throughout this time she has remained a close friend, and I am convinced that when her novel in progress is finished, it will be startlingly good.

Bruce Stewart was a contrasting figure: powerful physically,

Kawe Korero, a Guide to Reporting Maori Activities, 1985.

with a criminal record (he came to me from Wi Tako, where he had been incarcerated with, among others, drugs boss Terry Clark); but with a delicacy with words and a gentle manner. He was Ngati Haua, so I shared some knowledge of his Waikato people. At first he wrote with enormous energy but too much decoration. He was a quick learner, however, and once his prose became leaner and more direct, he wrote moving and powerful stories, many of which explored New Zealand sub-cultures unknown to the country's more genteel and fastidious writers. He too has been published and anthologised, and only his work with gangs and street kids — and his foundation of the Tapu Te Ranga Marae in Wellington — has prevented him from producing and achieving more as a writer. For Bruce, working with people will take a higher priority than working with words.

I tried too to be as supportive as I could of the work of other Maori writers, many of whom became established figures — Rowley Habib, Witi Ihimaera, Patricia Grace, Keri Hulme; and of Hone Tuwhare, who had been writing and publishing successfully long before I took an interest. These people needed no professional assistance. They are entirely at home in the world of imaginative writing. But I did what I could to encourage them as colleagues, to answer ill-informed criticism of their work, and to spread an awareness of it as widely as possible among Pakeha. Patricia Grace and Keri Hulme, whom I had known and admired a decade before publication of *The Bone People*, have been especially loyal and supportive friends.

Of all the things that happened in the years of the so-called Maori renaissance, the phenomenon that brought me most personal satisfaction was seeing Maori who had previously been cut off from their family or tribe, or who had had no previous appetite for their own history, recover an interest in their roots. Dozens of individuals came to me for information I had gathered when nobody else was interested, or for copies of tapes I had recorded with their elders, since deceased. I was happy to be able to supply this material. One such inquirer was a descendant of Ngakahikatea, the first kuia moko I had interviewed. Another wrote, after I had put her in touch with Maori relatives she hadn't known she had: 'I feel highly privileged to have had my history handed to me so easily. It makes up for all the years without family, just to know where you came from and who you resemble. It was a strange set of coincidences which led me to all this. And the family didn't know I existed either, until three weeks ago. Thank you for your part in all this.'

I have cited positive reactions to my own work only to illustrate that Maori opinion on this issue — as on others — is various. Some Pakeha have the impression now that *all* Maori are opposed to Pakeha participation in Maori activities, that a mood of separatism is evolving that will eventually lead to Maori and Pakeha living in their own enclaves. The impression is intensified by the fact that some Maori who hold separatist views are skilled publicists, and make them known with ease through the news media. The media help them by virtue of their own appetite for statements that are newsworthy rather than true (ludicrous and disproportionate comparisons of New Zealand with South Africa, for example). Most Maori, particularly those with moderate opinions, are still not happy about airing their views through newspapers, radio, or television, even to balance what they regard as distorted impressions created by others. There is still a tendency to regard promotion of opinion through the Pakeha media — with its inevitable concentration on personalities — as whakahihi or boastful behaviour. There is also a marked unwillingness on the part of some to be seen to be criticising other Maori in what is essentially a Pakeha forum. The inability of most journalists to sift wheat from chaff in this area has not helped. Maori opinion can not yet be gauged from newspaper and magazine stories. It has to be sought at hui ('oral newspapers', Bill Poutapu used to call them) and in consultation with individuals — lots of individuals. The percentage of Maori people who are genuine separatists is small. Most Maori want greater control over their own lives, and control determined by Maori concepts of relevance and values; this may even imply separate schools, separate treatment for criminals (and separate definitions of criminality). But it does not imply exclusion of Pakeha from such activities. It rejects Pakeha domination and Pakeha control, not Pakeha participation. The situation may change, but that is how I read it in the late-1980s.

I have never felt or been excluded from Maori functions. But I no longer believe that an interest in Maori affairs is sufficient justification to present oneself at a hui. I now attend such hui only at the direct request of tangata whenua. I miss the excitement of the mihi and whaikorero, and the mingling and gossiping with hosts and visitors. But I feel that such occasions are specifically Maori — organised by Maori for Maori — and that my presence would be an intrusion. I am not Maori, I don't wish to be considered Maori. In some instances my reluctance has been influenced by an unwillingness to provoke confrontations with individuals who are uninformed about or hostile towards the work I have done, and who (at a hui) might express this in terms that would be difficult for me to respond to in public.

It is ironic that some critics have interpreted this reluctance on my part as 'retreating back to the white world' after raiding Maoridom for professional advantage. It is nothing of the kind. It is an unwillingness to be a cultural gate-crasher, to be involved in ceremonial and decision-making that belong to Maori. I still attend tangihanga for friends. I try to keep in touch with Maori language and Maori issues by watching and listening to *Te Karere* and *Koha* on television and the Maori news on radio, and by letters and phone calls to and from Maori friends. I derive immense satisfaction from *Koha* and *Te Karere* in particular, because their existence and their success illustrates the validity of the case we made for Maori programmes on television at the time of *Tangata Whenua*.

It amuses rather than saddens me to see how rapidly New Zealanders forget their earliest models (a *Koha* programme interviewing Pirihita Pateriki of Matata was advertised as the first time a Maori woman with moko had talked about her tattoo on television — eight years after we had devoted an entire *Tangata Whenua* film to the topic). The programme in preparation as I write, *The Natural World of the Maori*, has been promoted as the first television series for which Maori elders had been consulted. All this constitutes good news and sad news. The sad news is that it confirms New Zealand culture as a sandcastle one: our many small constructions are completed, admired and then washed away, unknown to those who follow. A decade later other people do the same things, imagining that it is for the first time. Such a process — such cultural amnesia — handicaps us because it often prevents building on sound precedents or harnessing experience already tested.

It is good news, however, in that it reveals Maori journalists working confidently in television at least, selecting and presenting stories according to Maori criteria. This is no more than Maori viewers have a right to expect; and it is educative for a non-Maori audience, which until recently had always been surprised to witness evidence of Maori being Maori in their own country, as if such behaviour was novel or of recent origin.

For my part, I shall continue to comment on matters involving Maori-Pakeha interaction, because I am one of the partners to such interaction. As to the suggestion that historians like myself should concentrate on instances of Pakeha racism, there is no way such instances can be measured, except in Pakeha points of contact with Maori. I will continue too, to write about instances of misunderstanding or injustice in New Zealand history, on whichever side of the cultural fence I find them. And I will resist the notion that we should be monocultural in our view of New Zealand experience, whether the source of that cyclopic vision be Maori or Pakeha. To live with one another, and to be able to understand one another, we need the benefit of *all* the perspectives we share.

The prospect of further controversy from such activity — whether from a Maori or Pakeha direction* does not concern me greatly. I have always taken for granted that history is, as Pieter Geyl expressed it, an argument without end; that it is something apparently true of and for the time and place in which it is written; that different historians, of different cultures and generations, will not only come up with different answers —

*I have not talked in any detail here about adverse Pakeha reaction to my work. I have in fact received more criticism from that direction — from people who think that the registration of Maori viewpoints creates problems where none existed previously — than I have from Maori sources. There are still people in public life who believe that New Zealand is, or ought to be, a monocultural society.

they will ask different questions. What *has* saddened me is that Maori reaction to what I have written has tended to be wholly approving, or disapproving in *argumentum ad hominem* terms. I was warned a long time ago by Bruce Biggs that there was another side to aroha: 'A need some Maori feel to drag down and discredit people who rise above the iwi.' It is also descriptive of the reaction that sometimes greets Pakeha who try to conduct dialogue on Maori-Pakeha issues. It is a debilitating trait, far more so than division based on tribal feeling. It often prevents Maori causes from making progress as quickly as they otherwise might, because some spokespersons are far more active fighting their own people and their allies than they are confronting the real adversaries: those who felt threatened by mana Maori, and want it to make no further inroads on the national life (one thinks, for example, of the tragic break-up of the Matakite organisation after the highly successful Maori Land March of 1975).

What further inroads *ought* mana Maori make on the national life? The first, I believe, is that every possible legislative and social condition should be created to ensure the flourishing of Maori language, institutions and wider culture. There is a moral obligation on the part of the majority Pakeha culture to rectify the destructive policies of the past. The British have not been noted for their tolerance of the ways of other peoples; themes of racial and cultural superiority have been far too strong in their history. Ernst Dieffenbach recognised the traits that made them less than ideal colonisers when he wrote of New Zealand in 1843: 'The moving spirit of English colonisation is that of absolute individuality. It is unwilling in its contacts with foreign nations to acknowledge any other system but its own, and labours to enforce on all who are under its control, its own peculiar principles.' This was in marked contrast with nineteenth-century Austrians for example. However much one tries to view the past in the context of its own values, there is no longer any excuse for belief in racial or cultural superiority, on the part of any group. Experience in Nazi Germany and South Africa has shown us the ultimate development of master-race theories. All people are the sons of Adam and Eve (or Rangi and Papa), and all are subject to original sin or its mythological equivalent in other cultures. As individuals, men and women are as equally capable of selfishness and cruelty as they are of altruism and fellowship. History and tradition record examples of all four qualities in all cultures.

But that is very far from saying that all cultures and individuals have behaved in the same manner towards one another, or have simultaneously practised the same virtues and vices. While the English, as Dieffenbach noted, were exalting individuality in New Zealand, Maori society gave pride of place to communal virtues. While nineteenth-century Maori were open-mindedly exploring all the technology and ideas that European colonisation brought their way, most Englishmen were adamant that their system, their 'way', their institutions, were the only ones that constituted the ingredients of civilisation. In this attitude, and in the determination of European colonists to use any means to wrest land from the Maori, lay the seeds of the New Zealand wars. While all men may be potentially equal in their individual capacity for good or evil, therefore, they are not all equally to blame before the court of history for conflict. European (largely English) plans for the colonisation of New Zealand had the effect, as Bruce Mason put it, of 'tearing apart the formerly seamless robe of Maori society and shattering the ancient resonances. Simultaneously, European-introduced disease and weapons almost annihilated the Maori people physically. The fact that the representatives of the British Crown then signed a treaty with the Maori people promising (in one of several versions) to protect their 'lands, their villages, and all their valued customs and possessions', and then did not do so — all this implies larger obligations on the part of the Pakeha majority in New Zealand to the Maori than to other minority groups. Those other groups were not displaced or disadvantaged by links in the chain of Pakeha migration; in fact they came as later links in that same chain. More importantly, their language and indigenous culture are not under threat because of the former actions of the Pakeha majority in New Zealand; those of the Maori are.

To help restore balance to the scales of historical justice, certain simple things ought to be done at once. All lands taken illegally or unfairly from Maori owners should be returned to the descendants of those owners (one thinks of Bastion Point and the Waireia Block in the North — but there are dozens of others). All Crown land not currently in use should be returned to Maori ownership, especially where it contains wahi tapu or symbolic mountains or rivers (such as Hikurangi on the East Coast). The resources of the state should be thrown fully behind the revival of Maori language and culture, instead of simply permitting this to happen (here one thinks of the shockingly inadequate follow-up for the Kohanga Reo programme). The Waitangi agreement, as a blue-print for the kinds of race relations Maori and Pakeha want in the late twentieth century (as distinct from 1840), should be renegotiated. Affirmative action programmes should be instituted immediately to ensure that Maori are represented in business and the professions in the same proportions as they are in the general population. This latter step would do no more than harness the considerable communications, artistic and entrepreneurial skills already operating in Maori organisations and communities. Because of the way we have structured much of the country's professional life, these Maori skills are frequently denied the community at large. If our elected representatives can be pressured to take such measures urgently; if individual Pakeha continue to educate themselves in the fields of Maori history, language, values and sensitivities; if the majority of Maori remain patient a little longer in the face of Pakeha clumsiness and lingering intransigence; then I see grounds for optimism about the country's future cultural and social life. Already the nation's institutions have begun to bend towards Maori needs in certain areas: in the education system, the law, funding for the arts, recognition of Maori as well as Pakeha historic places. But this process needs to go much further with far more momentum if the imbalances of the past 150 years are to be corrected in time to save the fabric of New Zealand society. As I have remarked elsewhere, this process is not one of turning back the clock, but rather of setting it, belatedly, at the right time.

While these things are happening, Maori and Pakeha will have to approach the task of nation and culture-building in a spirit of reconciliation. This is perhaps the most difficult — but also the most important — part of the process. Pakeha people *must* acknowledge and attempt to rectify mistakes made by their representatives or their ancestors or the agents of their culture. For this gesture to bear fruit, Maori people must then accept such expressions of regret and not exacerbate past injustices the way one worries a sore tooth.

Surprisingly, interviewing people for two vastly different books — *New Zealanders at War* and my Maori social history — I found that former prisoners-of-war shared a trait with Maori who had suffered the sharp edge of Pakeha discrimination when they moved into New Zealand cities in the 1940s and 1950s. It was this: that those who had most to forgive tend to be the most forgiving; those who are angry on other people's behalf tend to be the least forgiving.

I encountered the same view through the writings of Laurens van der Post:

> The suffering which is most difficult, if not impossible, to forgive, is unreal imagined suffering. There is no power on earth like imagination, and the worst, most obstinate grievances are imagined ones. Let us recognise that there are people and nations who create, with a submerged deliberation, a sense of suffering and of grievance, which enable them to evade those aspects of reality that do not minister to their self-importance, personal pride, or convenience. These imagined ills enable them to avoid the proper burden that life lays on all of us. Persons who have really suffered at the hands of others do not find it difficult to forgive, or even to understand the people who caused their suffering. They do not find it difficult to forgive because out of suffering and sorrow truly endured comes an instinctive sense of privilege. Recognition of the creative truth comes in a flash: forgiveness of others as well as ourselves, for we too know not what we do.

With a preparedness to offer and to accept reconciliation must come a willingness to abandon the language of confrontation, 'which distorts truth, poisons the atmosphere and inflames passion. Abuse, the cheap imputation of the worst possible motives, treating people as scum in speech — all this pumps vituperation into the atmosphere and has a deep effect on the possibilities of physical violence.' Any destabilising of New Zealand society at this time by exaggerated claims* and physical confrontation will not only retard the process of reconciliation; it will make more likely a conservative Pakeha backlash that will halt and even reverse the corrective and healing process now under way. Maori impatience for social change — entirely justifiable — must nonetheless accommodate alliance with Pakeha individuals and institutions, and allowance for the cumbersome nature of those institutions in transition. For their part, Pakeha must remember that further Maori forbearance can only be bought with genuine acknowledgement and rectification of past mistakes, and public repentance for their occurrence. There can be no return to either the violently coercive policies of the nineteenth century or the benign inertia of our recent history. Maori expectations for change have been created and fed by the knowledge that change is possible. There is no way now that they can be diverted or suppressed.

---

*There are already ample skeletons in our historical closet. Regrettably, some writers, Maori and Pakeha, have chosen to caricature them or invent entirely new ones, a process which only serves to heighten confrontation dishonestly.

CHAPTER NINE
Being Pakeha

I NOTED AT the beginning of this book that — historically, if not in fact — New Zealanders are all immigrants. That is a portion of the truth. The other part, the larger part, is that however far the ancestral umbilical cord stretches, I and millions of Pakeha like me were born here. We are citizens of Aotearoa. We have no other home, no other turangawaewae, any more than Maori have in Tonga or Samoa, the Hawaiki of the Polynesians. The Gaelic culture of my forefathers in Ireland and Scotland was obliterated by the English. I possess neither that, nor the 'Britishness' offered as a substitute. The culture I have is my Irish-Catholic heritage, plus the ingredients from many other sources, especially Maori, which have attached themselves to me like iron filings to a magnet as I have grown up and continued to grow in New Zealand.

To be a citizen of Aotearoa in the 1980s, even a Pakeha one, is to be inevitably affected by the enlarging Maori presence and the renaissance of Maori rituals and values — something my European ancestors here never experienced. For some that effect may be limited to fear or rejection of those elements in New Zealand life. For most of us, however, they will penetrate our consciousness to some extent. For myself, the Maori presence has given the land on which I live an historical echo a resonance it would otherwise lack; it has put me in touch with symbols that may arise out of man's collective subconscious, but which here are Maori and therefore New Zealand in idiom; it has exposed me to concepts — the mauri of people and places for example — which I believe have universal value and application; and it has revealed to me more of life and death — and of living and dying — than I had encountered in twenty previous years of purely Pakeha existence.

None of which makes me Maori. In a sense, the emphasis of the latter part of this memoir on Maori experience has been misleading. Because what I have always been interested in is

New Zealand history, its Maori *and* Pakeha components. In the past decade I also wrote two general books on New Zealand, another on the post-war years, one on Auckland, one on the news media, a chapter for *The Oxford History of New Zealand*, a history of New Zealanders in combat, and a biography of an Austrian. I also contributed to dozens of other books, from short story anthologies to a manual on oral history. All these projects uncovered facets of the nature of my own country and compatriots; some, especially *New Zealanders at War*, explored themes that are central to our history. And I valued immensely the range of relationships I formed in the course of such research, with people as diverse as Ben Symonds, South African War veteran, John A. Lee, and Alister McIntosh, head of the New Zealand Prime Minister's Department for two decades.

But by the very fact of living and working in New Zealand, and especially of working on aspects of Maori history, it is inevitable that I have shared experiences with Maori and been as influenced by them as they have been by the presence of Pakeha in New Zealand. This is an entirely natural and inevitable process. It ought not to be a source of regret for either party, any more than one ought to object to the mingling of Jutes, Angles, Saxons, Celts, and Scandinavians in English history. What has happened has happened, and cannot be undone.

The five solid objects that lie on my desk, and the two that hang beside it, are representative of the randomness and variety of history and culture acting on one life, and on the lives of my fellow countrymen and women. Seeing them, touching them, provides reassuring evidence of connections with the past. One is a flint from the grounds of Hexham Abbey. One is the Roman coin Colin Hornig sent home to Paremata from North Africa just before he was killed. Another is a bullet from the New Zealand trenches at Gallipoli where my step-grandfather was one of the few New Zealanders to survive without wounds. I have a small piece of fossilised kauri gum, soul of a long-dead tree. I have a crucifix worn by one of the nuns who taught me, with a tiny skull and cross-bones at the base to remind the wearer of the inevitability of death. I have the heavy Taranaki mere from Father Kavanagh, its carved takarangi spiral

194

representing eternity. And I have a tiny argellite chisel I found in the sand dunes at the mouth of Porirua Harbour.

From childhood, I have always felt drawn to artifacts made by people long dead. To hold them in trust, to protect them, to touch them, has always seemed to me to be forming a relationship with the original makers and users. The palm of my hand tingles when I am in contact with them, as if some mauri radiates life from them. For these reasons, I respect them enormously. I respect especially the Maori objects, because it was encountering them that first made me curious about the relationship of the past to the present. The persistence of this curiosity created my imaginative and professional life; and the seed of those early Maori connections generated a larger interest in that part of our history than I might otherwise have had. From my time in Waikato, whenever I encountered Maori behaviour or phenomena that I did not understand, I set out to learn about them. And in trying to make them comprehensible to myself, I sought also to make them intelligible to a wider Pakeha audience. It never occurred to me that to do so might be inappropriate, nor that my presence in this role might eventually be unwelcome. I saw it as beginning to redress, in a small way, 150 years of Pakeha hostility or indifference to Maori things.

For the periods that I appeared to be involved more in Maori than in non-Maori activities, it was the chain effect of one project attracting or leading to another. I never felt that I was becoming Maori when I worked in Maori-related fields, nor did I want to. Piri Poutapu and Sally Marshall-Tuwhangai constantly told me that I had 'a Maori heart'. That was a compliment; it was well meant and well received. But it was no more true than their assumption that I was an adopted Waikato. My loyalties have always been first to family, and then to individual people and to truth as I have perceived it — never blindly to a tribe or a race, not even my own 'race', whatever that may be.

I feel nothing but sadness for Pakeha who want to be Maori, or who believe they have become Maori — usually empty vessels waiting to be filled by the nearest exotic cultural fountain — who romanticise Maori life and want to bask for ever in an aura of aroha and awhina.* These are the same people who crumple with disbelief and shock the first time somebody calls them honky or displays some of the more robust characteristics of Maori behaviour. They remind me of Quentin Bell's description of the kind of English writer who believes he knows the lower classes and is able to 'come down to their level'; he loves them so long as they play the role that he expects of them; but his affection changes to bitter disappointment and hatred when that role changes. We are what we are, physically and culturally, and we can't change sides.

We can, however, be more understanding of one another. There are things about Maori and Maori culture with which I can identify strongly, especially those things that were characteristic of all tribal peoples, my own Gaels included: a feeling of connection between living and dead; the sense of spirituality which recognises that people and places are more than mere physical presences; the conviction that the consequences of behaviour remain somehow embedded in the ethos of places, just as they do in the lives of people; a belief in the power of psychic communication in those who are open to such faculties; a need for ritual and tradition; emotional honesty; the fierce warmth of friendship and a lack of inhibition in the physical expression of it; an equal lack of inhibition in the expression of anger and grief. These are qualities I admire and in large measure share as a consequence of my own antecedents. They seem to me to be tika: right, proper, natural; they arise from patterns of heredity in whatever chromosomes we all share.

Such characteristics have become contentious only because people from Western, industrialised societies tried to remove them from their own lives through education and the secular sciences, and then to erase the ancient patterns of living and communication from the lives of indigenous peoples who had retained them longer. This latter process is the effect of colonisation I find most offensive, tantamount to cultural genocide. And it was allowed to proceed in New Zealand because notions

---

*I have known one exception. Tiraha Cooper of Te Awamarahi, of pure Pakeha descent but brought up by Maori from birth *was* Maori; she had moko and spoke no English.

of racial and cultural superiority were harnessed to technological pre-eminence, creating an almost unstoppable momentum for cultural change; *almost* unstoppable. In fact, Maori had the resilience and the adaptability to preserve the core of their culture and beliefs, and eventually to use Western technology selectively to strengthen them. That for me is yet another source of admiration for the Maori. So is the aesthetic beauty of Polynesian colouring and features.

There are other Maori characteristics I have found difficult to accept, however, because of my upbringing and education and the kind of person I have consequently become: the emphasis on oral expression and the low priority accorded written forms of communication; the highly socialised pattern of behaviour which values being with people — lots of people — above the occasional need for solitude and quiet contemplation; a stronger preference in some circumstances for talking about decisions than for making them. None of these features are Maori 'faults'. They are simply my perception of aspects of the culture with which I am out of tune, because of my own social and cultural conditioning.

I would judge that Maori have the same percentage of virtuous and non-virtuous people, of honesty and dishonesty, of reliability and unreliability, of achievers and non-achievers, as any other group of human beings — no more, no less. But the standards by which these things are measured — the virtue, the honesty, the achievements — are often different from those applied by Europeans, and this is the source of much needless misunderstanding between Maori and Pakeha. I have known Maori who have shared with their family and tribe resources which they held in trust, and gone to prison for it; I have known men who never wrote a report or answered a letter in the course of their bureaucratic employment who were powerhouses of energy and masterly communicators on marae with which they were associated; I have seen young people who dropped out of school after their third failed attempt at school certificate subjects become astute social workers and highly successful church ministers. I have also seen people who have done things like this shattered, because the accusation of failure levelled by the

Pakeha system of law, administration and education identified them as failures and then made them failures, by puncturing their self-esteem.

I don't romanticise Maori or Maori life. But I do say that the most persistent error Pakeha have made in their association with Maori is this: to measure them by European standards, find them wanting and declare them to be unreliable or unsuccessful, and then blame them for this. Such a system of measurement can create genuine failures because people who are written off by others tend to write off themselves and allow their talents and initiatives to bleed away; or such an experience may create rebels filled with hatred for a system that has chewed them up and spat them out.

It is not enough to say: the Chinese do well in New Zealand; the Vietnamese do well; Indians do well; the Samoans do well — why not the Maori? Because all these other people begin with the security of an identity and a culture that originates elsewhere and is not under serious threat. Maori culture and Maori survival have been under threat of slow annihilation since 1840. The only reason the race, culture and language have survived is because of the eventual acquisition of Maori physical immunity to European disease and eventual cultural immunity to the assumptions of European superiority. As Maori numbers continue to grow (towards a projected fifty percent of the New Zealand population in the twenty-first century), as mana Maori waxes, as Maori concepts of relevance are gradually introduced into the systems of law and education, then just as surely will Maori confidence, competence and levels of achievement in New Zealand life rise. And Pakeha will have to become accustomed to this escalation of expectation and achievement, because they will not be able to halt it or divert it any more than Canute could the tide.

All this is by way of saying what I admire about Maoridom, why I feel a fraternal association with it, why I have been influenced by it; but why I cannot and never will be an intimate part of those people and that culture. What kind of New Zealander am I then, as a consequence of genetic inheritance, upbringing and my own experiences in adult life? What destination have

I reached as a result of the journey described in part in this memoir? In search of some of the answers to these questions I once visited a professional palmist in a caravan in Soho. As I talked to him I was careful to reveal nothing about myself, to test his powers of divination. 'You're a Celt,' he pronounced after studying my palm for thirty seconds. 'How do you know?' 'By the shape of your hand and the markings on it. But you were born in New Zealand.' By now I was incredulous. 'Is that on my palm too?' 'No,' he said. 'That's your voice.'

Given the vulgar fractions of my genealogy — two grandparents of Irish origin and one Scot — he was right. But we had never been touched by pure Celtic culture. Our last connection with Gaelic language had died with my Irish great-grandfather; on the Scottish side of the family, it had long since been obliterated by the cultural imperialism of the English within the United Kingdom. Our tribalism too had died with the brutal attacks of Cromwell and Montrose. The final violence to the Celtic pattern of our ancestors lives had been accomplished by the combination of rural famine with the industrial revolution in the eighteenth and nineteenth centuries, which uprooted our ancestors from the villages and clan territories where their families had lived for centuries. It drew them to towns and cities that promised work and money, and delivered (for most of them) slums, poverty and squalor. The process was almost identical to that which the Maori were to undergo in a more concentrated manner a century later.

At the end of it, the Celtic branches of our family had no strong roots in the places in which they lived, no language of their forefathers, no sacred shrines other than the Catholic ones in the north of England. They had only the options of remaining displaced in England and Glasgow, trapped in the lower orders of the class system; or emigrating to a spacious country where individuals and families could make new beginnings and uplift themselves by the sweat of their brow. They chose the second option, as I have described. As a consequence the first and second generations of both sides of the family in New Zealand developed strong preoccupations with material security and social improvement, because they were sharply aware of the deprivations suffered by parents and grandparents.

My generation, the third in New Zealand, was not allowed to forget where we had come from. But consciousness of our Irish and Scottish origins was diluted by the passage of time, and by the wider British and European reference points imposed on us by secondary and tertiary education: New Zealand's history (as we learnt it) as a British colony; the dominance of European mythology and symbols in our lives, from the reading of Grimms' Fairy Tales to our summer Christmas cards with snow and holly; a suggestion that the great figures in history were British, and usually English (Nelson, Wellington, Scott and Churchill).

In spite of all this, the values we *lived*, the things that gave us cohesion as a family and a community, were those derived from the Irish and Catholic ingredients in our background. I remember thinking at the age of five or six that 'Roman' Catholic was an odd way to describe our religion. We were Irish Catholic or, perhaps, New Zealand Catholic. Subsequent experience grafted other cultural shoots — New Zealand, Maori, Polynesian, English, Jewish, French, American, Austrian, Polish, Asian — on to my Irish-Scottish stock. I have been especially admiring of and influenced by the refugees from Hitler's Europe, for example. The courtliness and intelligence of Kazimierz Wodzicki, the Renaissance breadth and the conversational capacity of Lisl and Paul Heller, the luminous artistic vision of Margot Phillips, the hospitality and entrepreneurial talents of Harry Seresin, the sheer industry of June Jungowska, the cultural and commercial enterprise of members of the Jewish community, some of them survivors of the Nazi death camps. All these people brought to New Zealand skills, sensitivities and insights unrepresented in our British and Maori heritages. They helped change our culture — our theatre, our music, our eating habits — and change it for the better. I am a different person and a richer person for having known them.

'My place is in New Zealand, New Zealand is my place.' While I find myself still most strongly engaged by those things — historical, cultural and political — which arise out of the country in which I live, the works of Austen, Eliot and Dickens, of Saul Bellow, Gabriel Garcia Marquez and Patrick White, jostle in my bookcases with those of Mulgan, Sargeson and Gee, with Ihimaera, Grace and Hulme. T.S. Eliot, Auden and Yeats share shelves with Baxter, Campbell and Tuwhare. I try to keep my French alive by reading Baudelaire, Gide and Camus. Bloomsbury biographies and ones of Gandhi and Nehru sit alongside those of Katherine Mansfield, Frances Hodgkins and Walter Nash. I listen still with exhilaration and sometimes tears to the music of Beethoven, Bach and Mozart; and yet something less complex but more fundamental wakens in me when I hear karanga, tangi and waiata tangi, or the songs of Tuini Ngawai and Ngoingoi Pewhairangi. In idle moments — driving, fishing, washing dishes — the Irish songs and ballads of my childhood burst to the surface of my mind, and I sing them with nostalgia and pleasure. I have been transfixed by the art of the Italian Renaissance and by seeing with my own eyes the paintings of French impressionists; yet I am stirred more powerfully by the canvasses of McCahon and Woollaston, by Hotere's landscapes of the spirit, by the old sculpture of the exhibition called Te Maori and the new of Matchitt and Whiting.*

My cosmology is an amalgam of Irish, Catholic and Maori elements, the latter ones compelling because they have arisen from their long association with the country in which I live, and from phenomena I have experienced directly. The manner in which I relate to people is conditioned by upbringing, by my family, and by the people with whom I have shared friendship and exchanged views of life — Heeni Wharemaru and Sally Marshall-Tuwhangai, Lei Lelaulu, Tony Haas, Lisl Heller, Maria and June Jungowska, my American brother-in-law. All these have brought their own values and life experience into fertile association with my own and extended the dimensions of what I know and feel. Pakeha New Zealanders — from Jim Baxter, Frank Sargeson, Keith Sinclair, Christine Cole Catley, George Fraser, Jack Shallcrass, Ormond Wilson — have done the same and reinforced my conviction that New Zealanders have the capacity to be a people characterised by sanity, imagination and compassion.

---

*I cannot, alas, afford the works of all the artists I admire. But the pictures on my walls, the Mervyn Taylors, Eric Lee-Johnsons, Don Binneys and Robin Whites, are all sources of satisfaction.

My sense of family — that thread of continuity that links us directly to the past and future — grows stronger as I grow older. I valued an increasing ease and depth of communication with my parents, who were spared to know their children and their grandchildren, not simply as relatives, but also as friends. I draw continuing pleasure from the company of my brother and sisters and from the fact that our lives and interests are complementary rather than identical. I feel deeply the loss of one sister, Geraldine, who has chosen to make her home in North America. I marvel at the passage of my own children from adolescence to adulthood, and enjoy with them the experience of an emotional umbilical cord that can never be severed. They too have grown from offspring to friends, a process that widens and deepens the feeling of kinship.

There *is* something special about us (the ingredients of our lives, the proportions of their combination), and there is not. There is something special about New Zealand, and there is not. As I complete this book, I am impressed not only by the singularity of our experience, but also by its universality. The novel I have just finished reading is one of Saul Bellow's on the European migrant culture of North America. Its elements are Russian, Polish, Italian and Spanish, tumbling about in the kaleidoscope of American society; its themes are the culture that this movement excites, the compulsion of people who have known deprivation to pursue physical security, the strength of immigrant family bonds, spiritual inheritance versus secular materialism, God versus Mammon. It is true of the unique combination of time and place from which Bellow writes. But it also resonates strongly in the circumstances, time and place in which I read.

That latter place illustrates another feature of life in particular and life in general: the circular patterns in which history and personal experience seem to arrange themselves. I write now from another piece of land for which I have formed a strong attachment, because of its geographical features and its associations. The limestone headland at my back, Maungarua-wahine was fortified 400 years ago with Maori-quarried stone. Fern, manuka and rangiora leaves filter light through my window. By day, wood pigeons swoop and loop on the air currents above me, and at dusk herons beat their way home to roosts in the surrounding trees. The estuary below, Wharekawa, is the one where Pei Te Hurinui's Maori mother and Jewish father lived and worked before they moved to Kennedy's Bay nearly 90 years ago, and where kauri was shipped out to world markets at the turn of the twentieth century. As Paremata was, this harbour is surrounded by terraced fortifications and middens, evidence of human occupation that bridges a thousand years. I am drawn to it for its shape, its colours and its estuarine life; and for its resemblance to that other place in which I grew up. Here as there one is always conscious of the past in the present, the two dimensions constantly rubbing against one another to produce a frisson and a friction — sparks that illuminate and animate everything one sees and feels.

As I watch this land and seascape, wrapped around by recollections of relationships and remembrance of times past, I find I am Pakeha, I am New Zealander, I am Irish, I am Scottish, I am European; and I am, in parts of my spirit, Maori. I am all these things simultaneously. Most of all, though, and most gratefully of all, I am human and I am alive. I rejoice in the gifts that my antecedents and associations have bequeathed me. 'Love,' says Saul Bellow in the book I have just put down, 'is simply gratitude for being.'

APPENDIX ONE

Taha Maori:
Things Pakeha Ought To Know

I allowed myself to become increasingly involved in Maori history because I felt that neither I nor the Pakeha majority of which I was a member had nearly enough information about Maori experience, nor about the pattern of race relations in New Zealand. The more I turned over the rocks of evidence, the more I found worms crawling about that most Pakeha dismissed as being long dead. It seemed to me obligatory to draw attention to them. My Maori contacts always encouraged me to do so. In the course of this work, however, I became increasingly conscious of how poorly equipped I was to carry it out — of how massively ignorant my education had left me about taha Maori, the Polynesian dimension of life in New Zealand. I am not competent to rectify that same ignorance in others. But I can look back over nearly two decades and recall some of the elementary things I have learnt, and which I subsequently wished I had known at the outset.

Being an historian, I start with history: because the past provides, if not answers, then at least perspectives on the present. Current affairs are always the outcome of history and are better illuminated in the light of history. This is especially so in the case of Maori affairs, because they are such a confusing outcome of acculturation, military defeat, land confiscations, contradictory legislation, population displacement, racism, personality conflicts and continuing cross-cultural misunderstandings; and because the past is always far more potently present in Maori life than it is in non-Maori. Conceptually, Maori look forward into the past and backward into the future: the dead tend to be remembered more sharply and more often, past grievances are frequently the key to present attitudes, history and proverb are quoted in discussion and marae debate in support of contemporary issues.

Cross-cultural misunderstanding in New Zealand reaches as far back as the first known contact between Maori and Pakeha. The Dutchman Abel Tasman had anchored in Golden Bay in December 1642. In the thickening dusk his crew exchanged shouts with brown men in canoes, whom they could barely see. Neither side understood the other in the slightest. When the Maori blew pukaea (war trumpets) at the Dutchmen,

Tasman had two of his own trumpeters play in reply. In effect, a Polynesian challenge to fight had been issued and accepted. The outcome was inevitable. The following day four of Tasman's men were killed by Maori when they attempted to row from one of their vessels to another. Ignorant of how this had come about, the navigator condemned the 'outrageous and detestable crime', named the region Murderers' Bay, and departed without setting foot on New Zealand soil. The Maori involved almost certainly believed they had won a fair battle.

James Cook displayed a better understanding of Maori behaviour 130 years later. He too was attacked, but he did not use such incidents as a ground for either departure or excessive retaliation. After only a fortnight on the New Zealand coast he noted that a canoe-load of Maori had dropped astern after the Englishmen had fired over their heads. 'Not I believe at all frightened . . . but content with having showed their courage by twice insulting us.' Cook recognised that bravado was a strong element in Maori competitiveness and capacity for survival. It led them to take the offensive in uncertain situations so as to encourage themselves, discourage potential adversaries, and hence make their own success and survival more likely. It was a long-established code of behaviour. Individuals and tribes who practised it *had* survived; those who had not had been erased from history.

Where Europeans took the trouble to try to understand Maori codes of behaviour and to identify Maori expectations, Maori-Pakeha relations in the nineteenth century were generally harmonious (at the many shore whaling stations established around the coasts of both major islands, for example). Where they did not, there were severe disappointments on the European side, accusations of Maori unreliability and treachery, and bloodshed.

The Maori people appeared to take up many of the gifts offered to them by missionaries: agricultural and pastoral techniques, literacy, Christianity itself. They would experiment with these things and then turn them to Maori purposes, determined by Maori concepts of relevance. Some aspects they would discard if they did not live up to Maori expectations; others they would use in distinctly Maori ways (new religions such as Pai Marire, for example; or new methods of fighting). Few Europeans understood this process. They believed Maori ought to be totally civilised (that is, Europeanised) or that they would remain barbaric; no other options were recognised.

From 1840 onwards, the nineteenth century is littered with instances of misunderstandings that arose from an inability on the part of most Europeans to distinguish between Maori and Pakeha expectations, or to even admit that Maori expectations existed. The Treaty of Waitangi is a notorious example. To most Europeans it was simply a legal mechanism to cede the sovereignty of New Zealand from Maori to the British Crown. Most Maori had no understanding of the concept of sovereignty, and they believed that the British Crown was undertaking to protect Maori 'chieftainship of their lands, their villages and all their property'. To make matters more complicated, there were separate and differing versions of the treaty in English and in Maori. All of which led to confusion in the succeeding decades, and helped make the treaty a controversial document 140 years later.

Most Europeans too did not understand Maori views of land ownership, and this was a major factor that led to hostility between the races and to war. When the New Zealand Company arrived at Port Nicholson (Wellington), for example, they tried to buy land off the Ati Awa chiefs who lived there. But Ati Awa had been allowed to settle there by the principal conquerors of the district, their more powerful allies the Ngati Toa. Te Ati Awa neither consulted Ngati Toa, nor shared the purchase price with them. Hence Ngati Toi did not recognise the validity of the transaction and offered armed resistance to European settlement. Such incidents were typical of those which led to the New Zealand Wars of the 1840s and 1860s.

After the fighting in the 1860s, the settler Government confiscated vast areas of Maori land in Waikato, Taranaki and the Bay of Plenty (most of these confiscations were later deemed unjust by a Royal Commission — but sixty years later the land could not be returned to its former owners). Maori in these areas withdrew from close contact with Europeans, laying the base for the situation that existed up to the Second World War: Maori living in rural communities characterised by Maori values and protocol; Europeans living in towns and cities whose values and conventions were Western and largely British-based. This segregation — geographical, social, cultural — was the artificial basis for New Zealand's reputation for sound race relations.

The relative isolation of Maori from Pakeha did allow for a consolidation of what Sir James Carroll called 'Maoritanga' — a feeling of and expression of Maoriness. Some leaders sought to recover Maori morale through Maori religious movements — Tawhiao and the Kingitanga, Te Kooti and Ringatu, Te Whiti and Tohu at Parihaka, Te Maiharoa in the South Island, Rua Kenana at Maungapohatu. Others, members of the so-called Young Maori Party, preached a more integrationist approach to things European: Sir Apirana Ngata, Sir Peter Buck, Sir Maui Pomare.

The scenario changed entirely after World War Two. A decline in the Maori rural economy coinciding with expanding employment opportunities in the towns and cities began a chain migration of Maori into urban areas. The scale of this movement can be emphasised by noting that in 1945, more than eighty percent of Maori still lived in rural settlements. By the 1980s, that percentage was less than ten. Nobody — Maori or Pakeha — was prepared for the consequences of the migration. The housing that most Maori went into in the cities was patently inadequate. There was a degree of anti-Maori discrimination in employment, accommodation and some hotel bars. Many migrants, with no preparation for city life, floundered economically and socially. Some youngsters born in the new environment, feeling neither Maori nor Pakeha, reacted in a strongly anti-social manner.

A group of urban-based Maori leaders began — from the early 1970s — to call for major changes in New Zealand life. They claimed that the path in New Zealand race relations had until that point been one-way. Assimilation and integration had always required Maori to become more Pakeha-like. The Maori had to learn everything about the English language and Western ways of living; there was no serious pressure on Pakeha to reciprocate by learning about Maori language and Maoritanga. As a result, Maori values and institutions had a lower status in New Zealand life than their Western equivalents, and many Maori felt whakama or even hostile about their Maori background.

By the 1980s, Maori leaders and organisations were working to reverse this trend, to turn the previously negative experience of being Maori into a powerfully positive one; to raise Maori esteem and competence in a variety of areas. This process was accompanied by a greater Maori presence in public bodies, a call for separate Maori educational facilities, a demand for the settlement of outstanding Maori land grievances, and a more strident condemnation of what is seen as 'institutionalised racism' in Pakeha organisations. None of this threatens Pakeha New Zealanders — it threatens only those features of New Zealand life which in the past made it difficult or impossible for Maori to identify and behave as Maori.

So much for a general perspective. In addition, Pakeha should bear in mind that understanding particular Maori issues or land disputes requires a detailed knowledge of the history of individual cases. An example which shows how complicated land disputes can be — is that of the Waireia block in Hokianga. It is characteristic of dozens of unresolved Maori claims throughout the country. In 1983 the former owners of the block were offered compensation by the Crown for the unjust valuation and selling of the land in 1914. This was to be given either as a lump sum, to be negotiated, or in the form of land for a base farm to benefit the district as a whole. At a series of meetings,

207

the descendants of former owners could not agree on these options Some wanted a lump sum to go direct to the descendants; some wanted a lump sum to go to the people in the district who were landless regardless of whether they were descendants of the original owners; still others wanted a lump sum to go to the Tai Tokerau District Maori Council for the benefit of the wider northern tribal regions; and some wanted the money to go to a new umbrella organisation, the North Hokianga Trust.

Settlement had to be deferred. Because there was no consensus about how the money would be used, a specific compensation sum could not be negotiated. To a Pakeha observer attending just one of the Waireia meetings, it seemed as though hapu rivalry, jealousies and personality conflicts were going to destroy a gracious government offer — a goose was to be hacked to pieces before it could lay a golden egg. In fact, as subsequent research revealed, the situation was highly complex. The ambiguity of the Maori responses to the government offer was the outcome of a series of deceptions, sharp practices, dishonoured promises and bureaucratic inertia spread over seventy years. The Waireia block was surveyed and its owners defined in 1913. In 1914, the Native Land Court was to meet to consider an offer by a European, Henry Martindale, to buy the block. Most owners were strongly opposed to the sale. They wanted to keep the land as part of their inherited turangawaewae; and there was the likelihood that its timber would fetch a good price when it was eventually milled. A local man, related to most of the owners, moved among them offering to act as their agent, asking for proxies and promising to prevent the sale of the land.

In May 1914, Judge Wilson of the Native Land Court declared the 4351-acre block sold to Henry Martindale for £5230. That was the first shock. The owners' agent had voted in favour of the sale and committed his proxy votes to this outcome. The second shock was that the substantial quantity of timber on the block was declared worthless by a Valuation Department assessor and the previous owners therefore received nothing for it. The third shock was that, six years later, this same 'valueless timber' was sold by the new owner to the Rangiora Timber Company for just under £2000.

Waireia's former Maori owners were furious. Eventually, after they had presented the Government with a petition calling for compensation for the way the matter had been handled, Judge Acheson of the Native Land Court was asked to prepare a report on the sale of the block for the Minister of Native Affairs. This report found that no valid resolution to sell was ever passed by the Waireia owners, that money which should have been paid for the timber was never paid, and that the Tokerau District Maori Land Board had failed to protect the interests of the owners. These findings were so sensational, particularly in view of the fact that most parties to the original transaction were still alive, that the minister concerned suppressed the report. It was never printed, nor made public, nor even made available to the former Waireia owners.

It was all these factors that made the Government's eventual decision to compensate the descendants of the former owners a controversial one. What constituted fair compensation for the land? How much had the timber really been worth? Should the descendants of the owner who had acted dishonestly also be compensated? Should people now living in the area but unrelated to the former Waireia owners be part of any settlement? Should the money be invested, to remove the act of the compensation from the various controversies surrounding it?

None of these questions had been settled at the time of writing. They are presented merely to show how complicated some Maori issues have become, and the degree of research and information which is required to understand them. And what is true of Waireia is equally true of Bastion Point, the Raglan golf course, the Motunui outfall, and dozens of other places that have been sources of contention in the 1980s. In almost every case the origin of contention is the consequence of Pakeha attempts to place Maori land and customs related to land under European forms of administration.

The second issue I want to consider is that of Maori language. In a society that professes to be bicultural, members of each culture ought to be fluent in the other's language. In practice, bilingualism is largely confined to Maori. As a first gesture, however, well-intentioned Pakeha should master correct pronunciation of Maori words and names, and become familiar with basic Maori vocabulary and concepts and common Maori expressions. It is not the function of this book to serve as a guide for learning the Maori language — that task must be undertaken elsewhere under Maori tuition. But the following advice will lay the foundation for learning.

Vowel sounds in Maori can be long or short; length may alter meaning or indicate singular or plural. With that proviso, A is pronounced as in father, E as in egg, I as in kiwi, O as in raw, U as in plural. For the non-native speaker, the most difficult consonants are NG as in 'ringer', and WH which denotes an aspirated W, but which is increasingly pronounced more like an F. Only guidance from a native speaker will ensure that the non-Maori student of the language is approaching pronunciation satisfactorily.

The following words are ones with which every New Zealander ought to be familiar, as art of a basic New Zealand vocabulary. They occur frequently in Maori use of English as well as in Maori. In Maori, plurals are conveyed by changing the definite and indefinite articles ('te' to 'nga', for example), not by adding an 's'. This means that in Maori English the singular and plural form of the word will most often be the same. Words used as nouns can also be used adjectivally.

Meanings given here are generally accepted ones. But they can vary according to context, and from district to district (so that the people of the north tend to use kaupapa in place of kawa, for example). Some English equivalents are approximations rather than exact translations; the variety of meanings and the application of a single word such as mana, for example, could only be conveyed fully in a lengthy explanation. The first step for beginners is to learn to say and to recognise the words, and with recognition will come a subsequent understanding of the range and contexts of their uses.

ariki	lord, leader of a federation of tribes
aroha	caring, love for the many
arohanui	much love
atua	spirit, god
awhina	assistance
haka	posture dance, chant of welcome or defiance
hakari	feast
hangi	earth oven and its contents
he	a (indefinite article)
hikoi	march
hongi	pressing noses as physical introduction
hui	assembly, meeting
ihi	capacity to inspire awe
iwi	people, tribe
kahui ariki	Kingitanga 'royal family'
kai	food
kai moana	seafood
kai tiaki	guardian
kainga	village, home
karakia	prayer, chant, church service
karanga	welcoming call
kaumatua	male elder
kaupapa	programme, procedure
kawa	etiquette, protocol
koha	gift

komiti	committee
koro	old man
koroua	male elder
korowai	ornamental cloak
kotahitanga	unity
kotiro	girl
kowhaiwhai	patterns on meeting house rafters
kuia	female elder
kupapa	Maoris on the European side during the New Zealand Wars
makutu	curse, black magic
mana	spiritual power, prestige, authority
manuhiri	visitors
Maoritanga	Maori culture
marae	open space in front of a meeting house; sometimes refers to a village around a meeting house
matakite	second sight
mate	death, deceased persons
mauri	ethos, life force
mihi	greeting
minita	minister
mokopuna	descendant
nga	the (definite article, plural)
noa	common, free from tapu
pa	village, in pre-European times a fortified settlement
paepae	threshold of meeting house, position of tangata whenua for ceremonial welcome
Pakeha	person of European descent
patu	club
poi	dance performed with small flax ball on string
poroporoaki	final farewell, often for the dead
poukai	Kingitanga hui
pounamu	greenstone, nephrite
powhiri	welcome
puha	edible sow-thistle
rahui	prohibition, reservation
rangatira	chief, aristocratic
runanga	council
taha Maori	Maori dimensions of life
take	cause, subject for discussion
tane	man
tamaiti	child

tamariki	children
tangata whenua	people of the land, hosts
tangi	cry for the dead, ceremony of mourning
tangihanga	ceremony of mourning
taniwha	water spirit
taonga	sacred relic
tapu	sacred, prohibited
tauparapara (tau)	ancient chant, formerly associated with launching canoes
te	the (definite article, singular)
teina	of junior descent
tihe mauri ora	sneeze of life (expression used to introduce a speech)
tikanga	custom
tohunga	expert, chosen one, priest
tuakana	of senior descent
tukutuku	panels inside meeting house decorated with patterns traditionally made from flax strands
tupapaku	corpse
tupuna	ancestor
turangawaewae	a place to stand, a sense of belonging, a home marae
tutae	excrement
urupa	cemetery
utu	satisfaction
waewae tapu	sacred feet, people entering a particular marae for the first time
wahi tapu	sacred place, usually a burial ground
wahine	woman
waiata	song, lament
waiata-a-ringa	action song
wairua	spirit
waka	canoe, tribal federation
wero	challenge
whaikorero	formal marae discussion, speech-making
whakama	awkward, shy
whakapapa	genealogy
whakatauki	saying, proverb
whanau	extended family
whare	house
whare kai	dining room
whare moe	sleeping house
whare puni	elaborate meeting house

Equally important, Pakeha ought to recognise and be able to respond to basic Maori greetings and conversational exchanges. The following are the more common:

Tena koe	Hello (more formal, to one person)
Tena korua	Hello (to two persons)
Tena koutou	Hello (to more than two persons)
Kia ora	Hello (more casual)
Kia ora tatou	Greetings to a group of which the speaker is a part
Kia ora koutou	Hello to a group of other people
Kei te.pehea?	How are you?
Kei te pai	Okay
Ka nui te pai	Very well
Ko wai tou ingoa?	What is your name?
Ko Pita taku ingoa	My name is Peter
No whea koe?	Where are you from?
No Akarana	From Auckland
E noho	Sit down
E tu	Stand up
Haere mai	Welcome, come forward
Haere atu	Go away
Haere ra	Goodbye (from the one staying to the ones going)
E noho ra	Goodbye (from the one going to the ones staying)
Kua mutu	It's finished, I've finished

The extent to which Maori words should be used in written English, and the manner in which they should be rendered in that language, are still matters of contention. As far as most Maori are concerned, however, Maori words which they use when speaking English ought to be considered as part of basic New Zealand English, as distinct from the Queen's English (hui for a Maori gathering rather than 'meeting'; karakia for 'prayer' and so on). They ought not be printed in italics which indicate a foreign language or an exotic expression — unless it is to avoid ambiguity with an identically spelt European word. An example of the latter would be *take* or *rape*.

Maori usage ought also to be taken into consideration in the case of plurals. As already noted, Maori plurals do not add an 's'. The plural is indicated in Maori by the changing of the definite article. It sounds peculiar to Maori ears, therefore, when Europeans place an 's' on a Maori word. It is preferable to render the plural in English without the 's' (one Maori, ten Maori) where context makes the meaning clear. Secondly, Maori words which begin with 'te' already have a definite article and shouldn't be given a further one in English. So that one should write about Te Ati Awa tribe, not the Te Ati Awa tribe; Te Kohanga Reo, not the Te Kohanga Reo movement; and so on.

There is disagreement about whether Pakeha should be capitalised in written English and Maori, just as there is disagreement about the word's origin and original meaning. Its accepted meaning today is simply 'non-Maori' — it is not a term of abuse. And the tendency in most publications is to use the upper case, even though it does not refer to a single ethnic group. It has as much right to be capped as Maori (which was originally only an adjective meaning 'ordinary') and it looks foolish to render one in the upper case and the other in the lower.

After mastering the meaning, pronunciation and use of basic Maori, the next thing Pakeha ought to know is how to behave at Maori functions — hui, conferences, tangihanga, weddings, and so on. Most of these will take place on a marae. Even where they do not, the kawa of the marae will usually apply, and this should be fully understood.

On nearly all such occasions, visitors will be put through a welcoming or 'decontamination' ceremony. This will vary in detail from district to district and from marae to marae. But the basic structure is the same and Pakeha visitors should be familiar with it, and understand it, so as to feel confident and to know how to respond if they are part of it. In some (but by no means all) instances, it will begin with the wero or challenge, carried out by a young man wielding a taiaha. The explanation that follows is given by an authority on Maori ceremonial, Ranginui Walker.

> The wero . . . is a cultural survival from the times of tribal conflict. Its purpose was to determine whether visitors came with friendly or hostile intent. Accordingly, as the challenging warrior went through his gestures of defiance he never took his eyes off the visitors — if they were hostile one of the fastest runners among them could break ranks and pursue to kill him before he made the safety of the pa. Today the wero is performed in honour of VIPs. The leader who picks up the dart placed before the visitors signifies peace, whereupon the party is led onto the marae.
>
> A party of visitors arriving at a marae may not enter unannounced because they are waewae tapu. They bring with them alien tapu and accompanying ancestral spirits which might be inimical to those of the tangata whenua, so they must assemble at the entrance to await the karanga. This is announced by the high-pitched wail of women paying tribute to the dead. As visitors walk on, their eyes are cast down in homage to the dead.

Once on the marae, the visitors halt with a clear space separating them from the hosts, where both stand for a few minutes in acknowledgement of their mutual bereavements as well as those of other tribes. At a signal from the hosts visitors are free to sit down. The elders sitting on the paepae (formerly the beam on the threshold of the meeting house but nowadays a bench off to one side) rise in turn to give their speeches of welcome.

The mihi (welcome) has a standard format. It begins with a tau (chant in poetic form which identifies the local tribe). Depending on the occasion the tau may be a tribute to the dead or a philosophic exhortation to the living to unite in harmony. The second part of the mihi is the eulogy to the dead. Reference is often made to recent bereavements of the hosts, visitors and other tribes. This part of the mihi is embellished by mythological allusions and figures of speech which indicate the oratorical prowess of the speakers. They are poetic, deeply spiritual and very touching.

The third part of the mihi is introduced by a clear separation between the living and the dead. The dead are farewelled and consigned to the spirit world. The orator then turns to greet the living. Greetings are extended to the canoes, the tribes, the four winds. Individual visitors of note are welcomed by name. At this point it is usual to make reference to the reason why the two groups have come together (kaupapa).

The mihi concludes with a waiata (song), often a lament but sometimes one that identifies the speaker's tribe and the notable landmarks in his territory. The whaikorero (speech in reply) by a visitor also follows the format of the mihi. At the conclusion of the speeches intimacy between the hosts and visitors is expressed by physical contact through shaking hands and pressing noses (the hongi). The food provided for visitors immediately after the formalities signifies the complete ritual decontamination of waewae tapu. The visitors are then free to mingle with their hosts.

If Pakeha visitors are participating in the mihi and are recognised and singled out for welcome, then they may be expected to reply as part of the visitors' whaikorero. It could be acceptable to do this in English. But it is infinitely preferable to speak in Maori, even if it is only a few appropriate sentences. A brief and suitable reply to a mihi could go like this:

Karanga mai! Mihi mai!	Thank you for your welcome!
Te whare e tu nei, tena koe!	The house that stands here, greetings!

Te marae e takoto nei, tena koe!	The marae beneath us, greetings!
Aku rangatira tena koutou, tena koutou katoa	My elders, greetings, greetings to you all
Nga mate, haere, haere, haere!	To the dead, farewell!
Te hunga ora, tena koutou, tena koutou katoa	To the living, greetings, greetings to you all
Tena koutou, tena koutou, tena koutou!	Greetings, greetings to you all!

After the speeches, the hongi can present problems for those unprepared for it. It is *not* a rubbing of noses, but a pressing. Take the extended hand of the person in front of you, press noses lightly, perhaps twice, and murmur a greeting: 'tena koe'. If the host knows you, or has recently suffered a bereavement, he or she might want to hongi longer and more intimately. Leave this initiative to the host and simply follow it. If you are unconfident about any of this, ask a Maori friend to practise the hongi with you before you enter a marae.

It has to be stressed — for this is one of the things that distinguishes a Maori function from many non-Maori ones — that unless he or she is known to the tangata whenua and has permission to do so, a Pakeha *cannot* simply bypass ritual and wander onto and around a marae as a free agent. To do this would be to offend seriously against tikanga. People who have done this in the past have attracted ill will towards themselves and towards other Pakeha who have followed them to the same marae.

Pakeha visitors must also observe basic etiquette while staying on a marae. The marae proper (the area immediately in front of the meeting house) is highly tapu. It should not be walked across, especially in the course of speeches. Visitors should *never* walk in front of a speaker — if it is unavoidable that they do so, they should stoop as they pass, to show respect and regret.

Special permission is almost always required to take photographs, from the person assigned this authority by the marae (it may be the chairman of the marae committee, a senior kaumatua, or a Maori warden). Once given, that licence should be used with sensitivity and discretion. It is usually permissible to photograph groups arriving, groups singing on the marae, an individual speaking. Remember, however, that according to Maori values, the head is the most tapu part of the body. Many Maori object to having a camera held close to their face. Some elderly people may object to being photographed at all. In their belief photography diminishes their mauri or life force and makes them vulnerable to sickness. If the photographer encounters such an attitude, he should respect it.

At tangi, Pakeha should observe general marae protocol, including the hongi with mourners around the open coffin. In some areas it is customary to hongi with the tupapaku, but a Pakeha visitor should not do this unless he was closely acquainted with the deceased. If in doubt, take advice from local elders. If the visitor speaks on the marae during the tangi, he should never turn his back on the tupapaku. And most families (but not all) would object to photographs being taken of an open coffin. This is another matter on which advice must be sought — and accepted — from the local people and the family immediately concerned. If visitors attend the burial service towards the end of the tangi, they should wash their hands as they leave the cemetery — a ritual removal of tapu.

If the Pakeha visitor is staying overnight or several nights in the meeting house, there are further rules of etiquette to be observed. Shoes must be removed on the porch. Generally speaking, no eating or drinking is allowed inside the house (and sometimes no smoking, but this depends on the preferences of local kaumatua; watch and see how they behave). Certain sleeping spaces in the house are reserved. Facing the house, the left-hand side is generally occupied by the tangata whenua, the right by manuhiri. The spaces on the right nearest the door are reserved for senior members of the visiting party. Visitors may also take positions at the rear of the house and those on the left not occupied by the hosts, starting from the back. A visitor should indicate his position by placing his baggage at the foot of the mattress allocated to him.

After the evening meal in the dining room, most of the time before sleep will be taken up with whaikorero in the meeting house. This will usually be about the kaupapa of the hui, or about particular *take* that individuals want discussed. Participants lie on their mattresses, covered by their blankets or sleeping bags if this makes them more comfortable. The evening's activity is likely to begin with a prayer, followed by further mihi, which usually proceed clockwise around the house. These formalities completed, the whaikorero proper begins.

All speakers should rise to their feet. They should greet the whole company and the previous speakers to the best of their ability, although a simple 'kia ora tatou' will suffice for those whose Maori is limited or non-existent. Speakers should not move about while they talk, but it is accepted that they can be as verbally provocative as they like. In fact a short whaikorero, with no spirited exchanges, is regarded as a disappointing exercise. One should not interrupt others while they are speaking (the time to reply is when you get to your own feet); and, as on a marae, it is regarded as bad manners to cross in front of a speaker. Either stay still until he has finished or move behind him. Traditionally the whaikorero finishes when everyone has run out of things to say, or when the majority of participants have fallen asleep.

Marae on which hui and tangi are held are most likely to be tribally based and organised, and it is useful for Pakeha to have some knowledge of the concept of tribe and the bases of Maori organisation. There are several words for kinds of tribe. Waka (literally 'canoe') represents a federation of tribes (such as Waikato-Maniapoto) who trace their descent from one canoe, *Tainui*. Iwi (literally 'people') is the tribe proper, such as Tuhoe. Hapu (literally 'to be pregnant') is the sub-tribe and the one with which most people have closest association. Whanau (extended family) is the smallest tribal unit, and the basis for marae organisation in formerly populous Maori rural districts, such as the Ruatoki Valley. Most tribal names are headed by a prefix meaning 'descendant of' (such as Ngati). A man or a woman from Lake Taupo might say, therefore, that they belong to the Ngati Turumakina hapu of Ngati Tuwharetoa (iwi) of the Arawa federation (waka). Each layer of tribe is a division of the other, from waka downwards. In fact, most hapu are not simply sub-tribes, they are sub-sub-sub-tribes, formed when groupings became too large to live in one place. They would be named after the rangatira who led his immediate followers and descendants away and founded the new hapu.

Because of the mobility of the Maori people since World War Two and the degree of inter-tribal marriage over a longer period, most Maori now trace descent from more than one tribe — though most also identify more closely with a single tribe than they do with all their ancestral options. The record of the genealogical links with ancestors and relatives is known as whakapapa.

Increased mobility has also meant that most Maori now live outside what were once the traditional boundaries of their tribes. Nevertheless those boundaries remain — things of the spirit rather than geographical barriers — and most Maori locate their turangawaewae within them. The accompanying map indicates where these boundaries lie, though they were often not fixed with precision. Te Aupouri occupy the top of the North Island, for example; Ngai Tahu and Ngati Mamoe the bottom of the South Island.

Tribal trusts are based on traditional tribal territory, although they may help to fund tribal activities occurring outside the traditional region. Most were set up to administer funds allocated by governments in compensation for land unjustly confiscated (Waikato, Taranaki), for other promises not honoured (Ngai Tahu) or in return for ownership of tribal territory which had been formerly taken by the Crown (Arawa).

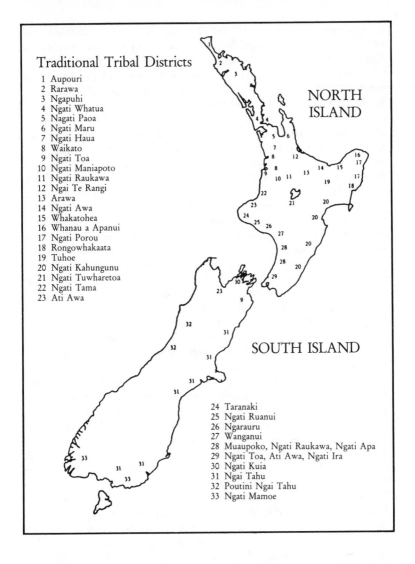

Traditional Tribal Districts

1 Aupouri
2 Rarawa
3 Ngapuhi
4 Ngati Whatua
5 Nagati Paoa
6 Ngati Maru
7 Ngati Haua
8 Waikato
9 Ngati Toa
10 Ngati Maniapoto
11 Ngati Raukawa
12 Ngai Te Rangi
13 Arawa
14 Ngati Awa
15 Whakatohea
16 Whanau a Apanui
17 Ngati Porou
18 Rongowhakaata
19 Tuhoe
20 Ngati Kahungunu
21 Ngati Tuwharetoa
22 Ngati Tama
23 Ati Awa

NORTH ISLAND

SOUTH ISLAND

24 Taranaki
25 Ngati Ruanui
26 Ngarauru
27 Wanganui
28 Muaupoko, Ngati Raukawa, Ngati Apa
29 Ngati Toa, Ati Awa, Ngati Ira
30 Ngati Kuia
31 Ngai Tahu
32 Poutini Ngai Tahu
33 Ngati Mamoe

These trusts are administered by elected representatives on behalf of the tribe and dispense funds for projects such as land development, marae reconstruction and educational assistance. They also, on occasion, act as spokespersons for the tribe as a whole.

Beyond tribal structures there is a thicket of Maori organisations or institutions with Maori membership and responsibilities. The following alphabetical list is not comprehensive but covers major ones:

Churches The Anglican, Presbyterian, Methodist and Roman Catholic Churches all have Maori sections, and the Church of the Latter Day Saints (Mormons) has a largely Maori membership in New Zealand. With the exception of the Mormons, they all have Maori clergy, and the Anglicans, Catholics and Presbyterians run church boarding schools. There is an Anglican Bishop of Aotearoa. The Anglicans and Presbyterians have separate Maori synods, and all churches hold huis, such as the Anglicans' annual Hui Topu. The degree of ecumenism among Maori has always been stronger than among non-Maori, and services, especially at hui and tangi, are often inter-denominational.

Cultural Clubs These exist to keep the Maori cultural heritage alive, especially haka, songs and language, and there are at least 300 throughout the country (the oldest being Ngati Poneke in Wellington). They may be based on a marae, a tribe or a district. In many cases they were established to keep Maori culture active in the cities, away from traditional roots in rural marae. There are a variety of competitions for these clubs, such as those held at the Kingitanga's Coronation Hui, and the biennial Polynesian Festival.

Department of Maori Affairs This arose out of the administration of the Native Land Court (established in 1865), and its organisation is still based on the Maori Land Court's districts. Its functions are to help with the identification of titles to Maori land, to administer and develop Maori and, and to oversee Maori housing and welfare. It also liaises with other government departments — especially Health, Education, Labour and Justice — to protect Maori interests.

Incorporations These are legal entities devised to assist the development and administration by the owners of communally held Maori land. The number of owners forming one can range from three to a whole tribe. Two of the best known (and most successful) are the Mangatu Incorporation on the East Coast, dealing in sheep and cattle, and the Puketapu Incorporation east of Lake Taupo, dealing largely in timber.

Kingitanga This is the Maori King Movement, formally established in 1858, but dating from an inter-tribal meeting called by Te Heu Heu of Ngati Tuwharetoa on the shore of Lake Taupo in 1856. The object of the Kingitanga has always been to unite Maori under the mana and tapu of their own King, and to complement the role of the British Crown in New Zealand. There have been five Kings (Potatau, Tawhiao, Mahuta, Te Rata, Koroki), and the present incumbent is Te Arikinui Dame Te Atairangikaahu. The ceremonial headquarters are at Ngaruawahia, at Turangawaewae Marae built by Princess Te

Puea Herangi; but the Maori monarchs live at Waahi Marae, Huntly. The Kingitanga has an annual Coronation Hui at Turangawaewae in May and a series of smaller loyalty hui known as poukai on marae that most actively support the movement (mainly those in the Tainui federation of tribes).

Kotahitanga This word means unity and the Kotahitanga Movement, originating from the Northland tribes in the nineteenth century, has always sought a degree of Maori self-government. It became a nationwide Maori organisation in the 1890s, with a Parliament at Papawai in the Wairarapa. In the 1950s and 1960s the movement was based on the East Coast. It was revived in 1983 to mount the hikoi to Waitangi in February 1984.

Mana Motuhake Literally, the separate mana or sovereignty of the Maori people. This too is a movement that has roots in the nineteenth century. The expression seems to have been used originally by Tawhiao, the second Maori King, and was revived by the prophet Tahupotiki Wiremu Ratana. It was adopted as the name for a new political party by the Hon. Matiu Rata, after he resigned from the Labour Party and from the Northern Maori seat in 1979. Calling for greater Maori self-determination, the party rapidly became the second highest polling party among Maori voters (after the Labour Party).

Maori Committees and Councils This four-tiered system of Maori leadership was set up in two acts of Parliament, in 1945 and 1962. It provides for Maori Committees in Maori communities, elected for three-year terms. These elect Maori executives on a regional or tribal basis. The Maori Executive Committees elect District Maori Councils (for nine districts), which in turn elect members to the New Zealand Maori Council, a national body. Although the Maori committees have some responsibilities for Maori welfare and nominate Maori wardens, the system has functioned largely as a means of forming and utilising Maori opinion regionally and nationally, and for purposes such as rewriting the Maori Affairs Act.

Maori International A private company with an all-Maori shareholding set up in 1984 to initiate joint ventures with the owners of Maori land and other Maori resources. According to its first managing-director, former Department of Maori Affairs Secretary Kara Puketapu, the company was initially interested in tourism and marketing Maori products. Later it would move into such areas as land development and forestry. In their prospectus, Maori International directors said they would act in joint ventures as 'advisor, manager, developer, investor, partner and financier'. The company aroused controversy before it even began operations because of its bid to take over the New Zealand

Arts and Crafts Institute at Whakarewarewa.

Maori Women's Welfare League The league was established by the Government in 1951, initially under the powerful leadership of Dame Whina Cooper. It was the country's first truly national Maori organisation, and its purpose was 'to unite Maori women in the common objective of homecraft and mothercraft and the general welfare of the Maori mother and child'. It has done this well, at local, regional and national levels, and it acted as the only major forum for national Maori issues until the formation of the New Zealand Maori Council in 1962.

Parliamentary Representation New Zealand has had four seats reserved for Maori electors since 1867. Until 1949 they were held by men, but since then there have been two Maori women MPs. The seats were dominated by the Labour Party-Ratana alliance from the 1930s to the 1960s. By the 1980s only two Maori MPs were members of the Ratana Church, though all four members were Labour. Three Maori members have been Ministers of Maori Affairs — Apirana Ngata, Matiu Rata and Koro Wetere — as have two Maori holding general seats, James Carroll and Ben Couch.

Ratana The Ratana Movement was founded by the Wanganui prophet Tahupotiki Wiremu Ratana after he had a vision in 1918. At first it concentrated on uplifting the spiritual and physical health of the Maori people, and preaching their kotahitanga (unity). From the late 1920s the movement went into politics. It formed an alliance with the Labour Party in 1935, and by 1943 had captured all four Maori seats. The movement is stronger in the 1980s as a church than as a political force.

Ringatu The Maori church founded by the prophet Te Kooti Te Turuki Rikirangi when he was being pursued by government forces in the late 1860s. It means upraised hand, a gesture members of the church make in prayer. It is strong still in the Bay of Plenty and East Coast regions, particularly among the Tuhoe, Ngati Awa and Whakatohea tribes. Members meet for a day of prayer on the twelfth of every month (Tekaumarua).

Sporting Associations Sport is a large feature of all specifically Maori communities, and of those with a large Maori population. The most popular games are rugby, rugby league, basketball, netball, softball, hockey, tennis and golf. There are specifically Maori tournaments in rugby, golf and tennis; and others in all sports held in association with Maori hui. The New Zealand Rugby Football Union has a Maori Advisory Committee; Maori rugby teams have toured overseas on seventeen occasions between 1888 and 1982, and they have played visiting international teams within New Zealand.

The other factor that should be considered in the context of Maori organisations, because it is often an enigma to Pakeha, is the question of Maori leadership. There are many bases for positions of authority within Maori groups. In pre-European times, leadership of hapu was hereditary and generally passed from oldest son to oldest son. This was because mana was deemed to be hereditary, and the achievements of each successful chief enlarged the degree of mana that could potentially be passed on to his descendants. But the practice was never inflexible. Where an older son was weak or withdrawing and a younger son a powerful orator or organiser, then leadership could pass to that younger son. Occasionally it passed to a forceful daughter. Such a process would never take place by election, but would evolve with the will of the people. Sometimes there were junior descendants, such as Te Rauparaha of Ngati Toa, who fought their way up the social scale by sheer determination and accomplishment. So while there was an expectation of what the anthropologists call male primogeniture, there was always a degree of flexibility, and Maori history is full of exceptions.

In contemporary times, mana is still a vital ingredient in Maori leadership — though it tends often to be interpreted as social and political standing as well as spiritual power. There are ariki (the Te Heuheu family of Ngati Tuwharetoa and the kahi ariki of Tainui) but they tend to communicate through nominated spokesmen. Increasingly it is the people with acquired rather than hereditary mana — organisational ability, communication skills, successful careers — who are emerging as spokespersons most acceptable to Maori committees and groups. These are not necessarily the same people who will be spokesmen on ceremonial occasions, which are regarded as taha Maori rather than taha Pakeha.

There are, therefore, a variety of bases on which Maori leaders are recognised. Some have inherited and acquired mana that make them universally regarded as national Maori figures (Sir James Henare, Dame Whina Cooper); some achieve recognition by virtue of their office (Race Relations Conciliator, Secretary of Maori Affairs, Director of Maori Education); some become leaders by virtue of elected office (Chairman of the New Zealand Maori Council, Member of Parliament); some, such as Mira Szaszy (former president of the Maori Women's Welfare League) remain powerful long after they have relinquished elected office; some have the mana of unchallenged tribal leadership (John Rangihau of Tuhoe); some secure leadership of a group concerned with a particular project (Eva Rickard and the Raglan golf course dispute); some have the mana of acquired expertise on a particular subject (Professor Hugh Kawharu on Maori land tenure); and some are leaders by election or consensus, of a particular marae or community.

Finally, when reading about the opinions or activities of Maori leaders or their organisations, Pakeha should note that there is no single Maori viewpoint or 'party-line'. Maori are as various as non-Maori, and are only likely to share identical opinions in the face of threats or insults; or on the broadest of topics, such as the retention of Maori land, culture and language. On the details of such issues and on strategies and tactics, opinions vary greatly according to age, sex, tribe, the region in which they live, their level of education, the organisations to which they belong, their politics, and so on. What a Maori leader says is likely to be true for himself and the immediate group he represents rather than for Maoridom in general. All this is stating the obvious for those associated with Maori organisations. But it needs to be emphasised: many Pakeha seem fixated by the notion that Maori are (or ought to be) of one voice, in a manner that is never expected of non-Maori. To quote John Rangihau of Tuhoe: 'To me there is no such thing as Maoritanga, because Maoritanga is an all-inclusive term which embraces all Maoris. . . . Each tribe has its own history, each person has his own history. And those histories cannot be shared among others.'

APPENDIX TWO

Sporting Contacts With South Africa

I've said little in this book about sporting contacts with South Africa. I have actively opposed such contact since my student days, because I believed it represented participation in the system of apartheid. And I believed that New Zealand, with its long-professed commitment to racial equality, should be the last country in the world to participate in such a legally entrenched system, to give comfort to its supporters, and to alienate countries of the New Commonwealth in the process. My information about conditions in South Africa, I should stress, always came from first-hand sources: from the National Union of South African Students when I was at university; and later from South African friends such as Joan Leech, whose father was an Anglican minister in Johannesburg and whose godfather was Trevor Huddleston.

I outlined the factors that led to my stance on Springbok tours when I spoke to the Hamilton Founders Dinner at the University of Waikato on 24 August 1981:

The question I hear supporters of the 1981 Springbok tour ask most often is this: Why should the South Africans have been welcomed to New Zealand so wholeheartedly in 1956 and be so reviled by a large section of the population in 1981? What has caused New Zealand to change so drastically in twenty-five years?

It is a fair question. In the heat of immediate confrontations it should be asked. And it should be answered to impose an overview and a degree of perspective on what is happening. I'm not aware that anybody has tried to answer it, methodically and coherently.

What I want to do — as an historian — is identify some of the significant things that have happened to bring about this change in climate. The glib would say — as a cabinet minister has said — that the Western world has changed in that time: that there is less respect for lawfully taken decisions of governments, less respect for law and order, less respect for individual rights; that professional agitators foment social disharmony with a view to bringing down democratic institutions.

The realities of history are always a more complex juxtaposition of issues and forces than a recipe such as this would suggest.

First, let's look at New Zealand. In 1956 only 35 percent of the Maori population lived in towns and cities. True, they were moving in that direction in increasing numbers. But by and large they were not a visible component of our cities. They tended to be in enclosed suburbs, and the contact between Maori and Pakeha outside country townships was minimal. This had been the story of New Zealand race relations throughout the twentieth century. The two major ethnic groups who made up the country's population — Maori and Pakeha — had been geographically and socially insulated from each other. The only areas of national life in which Maori had participated on anything like a large scale were warfare and rugby. A consequence of this absence of contact was an absence of conflict. Hence New Zealand had one of the best records of race relations anywhere in the world.

By the late 1950s, however, the social landscape was changing irrevocably. Maori continued to come to towns and cities in large numbers and where there was interaction between Maori and Pakeha there were also recorded instances of discrimination: in employment, in hotel and rental accommodation, in housing. And if such discrimination did not cause widespread comment or conflict at the time, it was largely because of Maori shyness or forbearance.

There was also, of course, the institutional bias of the New Zealand system of government in education, in the law, and in other applications of government policy through branches of the Public Service. Our institutions were designed to reflect Western European values, practices and priorities rather than Polynesian ones. I'm not saying for a moment that this was blameworthy — it was an inevitable consequence of the country's earlier history of conquest and subjugation. And, although successive New Zealand governments had talked about cultural integration as the national ideal, they had always meant that Maori must integrate with Europeans, not vice versa. There had been no serious pressure on Europeans to learn Maori protocol and ways of doing things.

In this whole situation, a degree of conflict was latent, and perhaps inevitable. Maori came to towns and cities whose Pakeha institutions and citizens were not prepared for them. Abrasion resulted. A generation of children grew up in a cultural vacuum. The Maori criminal offending rate shot up, and some people on both sides acted in an intolerant and even racist manner. And a growing number of forceful and articulate Maori began to demand radical changes in the structure of the country's national life.

How do we stand in 1981? Some 90 percent of the Maori population now live in towns and cities (and to appreciate the pace and magnitude of change remember that is an increase of nearly 130 percent in only twenty-five years). The institutions of national life have at last begun to bend towards Maori needs and aspirations in addition to Pakeha ones. This has been most dramatically apparent in the education system, in the funding of arts and literature, and in the activities of bodies such as the Historic Places Trust. The most conservative of Maori institutions — the New Zealand Maori Council and Maori parliamentary representation — now speak far more emphatically for Maori viewpoints than they did in the 1950s. And we have devised new institutions, such as the office of the Race Relations Conciliator, to mitigate racial and cultural conflict.

All this is praiseworthy and to be welcomed. We are now a less comfortable society than we were in the 1950s. But we are a more just and a more fully integrated one — and this is what our national spokesmen have told us for a long time we should be.

Throughout this period there has been another factor at work. The 1950s and early 1960s were, for most Pakeha New Zealanders, years of relative prosperity. Wool prices were high, goods and services were readily available, employment was secure, houses were easily and cheaply built, there seemed enough of everything to go around. After the austerities of the '30s and '40s, the country exuded contentment and relative tranquillity, once the sore of the waterfront strike had healed. Such prosperity, of course, always papers over the cracks in society. It's only in the discontent of hardship and apparent injustice, in the shrinking and withdrawal of resources that accompany recession, that the condition of minority groups becomes visible. It's then that the plight of Maori, Islanders, women, solo mothers, homosexuals and others tends to become apparent and tends to be talked about. The cry then raised — by the minority groups — is one of justice for all and not justice simply for the white middle-class business and professional few. In particular, growing unemployment has hit Maori families hard since the late 1970s. It has limited their capacity to take an equal place in New Zealand society, just when opportunities seemed to be opening up and expectations were raised. In some instances it has intensified a feeling of alienation from wider New Zealand life on the part of the poorly educated workless young.

Both sets of factors of which I have been speaking — the diminution of prosperity and the fight to incorporate Maori elements into the national life — have left a legacy. That legacy is a more urgent impatience on the part of many Maori and some Pakeha to continue the accommodation of Maori needs and aspirations. And a far greater scrutiny of and sensitivity to our national performance in the field of race relations than was apparent in 1956.

One measure of this increased sensitivity has been the fact that until 1960, public opinion allowed the New Zealand Rugby Football Union to despatch so-called nationally representative teams to South Africa that excluded Maori, with scarcely a ripple. In the years since 1960, however, this has not been possible. We have not permitted another country to dictate on racial grounds who should and who should not represent us abroad.

Parallel with these purely national developments, the country has been influenced by outside factors; by a currency of importable international feelings and ideas. The civil rights movement in the United States — the black-is-beautiful assertion of Negro identity — had reverberations here and gave impetus to the momentum of Maori reformist groups such as Nga Tamatoa, Te Reo Maori, Te Matakite O Aotearoa, and more latterly Mana Motuhake. In addition, many New Zealanders have become increasingly attuned to the sensitivities of Third World nations, particularly those in the Commonwealth. And we have heard their voices with increasing regularity and volume as they grow in confidence.

It is their view of racism that has been the key one. The so-called New Commonwealth — India, the African nations, the West Indies, the Pacific countries — were, previously, non-white peoples colonised by whites armed with technological pre-eminence. While the colonising authorities eventually gave them the political machinery and the education to conduct their own affairs — and few of them would want to reverse that process — it also left behind a memory of exploitation and of British assumptions of racial and cultural superiority. Only those who have been subjected to racism — malevolent and benevolent — can fully appreciate its ugliness and its crippling effects. It is the belief that a person's worth can be judged by the colour of his or her skin; it is the belief that people are superior or inferior according to such colour. It is a belief that exalts the perpetrator to cocky, bullying confidence and the victim to hopelessness and insecurity. The effects of cultural imperialism are scarcely less damaging.

While the antagonisms and inadvertent mistakes of the past should not be chanted like a never-ending litany of reproach, we should at least remain mindful that members of the New Commonwealth were victims of British imperialism and white racism in their recent past; and consequently they remain more sensitive to race issues than to any others. New Zealanders, from their cocoon of relative security, have to accept that this is so. They must try to understand why it is so, and they must act with sensitivity towards their Commonwealth brothers because it is so. The reason the Old Commonwealth was so cosy and so co-operative and never spoke of such issues was because it was a club of white masters, a club which — until 1960 — included South Africa, the only country in history other than Nazi Germany to enshrine and perpetuate racism in its legal system.

The climate in which the 1981 Springbok tour is taking place, therefore is a very different one from that which existed in 1956. It is a product of a relatively new and growing consciousness of race issues at home, combined with an awareness of and a sensitivity for the feelings of Commonwealth nations abroad.

The people I know who are opposed to this tour are not criminals, communists, proponents of mob violence, or the Prime Minister's rent-a-demonstrators. They are my friends, they are people like myself, they are myself. They are people who care passionately about New Zealand's race relations performance at home and her reputation abroad; they are people who are interested in and deeply involved in the multicultural aspects of New Zealand life, especially Maori-Pakeha activities. They are people who know and care about what is happening in Africa and South Africa and they are relatively well informed about those countries. They are not anti-rugby: most of the males I know have played it and followed it with pleasure, and look forward to the day when they can follow it again. They are people who are by nature gentle and law-abiding — who have never, in fact, broken a law in their life and never contemplated doing so. They are ordinary New Zealanders who just happen to be extraordinarily caring and informed about the race issue. And most of them are prepared to do anything short of violence to people to stop this tour, or if they cannot do that, to show the rest of the world that they object most strenuously to its taking place.

These are the kinds of people by whom the anti-tour movement must be defined — not by the handful of crazies or agitators who may from time to time appear in the frontline. This latter group has never been large enough to affect New Zealand life on a large scale.

The extent to which the national life is being affected now is symptomatic of the magnitude of the caring and committed group. There have always been such people in New Zealand. It is just that their numbers swell as education spreads and social conscience grows. One of the things we have to remember now — to preserve sanity and perspective, and because it will become apparent in retrospect as it has on earlier occasions — is that New Zealanders are basically decent and law-abiding people. When discontent and civil disruption take place on the scale they do now and did during the 1913 Waterfront Strike and the Depression riots, it is not because mob rule is imminent and the institutions of society are threatened. It is because such a degree of disruption is always the iceberg tip of far deeper discontents: it is a manifestation of issues far more profound than that of simply preserving the peace. And it is evidence that the government of the day has made a severe misjudgement in letting events accumulate and gather momentum.

APPENDIX THREE

Television and Maori Topics

The script notes below were written in 1972, as a basis for persuading the then NZBC to commission the *Tangata Whenua* series. I reproduce them here because I believe that what they had to say — about the need for Maori programmes and about their treatment, by Maori or Pakeha journalists — is as true now as it was then. I note too that, a decade after *Tangata Whenua* had screened, Television New Zealand has followed up with few, if any, hour-long documentaries on Maori subjects.

New Zealand is moving through a phase of cultural transition and reorientation. Ties with Europe that shaped our values and institutions are weakening. Many people, especially the young, are questioning the relevance of these values and institutions and looking for others with which to modify or replace them.

This process of readjustment is reflected in the styles of the so-called counter culture; in the use of drugs; in an interest in Eastern philosophies and religions; in the development of special interest groups pressing for changes in social legislation; in communal experiments; and, for the less adaptable, in crime rates and the incidence of mental illness.

While something like a cultural vacuum has been growing, the movement of Maori and Pacific Islanders from rural to urban areas has intensified to the point where the Polynesian race in New Zealand is now a predominantly urban group.

So two groups of young people born after World War Two are growing up alongside each other feeling degrees of cultural disinheritance: one whose links with Europe become more remote and who seek new definition of their identity as New Zealanders; the other, Polynesians who have been removed from the sources of their culture (in the case of the Maori, rural marae where the Maori language is spoken and holds traditional attitudes of the culture, and where social controls still operate), and who feel a sense of confusion about what they are: they are not Maori, in the sense that they have lost their language and a knowledge of their traditions, and yet they are not accepted as Pakeha in Pakeha-defined communities. This latter group has begun to react with aggressive assertions of coloured minority identity demonstrated through organisations like Nga Tamatoa, Polynesian Panthers and the Maori Organisation on Human Rights, and in the case of the less articulate, through gang and criminal activity.

At worst, these factors have brought expressions of racial tension to New Zealand on a wider scale than any seen since the armed conflict of the 1860s. At best, they have begun to produce modifications in the basically European-oriented systems of education, law enforcement and media communication.

What is needed more than anything else is an extension of awareness through the media of the *values and rituals* of Maori culture as they have survived in spite of government-sponsored programmes of assimilation; in particular, their use in coping with problems speaks very much to our times: their relevance to conservation, reconciling minority rights with those of whole communities; offering all kinds of people roles in their society and a consequent feeling of identity; and offering communities degrees of social cohesion.

Why a documentary series on Maori topics?

1. Because such programmes would be engaging for their thematic, visual and narrative appeal.

2. Because the media have done very little up till now to cater for the needs of people whose lives are directed more by Maori things than Pakeha. There is a need to redress an imbalance that many people, particularly minority groups, feel acutely. In some respects Maori have been treated as foreigners in their own country. Newspapers and television have not set out to reflect their interests and preoccupations anywhere near as energetically as they have European ones.

3. Because many Polynesians in New Zealand have been deprived of knowledge about their culture by the education system and by assimilation policies. A film series would go some way towards helping people get back in touch with things they believe should have been their inheritance, particularly by giving them access to knowledgeable people in isolated areas who have been deprived of their teaching functions.

4. Because many non-Maori are several generations distant from their cultural origins. The films would emphasise that there are other cultural roots open to them in New Zealand that they did not encounter through their home background or education.

5. Because most New Zealanders are not aware that there is a distinctive, intense and intact culture in New Zealand outside the majority one. They are unaware because they've had little contact with it: they have not eaten Maori food at a Maori table, heard a kaumatua

chant, or a group of old women calling to the dead. They have not, in fact, experienced the Maori being Maori.

6. Because in some areas of the country, Maori things have not only survived the processes of assimilation and urbanisation, they are actually growing in strength and confidence. Maori who are secure in the identity of their culture are more forthcoming than they have been in the past. There has begun an upsurge in the practical expression of Maoritanga.

7. Because by projecting the proposed subject matter of the programmes into the national consciousness, the films could help promote a blueprint for future and workable race relations. It could do this by contributing to the growth of life styles in New Zealand that are truly integrated — that have their basis in New Zealand, and in which Maori and Pakeha can share increasingly as Maori language is taught in schools and urban marae are established throughout the country.

Why a series now?

1. Because the social need and the demands for such programmes increase daily.

2. Because elderly people who are colourful and dramatic characters and authoritative sources of information are dying every month.

3. Because situations that were previously inaccessible (marae ceremonial, tangihanga, religious services and so on) are gradually and cautiously being opened to the media. This is happening because traditionally oriented communities are coming to terms with the technology of cameras and microphones, because they are beginning to accept television as part of their daily lives, because they are realising that they will have to use television to reach many of their young people long gone to cities, and because they are beginning to trust some of the people who represent the media (after some earlier disastrous encounters). The door is being nudged open gradually, and with care can be opened further.

Objectives

The series would set out to:

1. Meet the needs outlined earlier.

2. Hold up a mirror to areas of New Zealand life that most of its citizens are unfamiliar with; illuminate corners that will give people a more informed appreciation of what it means to be a New Zealander as distinct from something else.

3. Bring a television audience into situations — emotional and geographical — that they have had little or no contact with.

4. Show that Maori culture has adapted and grown from the time of European contact and continues to do so.

5. Reveal that this culture is not something homogeneous. It is not something that can be packaged and slotted into a tidy compartment and plucked out for educational use in the same form for every part of the country. Regional and tribal variations in history, protocol and dialect are considerable.

6. Suggest that people in New Zealand *do* have cultural options, that there is more than a single way of dealing with the basic experiences of life here and that people can and do participate in them.

None of these objectives would be stated explicitly. They would emerge from the content of the programmes through the discussions and behaviour of the participants.

Treatment

After almost a year of discussion with elders and communities all over the North Island about what subjects engage their attention most often, I feel the topics we have selected as focal points for the programmes are those closest to the surface of Maori consciousness.

I propose that we should:

1. Make the programmes about people and tribes rather than subjects. The subjects should emerge as themes. In particular, it is important that we show values and ceremonial in the *contexts* of particular times, places and purposes. The failure to do this in past television programmes has given many Pakeha and Maori viewers the impression that Maori culture is a distraction or an oddity unrelated to people's lives: that it is contained in concert performances and museum display cases.

2. Allow the participants to make their own choices about how they handle the activities filmed and the themes. The role of the film crew should merely be that of recording things as unobtrusively and faithfully as possible. It is essential, for example, that people speak in Maori if this is their most fluent form of communication.

3. Bend the technology of the film-making process to the needs and convenience of the participants. In other words, conform to the protocol of the situations we work in, not interrupt speeches and conversations, not ask for re-enactments, take care over the use of things like clapper boards.

4. Encourage the participants to explore subjects through anecdote and incident rather than through a didactic process.

5. Not set out to be comprehensive in coverage. That is not the way people deal naturally with topics. We should try to be suggestive rather than definitive: to evoke the feelings people have about things

rather than load the programmes with a mass of factual information.

6. Show patience and a lack of concern about time so that the people we are working with get to know us, understand what we are doing, trust us, and cooperate willingly. They must accept our goodwill and competence. This will usually mean discussions with elders, calling meetings of whole communities, and further discussions with the wider group and answering questions. It will also mean establishing social relationships with the participants: eating, drinking and sleeping with them. When we do film, there must be no doubt about our authority to be in a situation.

APPENDIX FOUR

The Treaty of Waitangi

In 1983, at the launching of *Maori — A Photographic and Social History*, I proposed a re-definition of the principles of the Treaty of Waitangi and a drawing up of a new race relations covenant for New Zealand.

Nationally, the Treaty of Waitangi is the most powerful symbol we have. For those who believe in its value, it is a symbol of New Zealand's commitment to racial equality; it is a standard against which the performance of governments and individuals can be measured and — if found wanting — criticised. For those who condemn it, the treaty is a symbol of Pakeha duplicity and oppression; this is the basis for the accusation that 'the treaty is a fraud'. But — and this is what I want to stress — in both instances, from both differing points of view, the treaty is a potent symbol; the name Waitangi and recollection of the ceremony which took place there strike powerful reverberations, positive and negative, in the public mind.

I happen to hold the first view: that the various texts of the treaty — with all their ambiguities and imperfections — represented the aspirations of decent and fair-minded people, Maori and Pakeha, to live equitably and harmoniously together. According to this view, the treaty is not a fraud — but it has been defrauded by the subsequent behaviour of Pakeha governments and individuals who sought to deprive Maori of much of their territorial and cultural resources.

I do not believe, however, that the differing viewpoints on the nature and value of the treaty can be reconciled. Not only have these arguments not been reconciled, they are more sharply and more irreconcilably stated in the 1980s than ever before, and the very notion of celebrating the Waitangi anniversary is under more threat than ever before.

Symbols, however, remain powerful. They reflect fundamental truths about individuals and nations. They are not easily discarded, nor can they be discarded without risk of psychological damage. What I believe is needed now more than anything else is a reconstruction of the Waitangi symbol in a manner that speaks to our time — a manner that highlights what people of goodwill on all sides want for New Zealand, and a manner that reconciles viewpoints that currently conflict. I propose that a new Waitangi agreement be drawn up, that it be called the Waitangi Covenant, that it embody the principles that all parties believed were or should have been in the Waitangi treaty, and that it be signed by all members of Parliament as the current representatives of Maori and Pakeha people.

This agreement would not be a legal document, because the effects of a legal treaty on existing and future laws would lead to interminable and non-productive argument. Instead, it would be a solemn statement of principles governing cultural and race relations to which New Zealanders — through their elected representatives — wished to commit themselves in the interests of fair play and genuine equality.

It should include wholehearted acceptance of the Maori right to retain the Maori language and Maori culture; acceptance of the Maori right to control and dispose of remaining Maori land and its resources according to Maori wishes; and recognition of traditional practices associated with land ownership, such as food gathering and the protection of sacred places. It should affirm the right of people to identify as Maori or Pakeha citizens of New Zealand, and the right of access to all the cultural resources and legal remedies which such an affirmation implies.

It should include the name Waitangi, to remind us of the promises made and accepted in good faith in the Bay of Islands and elsewhere in 1840; and to remind us that these initial promises were frequently dishonoured. And it should be called a covenant because it is a morally forceful agreement on principles, rather than a legal document subject to narrowly legal interpretations and subsequent litigation and amendment.

It should be signed by members of Parliament because Parliament — with its elective foundation — is more representative of the values and aspirations of New Zealand life than any other single body. But after a solemn and ceremonial parliamentary signing, or after a suitably Maori ceremonial which would include the signing, there is no reason why the covenant should not then be signed by other organisations and individuals, Maori and Pakeha. Additional signatories would intensify an unequivocal commitment to genuine racial and cultural equality after more than a hundred years of equivocation.

It is up to others to take up this proposal or reject it. I have put it forward because I believe that the need to resolve racial issues is a race against time, because I believe it is one that could find acceptance from all parts of the political and ideological spectrum, because I believe it does reconcile current points of contention, and because I believe that, more than ever before, we all want racial harmony as a foundation for a fruitful national life in Aotearoa.

Acknowledgements

Much of this book has been written from diaries or interview notes made at the time of the events described. Accounts of some incidents have been published elsewhere in somewhat different form. For permission to republish such material, I am indebted to the editors of the New Zealand *Listener, Landfall, Natural History, Comment,* to Hodder and Stoughton, publishers of *Te Puea* and *Whina,* and to Alister Taylor, publisher of *Moko — Maori Tattooing in the Twentieth Century.*

I want to thank those to whom I owe the largest debt of gratitude: members of my family, for allowing me to expose parts of their life to public gaze, for prodding my recollection of events remembered only indistinctly, for telling me stories about incidents that preceded my birth, for supplying me with photographs I did not have. In particular, my thanks to Eleanor (Tierney) Smith, Martha McMenamin, Lewis and Nell King, Louise Hoobin, Terry King, Gerri Judkins, Madge Waring and Peter Rodgers; and to Maria Jungowska for sharing and bearing my enthusiasm for family matters.

My thanks too to a range of friends, Maori and Pakeha — too many to specify — for introducing me to and participating in many of the experiences described here, and for checking much of the material for this book. If anyone is offended by what they read, I can only apologise for an effect that was unintentional; I repeat, everybody I have written about has my respect and admiration.

All the photographs published here are the property of Michael King or the King family, unless identified otherwise. The Maori photographs were all taken in 'authorised' circumstances — that is, with the permission of the subjects. They include two (of Makere Hose and Nohinohi Heu) who had declined to be represented in my book on moko, but who agreed subsequently to be photographed for publication and for posterity at Turangawaewae Marae. Both women were also filmed the same day by Reynolds Television Ltd with the approval of Queen Te Atairangikaahu.